Y0-CKL-117

# A Higher Score, Guaranteed

This book is the product of hundreds of hours of test preparation and research, and represents the best system of preparation for the ACT English exam on the market. Therefore, we want to back that up with a guarantee. If you, the student, complete this book, and the preparation does not help to improve your score, we will happily refund your money. Send an email to testprepbystep@gmail.com to make arrangements, which will require images of the completed book, the original sales receipt, ACT English scores before and after completing the book, and a written explanation.

All claims for refunds must be received within six months of original purchase

# The ACT English *System*

*A step-by-step, first-things-first, systematized, secret-free,*

*no gimmicks, no tricks, no wasted time guide to the ACT English test*

Philip J Martin

# THE ACT SYSTEM

ACT® is a registered trademark of ACT, Inc

Published by Test Prep by Step, LLC

For special group pricing, please email testprepbystep@gmail.com

ISBN: 9798482516133

www.theactsystem.com

www.philipmartinact.com

# Table of Contents

Introduction ............................................................................................................... 1
Step 1 ........................................................................................................................ 6
Step 1 Practice ........................................................................................................ 11
Step 2 ...................................................................................................................... 20
Step 2 Practice ........................................................................................................ 23
Step 3 ...................................................................................................................... 32
Step 3 Practice ........................................................................................................ 40
Step 4 ...................................................................................................................... 51
Step 4 Practice ........................................................................................................ 55
Step 5 ...................................................................................................................... 66
Step 5 Practice ........................................................................................................ 71
Step 6 ...................................................................................................................... 82
Step 6 Practice ........................................................................................................ 88
Step 7 ...................................................................................................................... 96
Practice Test 1 ....................................................................................................... 100
Practice Test 2 ....................................................................................................... 114
In Conclusion ........................................................................................................ 129
Answer Explanations ............................................................................................ 131
Score Conversion Chart ........................................................................................ 189

# Introduction

Have you looked through your average ACT prep book lately? It looks and feels more like the instruction manual for running a factory than it does a test preparation book. Frankly, you don't need to memorize or read about the technical names of the various types of ACT questions, their categories, the psychology behind the questions, etc. That knowledge is good for behind the scenes, but for you, it's a waste.

Also, if I hear another book or teacher promise to give all of the "tips, tricks, and secrets" to succeed on the ACT I think I'll scream. You don't need "tips, tricks, and secrets;" phrases like that are gimmicks that, at least I think, are big on promise but short on return. Not to mention, the ACT test makers are aware of each and every pattern and conceptions of patterns; as soon as it's circulated that "the shortest answer is almost always right," or whatever the case may be, the test makers will switch it up and defy the pattern. My nearly 600 hours of ACT classroom experience have taught me that you, the student, need three things, especially when it comes to the ACT English test: content knowledge, strategy, and skills. This book will get you there.

Additionally, anxiety is already high enough, so why are so many students preparing for the ACT English test trying their hardest to memorize very specific, unlikely to be asked about English rules? For example, many students sweat over the who/whom distinction, when the odds of a question requiring your knowledge of this is less than 1%; many are researching whether or not the oxford comma (the second comma in a series) is required or optional, and are getting confused by the strong opinions of English teachers and counselors. These topics are important, but unless you have already scored a 33 or higher in ACT English, they are a waste of mental energy. We'll get to those topics in this book, but in due time; we'll put them and the preparation they require where they belong.

The purpose of this book is clear: to focus your attention on the content and skills *most needed in ACT English to raise your score*, and to do so *one at a time*. In other words, those that, simply, are most tested across the ACT English test. The closer a Step is to Step 1, the more important; the further a Step is away from Step 1, the less important (and by less important, I simply mean less likely to be tested on ACT day). For example, you won't find the who/whom distinction near the front of this book! As a Step is learned, it is continually refreshed throughout the book so as not to be forgotten, but rather built upon. This preparation culminates in two full-length practice tests (the final Step!).

# How to Use This Book

Use of this book is simple. Review the Step, then work your way through the practice that follows. The practice contains questions that reflect the current Step as well as previous Steps. Why not simply focus on this current Step's material only? Because again, we want to treat the ACT English test as cumulative, testing both skills and content, and want to continually build upon the most important and work our way to least. This kind of guided *practice* (as opposed to blindly studying) will reveal specific problem areas, thus heightening your focus.

In addition, the vast majority of the practice offered to you in this book is within the context of full-length passages. This is to train your mind to pay attention for that span of time and to become used to the real-life length of ACT English passages. Following each practice section you will find a list of answers. However, the back of the book contains a written explanation for each and every question; these explanations review rules and strategy while giving the reasons behind each correct and incorrect answer.

In a time crunch? Don't have time to use this entire book from start to finish? In that case, complete as many steps as possible, then skip ahead to the two practice tests in Step 7.

# Timing

Each ACT English test is 5 passages in length, and you are given 45 minutes to complete the test. This equates to 9 minutes per passage. Before the final practice tests (which are comparable to real ACT English tests), we will return to timing because this is a crucial skill for the ACT exam. For the first six steps, however, timing will be inaccurate because the passages are customized to teach certain skills and content.

# Overview and Basic Strategy

The ACT English Test is the first of four and is followed by Math, Reading, and Science, respectively. The English Test is designed to test just that: your ability to recognize either the *correct answer* (as in a question of grammar) or the *best answer* (as in a question of context).

It consists of 5 passages, or essays if you will. Each essay is roughly 340 words in length and contains 15 questions. Most of the questions reference an underlined portion of a sentence or sentences and ask you to choose the correct or best answer from four choices. Other questions may refer to a paragraph, asking for the best placement of a certain sentence or an appropriate sentence to finish or begin that paragraph. Further still, some questions refer to the passage as a whole, and could be categorized as something more like "reading comprehension."

**Your best-bet basic strategy is this: <u>Answer questions as you go, but in context</u>**. Read everything, and answer questions as you go. "Read everything," means *do not* skip over paragraphs, sentences, or pieces of sentences that are not underlined. You will need that information (more than you know!). "Answer questions as you go," means you should stop and answer questions while you read. However, this comes with a caveat: you will likely need greater context than just an underlined portion to answer a question correctly, such as the sentence as a whole, the sentence before, the sentence after, etc. More on that in a later lesson!

# Question Breakdown

I break down ACT English questions into two types: grammar and context.

## Grammar

Questions of grammar are questions that, like math, have a right or wrong answer. Take, for example, number 23 below:

I went to the grocery store <u>today, I forgot</u> to buy cheese.
                              23

This question is a question of grammar because, as written, *it is wrong*. In other words, the right answer doesn't depend on the flow of the paragraph, the author's intention, the greater context, the previous sentence, or the purpose of the essay or paragraph. There are a handful of ways that you can combine these two complete sentences (called *independent clauses*) into one, but no matter the way, we need one that is grammatically correct (*more on that later!*).

## Context

You know how sometimes your teacher marks your answer wrong not because it is technically incorrect, but because it isn't the "best answer"? Well, ACT English does the same thing. Based on the sentence that the question is in, or the preceding sentence, or the sentence that follows, or the paragraph as a whole, or even the entire essay, there can be an answer that is *best* as opposed to just grammatically correct. Think about number 24 below:

I went to the grocery store today. <u>Because of this,</u> I forgot to buy cheese.
                                      24

You will notice that "Because of this" is underlined. As an introductory, dependent clause, it is grammatically correct in that it is set off from the independent clause of the sentence ("I forgot to buy cheese"). But, does it *work*? Is it *the best* choice of words? It isn't going to the store, though, that *caused* me to forget to buy cheese. Can you think of a word or phrase that would be *best* to link these thoughts?

*Introduction* 5

# STEP 1

*Sentences and Phrases in Context*

It is undeniable that there is a skill that, if mastered, can move the needle on your ACT English score more than any other, and that is this: <u>placing, rejecting, and organizing phrases and sentences properly in a paragraph based on greater context</u>.

Again, it doesn't matter now if you know what that means or not; the purpose of the book is to teach you these things *through* practice.

Read the following paragraph:

> In the year 2000, the coffee farmers had had enough. Each felt individually taken advantage of by middle-men who would barter the prices of their beans to international distributors. Under this new venture, the farmers would hire a representative who would negotiate prices on their behalf. In this way, the representative worked for the farmers: not the other way around!

Notice anything missing? If not, *read it again, slowly*. Don't sweat if you don't: fortunately, the ACT English test is multiple choice, so you do not need to recognize these things blindly. But does something about this sentence strike you as odd? It should. You should be asking yourself this question: *what new venture*? You see, in the third sentence, "this new venture" is mentioned as something the farmers are doing. However, the venture has not yet been brought up or alluded to before that. This is the kind of recognition that is vital to your ACT English success.

The following page demonstrates how this paragraph might appear on the ACT. See if you can correctly place the sentence, and then try your ability to do so in the following paragraphs as well. If you want to test your abilities, cover up the questions in the right column, read the paragraphs, and ask yourself, "What does this paragraph need to function properly?"

In the year 2000, the coffee farmers had had enough. Each felt individually taken advantage of by middle-men who would barter the prices of their beans to international distributors. |1| Under this new venture, the farmers would hire a representative who would negotiate prices on their behalf. In this way, the representative worked for the farmers: not the other way around!

1. At this point, the author is considering adding the following true statement:

   In response, the farmers united and created their own, joint business.

   Should the writer make this addition here?

   A. Yes, because it creates feelings of sympathy in the reader.
   B. Yes, because it creates a logical transition to the next sentence.
   C. No, because the farmers' response is not relevant to the paragraph.
   D. No, because the information is already provided in the paragraph.

[1] To this day, the status of the Ivory-billed Woodpecker remains a mystery. [2] Some say that it has been spotted dozens of times. [3] I, on the other hand, prefer a position somewhere in between. [4] I believe my grandfather when he says that, as a young man, he spotted the bird, which today carries on indiscreetly as an endangered species. [5] Others maintain that the bird is extinct. |2|

2. For the sake of logic and cohesion, the best placement for Sentence 5 would be:

   F. where it is now.
   G. after Sentence 1.
   H. after Sentence 2.
   J. after Sentence 3.

|3| Well, did you also know that in 1484 he asked John II, King of Portugal, to finance his voyage? For various reasons, John II denied Columbus twice. This forced him to seek funding from neighboring Spain.

3. Given that all of the following statements are true, which one, if added here, would most effectively introduce the topic of this paragraph?

   A. You probably know that, as the rhyme goes, "In 1492 Columbus sailed the ocean blue."
   B. In the days of Christopher Columbus, most of Europe lived under a monarchy.
   C. Have you ever felt like a failure?
   D. Sailing seems timid and easy, but have you sailed across the open ocean?

Did it come naturally to you to see not only that each of these paragraphs was imperfect, but that each was missing something? If so, that is a good sign; follow that instinct! If not, the practice that follows in this Step will be beneficial and will teach you to notice clues that can help you nail down the answer.

## Explanations

**# 1.** The correct answer is **G**. As we said on the previous page, and as written, there is simply no reference point for the phrase "this new venture," especially one that attributes it to farmers. Thus, the paragraph needs a sentence that does so. The "joint business" is this venture. The answer is not **F** because, while these positive feelings may exist, that is not the primary function of the sentence relative to the rest of the paragraph. The answer is not **H** because the farmer's response is relevant in that it itself *is* the venture. The answer is not **J** because the information is not provided in the paragraph, which is why it is needed.

**# 2.** The correct answer is **C**. This time, the question asked you to properly place a sentence. The sentence that needs proper placing begins with the word "Others." This is the context clue that you need to place it correctly. "Others"…compared to who or what? "Some," which is why this sentence pairs with Sentence 2 and, along with Sentence 2, forms a complete thought.

**# 3.** The correct answer is **A**. This time, the paragraph is searching for a sentence to properly introduce a paragraph. We need to look for clues that will help us to do two things: a) Link the proposed sentence to the second sentence, and b) Notice which sentence introduces the topic of the paragraph as a whole. Notice that the second sentence says, "did you *also* know…" That's our clue: we need an opening sentence that references our knowledge of a topic. This is why **A** is correct; it does just that and, if you read on, you'll notice that the rest of the paragraph is also about Columbus. The answer is not **B, C, or D** because none of them reference what we know about something. **D** may be tempting because it properly is in the second person (it is speaking to "you"), but the paragraph is not about the dangers of sailing.

Easy enough? I hope so. We'll put this skill to the test after a mini-lesson!

# *Step 1 Mini-Lesson: Yes or No*

OK, I will admit that it feels a bit like cheating to tuck a mini-lesson into a greater lesson. But it is related and beneficial to do so here. Roughly three questions on every ACT English test your overall comprehension of an essay by asking you *Yes* or *No* after the essay has finished. These questions look something like this (I ask one here following a paragraph to get you thinking the right way; the subject of the essay is a fictional town, Shady Gulf, FL, and all it has to offer for tourists):

Visitors to the quaint beach town will be pleasantly surprised by the number of activities available to them. Many people, for example, have ridden a zip line. Few, however, have ever done so over beautiful bays that can sometimes feature dolphins or manatees. In addition, the In The Zone Arcade features more arcade games than any other single location in the entire state. Locals and tourists alike save up tickets won over weeks or months to trade them in for amazing prizes. If your summer plans are up in the air, pay a visit to Shady Gulf, FL; you'll be glad you did!

15. Suppose the author wishes to add a paragraph to the end of the essay about the biological differences between manatees and dolphins. Would such an addition be appropriate?

    A. Yes, because the reader is likely receptive to more information about these amazing sea creatures after reading about Shady Gulf, FL.
    B. Yes, because as it is currently written, the essay is incomplete.
    C. No, because the subject of the essay is Shady Gulf, FL, not the animal life in and around the town.
    D. No, because there is no mention in the essay of the sea life in and around Shady Gulf, FL.

The answer is **C**. The main reason I am teaching you about these comprehension questions is because your ability to get these questions correct on the ACT: 1) Will set you apart, as these questions are among the most missed, and 2) Depend upon a skill *that we are starting to practice now*. This skill is the ability to pay attention to the paragraph or essay as a whole while you read along answering questions.

On the pages that follow you will find passages and questions that test these skills. Do not worry if you do not have them perfected now…that is why you have this book! We are beginning to *build a skill*.

## PASSAGE I

**Flannery's Childhood Home**

Those who know of the Southern Gothic writer Flannery O'Connor likely remember that she lived much of her life on a farm in Milledgeville, GA. It was on this farm where she lived as an adult, raising peacocks and writing stories. |1| However, the award-winning author spent her most formative years as a child in Savannah, a charming town on the East Coast of the same state. |2|

The charming home is tall and thin, reaching three stories in height, and overlooks Lafayette Square. Today, the square is shaded by beautiful oaks, but in the early 20th century (when the O'Connor family occupied the home) the square was completely grassed and served as a play space for the hundreds of school children who were educated in the area.

1. At this point, the author is considering adding the following true statement:

    Peacocks are male peafowl known for their beautiful plumage.

    Should the writer make this addition here?

    A. Yes, because it introduces a crucial distinction between peacocks and peahens.
    B. Yes, because it creates a logical transition to the next sentence.
    C. No, because the sentence detracts from the main focus of the paragraph.
    D. No, because the information is already provided in the paragraph.

2. Given that all the choices are true, which one most effectively introduces the reader to the fact that the house she grew up in is still standing and open to the public?

    F. The real estate market in Savannah, GA is thriving, as many prospective citizens seek work in the beautiful city.
    G. Today, the writings of Flannery O'Connor continue to both shock and inspire readers of all ages.
    H. Savannah, GA is a relatively short drive from Charleston, SC.
    J. Her childhood home in that city is preserved to this day, and has in recent decades been converted into a museum.

[3] Flannery was one of these children, but her mother preferred to have friends over for play-dates rather than permit her only child to aimlessly roam around the square. [A] Thus she spent much of her time reading and playing with friends in rooms on the second floor. [B] When they were ready to take a break from these activities, Flannery would read out loud to her guests. [C] However, the stories she found most interesting (such as *Grimms' Fairy Tales*) were not the most appealing to the little girls who came to visit. [D] |4|

Flannery also spent time <u>dreaming about future fame</u>. Though the space was small, it ran up against a back alley, which was primarily used by workers and servants; at the very least this space, meant first and foremost for growing different plants, must have been at least moderately entertaining for the young girl! However, the family also used the space to raise chickens. Flannery, an imaginative child, had other

3. The writer is considering deleting the preceding sentence. Should the sentence be kept or deleted?

   A. Kept, because it gives us a window into the everyday childhood environment of Flannery O'Connor.
   B. Kept, because it makes clear that trees are more valued today than in the past.
   C. Deleted, because it doesn't make clear whether or not Flannery O'Connor ever played soccer in the square.
   D. Deleted, because it it not specific enough about the century in which Flannery O'Connor was born.

4. The writer wants to add the following sentence to the preceding paragraph:

   > Like all girls their age, they would draw and play make-believe.

   This sentence would most logically be placed at:

   F. Point A.
   G. Point B.
   H. Point C.
   J. Point D.

5. Which choice best introduces the subject of the paragraph?

   A. NO CHANGE
   B. in the backyard garden.
   C. lounging in the backseat of their car.
   D. gathering eggs and cleaning the coop.

plans for them beyond laying eggs. |6| In fact, she was given a small taste of fame when a crew came to film the fowl she had trained to walk backwards!

[1] In those days, there was no air conditioning. [2] The most common reprieve from the heat was the simple opening of windows. [3] Today, fans of O'Connor speculate just what kinds of people and conversations she saw and overheard on the streets below her home. [4] Surely early inspirations for her over-the-top characters can be traced to this time and place. |7|

6. At this point, the author is considering adding the following true statement:

> Like other families of the time, the O'Connors would eat eggs and the chickens that laid them.

Should the writer make this addition here?

F. Yes, because it shows how the O'Connor family was similar to other families.
G. Yes, because it logically bridges the previous sentence to the rest of the paragraph.
H. No, because at this point in the essay the reader does not need more information about Flannery O'Connor and her childhood home.
J. No, because the information provided, while not explicitly stated, should be assumed to be true.

7. For the sake of the logic and coherence of this paragraph, Sentence 2 should be placed:

A. where it is now.
B. before Sentence 1.
C. after Sentence 3.
D. after Sentence 4.

Question 8 asks about the preceding passage as a whole.

8. Suppose the author's main purpose had been to compare and contrast the characters of Flannery O'Connor's fiction. Would this essay accomplish that purpose?

F. Yes, because it discusses the kinds of people she likely heard outside her window.
G. Yes, because the characters she created in Savannah stayed in her mind when she was forced to move to Milledgeville.
H. No, because the essay describes the history of Savannah in tedious detail.
J. No, because the essay provides an overview of her childhood home and what it was like to live there.

*Step 1* 13

# PASSAGE II

## The Texas State Fair

[1]

They say that everything is bigger in Texas. I got to witness this first-hand when my family was vacationing in the Dallas area. It all began when my father playfully asked us children, "How about a turkey leg for dinner?" |9| My little brothers and I did not understand what he meant until we saw the spectacle for ourselves. [A]

[2]

We began to get excited when we heard our father's stomach rumbling. We were going to the fair! After we parked the car we made our way through the hundreds of vendors lining the entrance. My brothers had to stop at every other booth, and they begged my mother and father to buy them all sorts of toys and pets we did not need. [B] Finally, we emerged into the open air and witnessed hundreds of rides and games to play.

9. The writer is considering deleting the preceding sentence. Should the sentence be kept or deleted?

   A. Kept, because it deepens the reader's understanding of the father's desires.
   B. Kept, because it helps to build anticipation that is fully realized in the next paragraph.
   C. Deleted, because it adds a level of technical detail that is unnecessary at this point in the essay.
   D. Deleted, because it detracts from the lighthearted tone of the rest of the paragraph.

10. Which choice most effectively explains the excitement of the children and logically coheres to the sentence that follows?

    F. NO CHANGE
    G. glimpsed a giant carousel from a distance.
    H. fell asleep in the backseat, only to be awakened a few minutes later in a large parking lot.
    J. when the excitement began to build.

[3]

My father bought us packs of little tickets, which were used as currency to get on the various rides. |11| My brothers used almost all of theirs on a small dragon roller coaster. [C] I, on the other hand, was looking for something a little more daring. It's not everyday that I get to choose from so many different thrills!

[4]

When I first laid eyes on the Starspinner 5000, I knew it was what I had been searching for. My father and I waited in line for what felt like an eternity. |12| Finally, when we reached the ticket-taker, we paid 4 tickets apiece, entered the large circle, and took our places. [D] We were instructed to stand with our backs to the padded walls, and we quickly learned why.

[5]

<u>All of a sudden the room started to spin</u>: faster
       13
and faster it spun until we were pinned to the walls behind us. As we increased speed, the walls themselves slid upwards, lifting us up from the floor. At first I was worried for my father, thinking that at his age he couldn't handle it. However when I looked

11. At this point, the writer is considering adding the following true statement:

> Although my brothers chose cotton candy, the sweet smell of frying dough urged me to order a funnel cake topped with powdered sugar.

Should the statement be added here?

A. Yes, because it adds a fun detail to what is already a lighthearted essay.
B. Yes, because it answers previously raised questions about what the family would eat that evening.
C. No, because most readers are unfamiliar with food commonly found at a fair.
D. No, because it provides details that interrupt the logical flow of the paragraph.

12. If the writer were to delete the preceding sentence, the paragraph would primarily lose:

F. a transition from the narrator's initial desire to ride to the fulfillment of that same desire.
G. an unnecessary exaggeration.
H. a contextual detail that helps provide context for the fear that both father and daughter are experiencing.
J. a detail that teaches the reader that it takes time to count tickets and ensure you have enough of them to board the ride.

13. Which choice provides the most effective transition to Paragraph 5?

A. NO CHANGE
B. My stomach was churning
C. I could hear my father screaming with excitement next to me
D. I was seeing stars

over, he was grinning ear to ear. |14|

14. Given that all of the statements are true, which one, if added here, would best conclude the paragraph and the essay by referring back to the opening paragraph?

   F. Maybe we should have ridden the carousel after all!
   G. The book of tickets slipped out of his pocket, flew into the air, and were out of reach until the ride finally came to a complete stop.
   H. "I think I'll skip out on the turkey leg!" he yelled, which made me chuckle.
   J. My brothers had no idea what they were missing out on; dragon roller coasters could never create a thrill like this!

---

Questions 15 and 16 ask about the preceding passage as a whole.

---

15. The writer is considering adding the following sentence to the essay:

    To them, it was beyond exciting to go up and down the simple track at high speeds.

    If the writer were to add this sentence, it would most logically be placed at:

    A. Point A in Paragraph 1.
    B. Point B in Paragraph 2.
    C. Point C in Paragraph 3.
    D. Point D in Paragraph 4.

16. Suppose the author's main purpose had been to write about a fun family memory as a gift for her father. Would this essay accomplish that purpose?

    F. Yes, because the essay focuses on an exciting experience shared by the author and her father.
    G. Yes, because the essay discusses many fun activities the family did together, such as snorkeling, camping, and playing charades.
    H. No, because the essay is designed to scare readers away from riding the Starspinner 5000.
    J. No, because the essay rarely mentions the author's father.

# Step 1 Correct Answers

I'm going to go out on a limb here and guess that that wasn't the most fun you've ever had. It might have been a little painful, tense, and tedious, but that is good: *we are building a skill*. The format of each question is based on real, recent ACT English questions. Here are the answers for all 16 questions.

**Passage I**

1: C
2: J
3: A
4: G
5: B
6: J
7: A
8: J

**Passage II**

9: B
10: G
11: D
12: F
13: A
14: H
15: C
16: F

Stumped on any? You will find the explanations for each answer beginning on page 131.

# STEP 2

*Verbose and Redundant*

In the last Step, we used context clues to correctly place or delete sentences or smaller phrases. Here, we will keep up the very basic idea that, on ACT English, there is often a *best* answer. Specifically, we will learn two new concepts (all while building upon Step 1):

**Verbose** - here's a rule of thumb: less is more. What does that mean? It means that if something necessary can be said in less words, it is better. Check out this sentence:

I chewed, swallowed, and digested my hamburger last night.

Any grammar errors? Nope. But notice anything wrong? Hopefully you see that the words "chewed, swallowed, and digested" could be replaced with one word: *ate*. Recognizing when phrases or sentences are overly wordy, or more specifically which combination of words says the right thing with the least number of words, is a fundamentally crucial skill to move the needle.

**Redundant** - one thing the ACT wants you to recognize is when an underlined portion is: a) Saying the same thing twice, and b) Being redundant (see what I did there?). Check out the following example:

Eventually, I will clean my room at some point.

At first glance this sentence seems fine. But do you notice the redundancy? "Eventually" and "at some point" are synonyms: they mean the same thing, and both imply that a day is coming in the future on which the author will clean his or her room. The ACT will want you to notice that this portion of the sentence should be deleted and the sentence should be ended after "room."

# *Step 2 Mini-Lesson: Best Word/Phrase Placement and Jumbled Words*

We are working on recognizing *best* answers. Here's a strategy that you MUST be aware of: **_LISTEN_**. That's odd advice for a test taken in a silent room, but if a group of words or a sentence "sounds" (in your mind, that is) off or strange, ***it probably is***. Even if you don't read a lot, you've absorbed a lot of well-written English over the course of your life. Here are two types of questions that test your ability to listen.

1) **Best Word or Phrase Placement** - One type of less-asked-about-but-related-question that I've seen is the *best* location of a word or phrase within a sentence. Check out this example:

   Gilbert J. Smith, a reporter for the *Washington Wire*, reached a surprising conclusion after <u>financially</u> interviewing hundreds of successful business owners as to how to achieve lifetime stability: read often!

You should be asking yourself: how can someone financially interview another person? It doesn't really make sense. Thus, the ACT will want you to read and reread the sentence with the word or phrase in a proper place; in this case, one proper place for the adverb "financially" could be before "successful."

2) **The Jumbled Up Words** - A second type of less-asked-about-but-related-question that I've seen is the jumbled words kind of question. Look at this example:

   My brother will <u>be the one being coming near by</u> to pick me up.

Umm...what? That should "sound" off, because it is. We need a less wordy phrase that actually makes sense to replace this jumble. That would be "be coming."

Without further ado, let's get into it; this book, after all, is about maximizing the productivity of your time. The following three passages test skills from Step 1 as well as the current Step.

# PASSAGE I

## Uluru

[1]

In late July, 1873, William Gosse spotted a large, almost mountainous rock rising from the Australian landscape in July. He named it Ayers Rock after Sir
¹
Henry Ayers, who at the time was the Chief Secretary of South Australia. |2| Unbeknownst to Gosse, the rock already possessed a name: Uluru. [A] This latter

1. A. NO CHANGE
   B. landscape in late July.
   C. landscape in late July, 1873.
   D. landscape.

2. The writer is considering deleting the preceding sentence. Should the sentence be kept or deleted?
   F. Kept, because Ayers, as the discoverer of the rock, deserves more recognition.
   G. Kept, because it gives a detail that contrasts well with the formation's other name.
   H. Deleted, because it gives unnecessary details about Sir Henry Aires, which detracts from the paragraph's purpose.
   J. Deleted, because it it raises questions in the mind of the reader that are left unanswered.

name, it being Uluru, was given to it by the
         ³
Pitjantjatjara, the aboriginal people who regard the rock as sacred.

3. A. NO CHANGE
   B. Uluru
   C. , it is Uluru,
   D. DELETE the underlined portion

[2]

Uluru is an inselberg, a hill or mountain composed of rock that emerges from the surrounding landscape like a mountain. [B] Needless to say, one
              ⁴
of the reasons Uluru is so attractive to tourists is its absolute segregation from other hills, peaks, or mountains. In fact, the closest and nearest similar
                                    ⁵

4. F. NO CHANGE
   G. that surrounds it.
   H. while being made mostly of rock.
   J. in an isolated fashion.

5. A. NO CHANGE
   B. nearest, and closest
   C. closest
   D. most in proximity

formation is Mount Olga, <u>which is pretty close by.</u>
                                        6

[3]

For the most part, Uluru is composed of arkose. [C] This is a type of sandstone, the composition of which is at least 25% feldspar. It is believed that Uluru is a <u>remnant</u> of a mountain building event
                  7
called the Peterman Orogeny. [D] While other smaller arkose formations have since dissipated, Uluru has survived the test of <u>time that has passed by.</u>
                                                 8

[4]

Many animal species are native to the park in and around Uluru. For example, 7 different <u>species
                                                 9
and types</u> of bats take advantage of the rock
     9
formation for roosting during the day, and <u>at least 70</u>
                                              10

species of reptiles have been documented as well. |11| Some species, such as the black-flanked rock-wallaby and the common brushtail possum, are historically native to the area, but are locally extinct. That is not

6. Which choice most effectively illustrates the precise distance between Uluru and Mount Olga?
   F. NO CHANGE
   G. which lies 16 miles to the West.
   H. which is not too far away.
   J. which, by today's standards, is accessible by car.

7. A. NO CHANGE
   B. remnant, meaning a leftover,
   C. small remaining quantity of something
   D. remnant, remainder, or leftover

8. F. NO CHANGE
   G. time that has passed.
   H. time.
   J. time that, to this day, is still passing.

9. A. NO CHANGE
   B. species
   C. types:
   D. categorical types

10. F. NO CHANGE
    G. 70, or maybe more than 70,
    H. 70, 71, 72, or maybe even more
    J. as of today, up to, or perhaps exactly, 70

11. At this point, the writer is considering adding the following true statement:

    Snakes are an example of a reptile.

    Should the statement be added here?

    A. Yes, because it answers a question asked earlier in the essay.
    B. Yes, because it gives a detail that deepens the reader's understanding of the vast amount of animal life around Uluru.
    C. No, because it gives a detail stated elsewhere in the paragraph.
    D. No, because gives information about animal species and not about Uluru.

all: various species of bats also call Uluru home. |12|

[5]

In order to accommodate both the native history and English discovery of the inselberg, the Australian government named the rock Ayers Rock/Uluru in 1993. However, this was reversed in 2002 and it is now and henceforth will be known as the Uluru/
                                    13
Ayers Rock. This dual name signals to tourists that the formation is of historical significance.

12. The writer is considering deleting the preceding sentence. Should the sentence be kept or deleted?
    F. Kept, because it details another species of animal that lives in or around Uluru.
    G. Kept, because it builds sympathy for Uluru and the animal species living there.
    H. Deleted, because it gives information that has already been stated elsewhere.
    J. Deleted, because the topic of the sentence fits better with an earlier paragraph

13. A. NO CHANGE
    B. now known as
    C. referred to by the name of
    D. called a name that is the result of this reversal:

---

Questions 14 and 15 ask about the preceding passage as a whole.

14. The writer is considering adding the following sentence to the essay:

    This episode took place as early as the Cambrian period 530 million years ago and as late as the Neoproterozoic Era 550 million years ago.

    If the writer were to add this sentence, it would most logically be placed at:

    F. Point A in Paragraph 1.
    G. Point B in Paragraph 2.
    H. Point C in Paragraph 3.
    J. Point D in Paragraph 3.

15. Suppose the author's main purpose had been to write a brief essay about the history, importance, and geological makeup of an Australian landmark. Would this essay accomplish that purpose?

    A. Yes, because the essay details the author's firsthand experience visiting Uluru.
    B. Yes, because the essay speaks of Uluru's discovery, meaning, and scientific composition and importance.
    C. No, because, while the author mentions that Uluru is composed of arkose, he or she never discusses Uluru's history.
    D. No, because there is not enough information about Sir Henry Ayers, after whom the rock was named.

---

## PASSAGE II

### The Palace of Versailles

[1]

Extravagant palaces were a common fixture of
                                      16
royalty throughout European history. Massive homes filled with expensive décor illustrated a monarch's

16. F. NO CHANGE
    G. commonly regular feature
    H. feature that was common
    J. regular, and ordinarily common

wealth, power, and money. They could often host
opulent parties for hundreds of guests. Several of

these centuries-old structures standing remain still
today, and many have been re-purposed as historical

landmarks or tourist attractions. |19|

[2]

Located near the village of Versailles in France,

the Palace of Versailles uniquely stands apart for both

its beauty and history. The Hall of Mirrors, a massive

mirror-filled room built for entertaining, is perhaps

the best-known large feature of the Palace. Other

extravagant features include the massive Garden of

Versailles and the Royal Opera. |22| With ornate

statues and decorations around every corner of the
Palace, the Palace of Versailles is often
described as one of not only Europe's but the world's

17. A. NO CHANGE
    B. wealth and power.
    C. wealth, power, and control.
    D. powerful hoards of gold and money.

18. F. NO CHANGE
    G. today standing remain still,
    H. remain standing today,
    J. remain standing still today,

19. Given that all of the following statements are true, which one, if added here, would most effectively end Paragraph 1 and transition to Paragraph 2?

    A. While all of these former homes are significant, few are as well known as the Palace of Versailles.
    B. On the other hand, some of them have not survived the test of time and have been destroyed.
    C. Historical landmarks are all over Europe, and many of them have extravagant gardens.
    D. Many groups in and around not only Europe but the whole world are forming to raise funds to save many of these sites.

20. F. NO CHANGE
    G. stands apart
    H. stands uniquely
    J. stands

21. A. NO CHANGE
    B. Palace.
    C. feature of the Palace.
    D. giant, mountainous, humongous feature of the Palace.

22. If the writer were to delete the preceding sentence, the paragraph would primarily lose a statement that:

    F. makes clear the availability of the Palace to visitors.
    G. indicates the tragic implications for Europe if the Palace were to be forgotten.
    H. guides visitors as they tour the Palace from the Eastern half to Western half.
    J. concludes a summary of the grander features of the Palace.

23. A. NO CHANGE
    B. each and every decorated corner,
    C. each and every Palace corner,
    D. each corner,

most beautified and aesthetically pleasing places.
24

[3]

The beauty of the Palace of Versailles continues to attract visitors from all over. To this day, the Palace remains one of the most popular destinations in Europe. Travelers also come to learn about the
25

historical significance of the Palace. |26| After the Revolution, the Palace saw many uses, including as a diplomatic meeting place. Heads of state would meet at the Palace to discuss global issues. Arguably the most famous diplomatic document signed within the Palace walls was the Treaty of Versailles, which ended World War I.

[4]

For roughly a century, the Palace of Versailles
27
was only used as the home of the French monarch for about 100 years. In the years after the Revolution, the Palace went through disrepair and many phases of
28
restoration. It has served as a museum, a diplomatic hall, and even a storage space. Today, the Palace of Versailles is a UNESCO World Heritage site and is open to visitors, roughly 8 million of which pass through its doors each year. All guests come to admire the Palace's splendor while learning about the

24. F. NO CHANGE
    G. easy-on-the-eye
    H. attractively pretty
    J. beautiful

25. A. NO CHANGE
    B. being one of the utmost
    C. much like that of some of the most
    D. to be among the highest

26. At this point, the writer is considering adding the following true statement:

    It was the seat of the French government from 1682 until the French Revolution in 1789.

    Should the statement be added here?

    F. Yes, because it provides specific evidence of the historical significance mentioned in the previous sentence.
    G. Yes, because the author previously stated that it was the French Revolution that was responsible for the Palace's destruction.
    H. No, because the beauty of the Palace has already been stressed enough in the essay.
    J. No, because it fails to connect the preceding sentence to the sentence that follows in a logical way.

27. A. NO CHANGE
    B. As a home for kings, queens, and other royalty, the Palace
    C. The Palace
    D. Palace

28. Which of the following placements for the underlined portion makes it clear that the physical condition of the Palace has improved and worsened multiple times since the French Revolution?

    F. Where it is now
    G. After the words *In the*
    H. After the word *through*
    J. Before the word *Palace*

history that took place within its four walls.
                              29

29. A. NO CHANGE
    B. within.
    C. beneath its ceiling and above its floors.
    D. DELETE the underlined portion and end the sentence with a period

> Question 30 asks about the preceding passage as a whole.

30. Suppose the author's main purpose had been to compare and contrast various historic European buildings. Would this essay accomplish that purpose?

    F. Yes, because the Palace of Versailles is one of many such buildings.
    G. Yes, because the first sentence of the essay mentions the "Extravagant palaces" of European history
    H. No, because only the Palace of Versailles is detailed and described in the essay.
    J. No, because the essay says nothing about other European palaces or buildings.

# Step 2 Correct Answers

**Passage I**

1: D
2: G
3: D
4: J
5: C
6: G
7: A
8: H
9: B
10: F
11: D
12: H
13: B
14: J
15: B

**Passage II**

16: F
17: B
18: H
19: A
20: G
21: C
22: J
23: D
24: J
25: A
26: F
27: C
28: H
29: B
30: H

Stumped on any? You will find the explanations for each answer beginning on page 134.

# STEP 3

*Commas*

We are now starting to enter the territory of what I defined before Step 1 as "grammar," meaning the kinds of questions that have a right or a wrong answer. In this case, we are talking about commas.

When I was in high school, I remember getting some advice from a counselor at my school about this. She said regarding commas, "When in doubt, take it out." However, I don't think that advice is very helpful. After all, it could very well be the case that you, the student, need to recognize that a comma (or two!) belongs when there is not one shown or used.

I have different advice: in ACT English, *every comma is **deliberate***.

What does that mean?

That means that commas aren't thrown into sentences to create "pauses" just so people can take a breath. Of course commas create pauses in a sentence, but that doesn't mean that every pause *in your mind* or every pause *in your speech* needs a comma. It also doesn't mean that, just because a pause "sounds nice," that a comma belongs there or is *better* there. Again, with commas, we've left the realm of the *best* answer. Now, the ACT expects you to recognize the *correct* answer. Think about the following sentence:

There typically are a vast and overwhelming number of stainless-steel appliances that provide husbands and wives the ability to spend more of their time doing what they love to do and less of their time doing the things around the house that they do not want to do in just about 86.574% of households on the Southeastern point of reference on an official map of the Continental United States of America.

While that sentence makes almost no sense (I made it up off the top of my head), there is one thing about it you should know: it is grammatically correct, and it needs no commas. I'm trying to show you that just because a sentence could use a pause when spoken or even thought, it doesn't mean that one belongs on the written page.

The first time I wrote this Step, I had to remember that the purpose of this book is for you not to feel like you are reading a technical manual. I deleted pages of very specific rules about commas, phrases, etc. English teachers may not like that, but I want you to improve via *practice*. Thus, my explanations and lessons will be kept to an absolute minimum.

We will begin, of course, with the comma usage most likely to be tested on the ACT and end with the comma usage least likely to be tested (though still tested, and thus important).

## 1) <u>Setting off nonessential words or phrases</u>

The most-needed comma skill on recent ACT English tests is the ability to set off nonessential words or phrases with a pair of commas. In this case, commas act kind of like parentheses. The word or phrase that is offset is disruptive. Before we get to examples, think of it like this: imagine you are driving down the highway at 60 MPH and decide to take a detour off the main road to see the world's largest ball of yarn without stopping. You slow the car down as you exit and drive slowly past the yarn ball before getting back on the highway. The detour isn't essential to the trip you're taking, and you never stopped. That is what happens to a sentence when a nonessential word or phrase is inserted into it. Check out the following sentences. "Before" means no comma is necessary. "After" means a nonessential word or phrase has been added and has to be set off by commas.

<u>Before:</u>    The Auburn Tigers are my favorite football team.
<u>After:</u>    The Auburn Tigers, **not the Alabama Crimson Tide,** are my favorite football team.
<u>Before:</u>    My neighbor has trophies scattered throughout her home.
<u>After:</u>    My neighbor, **a former college athlete,** has trophies scattered throughout her home.
<u>Before:</u>    There are no snakes in Ireland.
<u>After:</u>    There are no snakes, **however,** in Ireland.

Your ability to spot these disruptive phrases, and to know that they are set off with commas (like parentheses…like this!) is comma necessity #1.

## 2) Setting off introductory word, adverb, or phrase, and setting off other dependent clauses

Before we begin, we need to define a couple of terms. I've mentioned them before, but now is the time to understand what these things mean. You may already know, and that's great, but in case you don't…

**Independent Clause** - for our purposes an independent clause is simply a complete thought or, you might say, a complete sentence; a thought that can stand alone as a sentence. We don't need to get too technical because this, after all, is an ACT English prep book and not a high school English book. Here are some examples of such clauses:

   a) Claudia went to the grocery store.
   b) One-third of hippopotamuses have no front teeth.
   c) Getting nauseous is my new normal.
   d) It rained on our wedding day.

**Dependent Clause** - for our purposes, when I say "dependent clause" I mean a phrase that can't stand alone as a sentence. Remember the strategy or advice to *listen* and simply determine which sounds strange? That can help you to identify when something is not a complete thought or sentence. Check out the following dependent clauses and notice how strange they are when treated like an independent thought or sentence.

   a) Because she needed an ingredient for her recipe.
   b) Despite brushing daily.
   c) Whenever I eat shellfish.
   d) Which is unfortunate.

It ought to irritate you a bit to see these clauses treated like complete sentences and ended with a period. That is the kind of recognition you will need to ace many ACT comma questions. Depending on how you try to combine clauses, they may or may not need commas.

- **a)** Claudia went to the grocery store because she needed an ingredient for her recipe.

    Because she needed an ingredient for her recipe, Claudia went to the grocery store.
- **b)** One-third of hippopotamuses have no front teeth despite brushing daily.

    Despite brushing daily, one-third of hippopotamuses have no front teeth
- **c)** Getting nauseous is my new normal whenever I eat shellfish.

    Whenever I eat shellfish, getting nauseous is my new normal.
- **d)** It rained on our wedding day, which is unfortunate.

Putting the first three of these clauses at the beginning of sentences disrupts the flow; they need to be offset by a comma. Some clauses (like the last one that says "which is unfortunate") only work at the end of a sentence after a comma (in fact, unless it is beginning a question, the word "which" will usually come after a comma, and always if beginning a clause).

Again, *listen* to the sentence. Does it flow? Does it need a pit stop? We can talk all day about the hundreds of technical English rules regarding clauses and subordinating conjunctions and exceptions to rules, etc. That is not going to be helpful for most people because *practice creates recognition.*

One last thing about this comma usage: if a sentence begins with an adverb (usually they end in *ly*), it must be set off by a comma.

**Incorrect**: Unbelievably the cat lived to be 22 years old.

**Correct**: Unbelievably, the cat lived to be 22 years old.

PS I have no idea how many hippos are actually missing their front teeth.

3) <u>**Setting off adjectives in a series**</u>

Simple rule here: adjectives in a row that describe the same word often need commas to separate them. You don't need one after the last adjective. For example:

    There's a mean, scary monster under my bed.

See what I did there? We need an adjective after "mean," but not after "scary." However, I said a second ago that this is "often" the case. There's an exception. If the adjective *can't be detached* from the noun, because it is essentially a part of the noun, it is treated like a part of the noun. This is better illustrated with an example:

    It's not a monster. That's just my smelly little brother.

See how there's no adjective after the word "smelly"? That's because "little brother" itself acts like a noun. To test this, rearrange the adjectives in the phrase. If it still "works," you need commas. If not, you don't. Look at this example:

    <u>Before</u>:    That's just my smelly little brother.

    <u>After</u>:    That's just my little smelly brother.

The change doesn't work; now it sounds like my brother is physically little, like a leprechaun, instead of "younger." There are lots of noun/adjective combinations like this. Bowling ball. Cheddar cheese. Etc.

4) <u>**Combining two independent clauses**</u>

Use a comma to combine, essentially, two sentences into one. Before I get to an example, what must follow the comma is a conjunction, which can be remembered by the acronym FANBOYS (for, and, nor, but, or, yet, so). Let's combine these two sentences into one.

    <u>Before</u>:    I went to the grocery store. I forgot to buy cheese.

    <u>After</u>:    I went to the grocery store, **but** I forgot to buy cheese.

Simple enough. Remember that what might be asked for is the *correct* conjunction. If our new, complex sentence said this, it wouldn't make sense: "I went to the grocery store, **so** I forgot to buy cheese." **But** is the appropriate conjunction for this pair of clauses.

# *Step 3 Mini-Lesson: Linking Independent Clauses and Related Grammar*

There are multiple ways to link two sentences together into one complex sentence. Let's look at those ways and the other ways to use the punctuation this brings us: semi-colons, em dashes, and colons.

### Semi-colon

The semi-colon has one use: to combine two independent clauses into one (but no FANBOYS allowed!)

    Correct: I am tired of typing; writing is tedious.

    Incorrect: I am tired of typing; and writing is tedious.    *-can't have that "and" in there!*

### Em-dash

This is just a long dash, like a double hyphen, this thing: —

You have to know it can do two things: combine independent clauses and replace parentheses.

    Correct: I am tired of typing—writing is tedious.

    Correct: The strength required to mountain climb—gained by months of training—is unbelievable.

    Incorrect: The strength required to mountain climb, gained by months of training—is unbelievable.

Why incorrect? When used like parentheses, em dashes must come in pairs. The comma should be an —.

### Colons

Colons have many uses (combine independent clauses, set off lists or quotes, set off dramatic nouns or phrases, etc.). Here's what you need to know: they *always* follow a complete sentence or thought.

    Correct: I am tired of typing: writing is tedious!

    Correct: I have three friends: Mom, Dad, and a tree.

    Correct: The politician began his stump speech: "Please vote for me."

    Correct: I reeled in the fish and couldn't believe what I caught: a shark!

    Incorrect: Physical labor: believe me it is demanding!    *-This colon doesn't follow a complete thought!*

*OK....give the following practice your best shot! It is heavy on Step 3 but strengthens Steps 2 and 1!*

## PASSAGE I

### Unity Through Tragedy

[1]

Like <u>many Americans I</u> remember where I was
    1
on September 11, 2001. That day started off as

normal as usual. I <u>woke up</u> to an alarm at 6:15 AM,
             2
got ready for the school day, and was picked up by a

<u>down the street good friend.</u> I attended my high-
          3

school <u>classes unaware of what was happening in</u>
                              4
<u>New York</u> through mid-morning. [A]
    4

[2]

When I arrived in English class, my teacher put

aside the lesson for the day and simply turned on the

television. [5] The first of the two towers of the World

Trade Center had already been struck by the plane,

and at this point there was speculation that this was

no mere accident. Horrifyingly, I watched as the

second tower was <u>struck, and</u> as the Twin Towers
                        6
then collapsed one after another.

1. A. NO CHANGE
   B. many Americans, I
   C. many, Americans I
   D. many, Americans, I

2. F. NO CHANGE
   G. rose up from my mattress
   H. awoke up
   J. woke up, not down,

3. A. NO CHANGE
   B. down the street, good friend.
   C. good friend down the street.
   D. DELETE the underlined portion and end the sentence with a period.

4. F. NO CHANGE
   G. classes unaware, of what was happening, in New York
   H. classes unaware of what was, happening in, New York
   J. classes, unaware of what was happening in New York,

5. At this point, the writer is considering adding the following true statement:

   > In a 9th grade English class, a student can expect to study vocabulary and grammar, among other things.

   Should the statement be added here?

   A. Yes, because it provides much needed context for the author's lived reality.
   B. Yes, because it creates a contrast between what was normal and the events of the day.
   C. No, because the sentence shifts the focus of the paragraph away from the author's lived experience.
   D. No, because the paragraph's focus is on Math class, not English class.

6. F. NO CHANGE
   G. struck, but
   H. struck
   J. struck and

Step 3    40

[3]

There are no words that can describe what happened to United America that day. It was a
                             7
moment that defined a generation. [B] This is particularly true for the families of the nearly 3,000 Americans who lost their lives. However, what took place in the United States in the months following the terrorist attack is something that those not only my age, but also those from a generation before me—will
 8
never forget: unity.
      9

[4]

Political squabbles, divergence of opinion, and differences in creed were all set to the side in favor of a simpler truer identity statement: *I am American!* [C]
   10
Honor due to veterans was renewed. American flags, once readily available at stores, were on backorder due to a seemingly unending demand at retail
                                                  11
locations across the country.
         11
[5]

When I look back on that day, I am horrified at the atrocities that took place by the work and evil schemes of only a small handful of people. Because more than twenty years have passed since these awful, terrorist attacks, I have noticed, unfortunately,
          12

7. A. NO CHANGE
   B. America
   C. the nation north of Mexico and south of Canada
   D. the United, America

8. F. NO CHANGE
   G. age but
   H. age—but
   J. age (but

9. A. NO CHANGE
   B. forget; unity.
   C. forget: being a united people.
   D. forget, unity.

10. F. NO CHANGE
    G. simpler, truer identity
    H. truer simpler identity
    J. identity, simpler truer,

11. A. NO CHANGE
    B. for American flags.
    C. when once they were easy to purchase.
    D. nationwide.

12. F. NO CHANGE
    G. awful terrorist attacks,
    H. awful, terrorist, attacks,
    J. awful terrorist attacks

Step 3   41

that the pride and unity that strengthened in the
               13
months following has slowly faded away. [D] Many

have forgotten that what unites a nation ought to

transcend everyday and political differences.

13. A. NO CHANGE
    B. pride, and unity,
    C. pride, and unity
    D. pride and unity,

---

**Questions 14 and 15 ask about the preceding passage as a whole.**

14. The writer is considering adding the following sentence to the essay:

    People of all walks of life came together over dinner.

    If the writer were to add this sentence, it would most logically be placed at:

    F. Point A in Paragraph 1.
    G. Point B in Paragraph 3.
    H. Point C in Paragraph 4.
    J. Point D in Paragraph 5.

15. Suppose the author's main purpose had been to write a history of the United States of America. Would this essay accomplish that purpose?

    A. Yes, because the essay details an important, though tragic, moment in American history.
    B. Yes, because the essay is chronological like all historical accounts.
    C. No, because the essay says nothing about events within the history of the United States.
    D. No, because the essay describes only one event of American history from a personal perspective.

---

## PASSAGE II

### The Colosseum

Few archetypes of ancient civilization are better

known than the Colosseum. An iconic symbol of

Roman history the Colosseum, was first constructed
            16

nearly 2000 years ago. Today, only about one-third of

the original massive amphitheater still stands; what
                                              17

does remain demonstrates the enormous scope of the

original structure. Looking at the ruins, it is not

16. F. NO CHANGE
    G. Roman, history the Colosseum
    H. Roman history, the Colosseum
    J. Roman, history, the Colosseum

17. Which of the following alternatives to the underlined portion would NOT be acceptable?

    A. stands. What
    B. stands—what
    C. stands, but
    D. stands; but

Step 3    42

difficult to imagine inside a mind the size and
majesty of the amphitheater at its peak.

Construction of the Colosseum first began around 70 A.D. under the Roman Emperor Vespasian. He decided to construct the amphitheater near the center of the city on the site of a palace that had been destroyed in the Great Fire of Rome. Funds for construction were generated by the Roman siege of Jerusalem in the same year. The Colosseum was fully constructed after ten years which was considered very fast for such a structure in the first century. [22]

The Colosseum is a free-standing stone structure. Builders used ancient forms of concrete to create certain parts, pieces, and sections of the main building. The amphitheater, overall, covers about 300,000 square feet. It once hosted gladiator battles, animal fights, mock military maneuvers, and other forms of popular entertainment. For centuries, the Colosseum was the largest amphitheater in the entire

18. F. NO CHANGE
    G. imagine inside your mind
    H. think up well
    J. imagine

19. A. NO CHANGE
    B. Roman, Emperor Vespasian.
    C. emperor, Roman, Vespasian.
    D. Vespasian, who was both Roman and an emperor.

20. F. NO CHANGE
    G. were to be being gotten
    H. being brought forth
    J. generated, were those

21. A. NO CHANGE
    B. after ten years;
    C. after, ten years,
    D. after ten years,

22. Given that all the choices are true, which one most effectively introduces the reader to the fact that the Colosseum was overseen by consecutive emperors?

    F. The Emperor Vespasian was not born into a noble family by any stretch of the imagination, but earned his way to the throne by military prowess.
    G. During this time, much of Europe, Northern Africa, and even parts of Asia were increasingly dominated by the Roman Empire.
    H. Although Emperor Vespasian had died the year prior, it was his son, Emperor Titus, who opened the Colosseum with a large festival in 80 A.D.
    J. Other projects on that scale often took decades or even centuries to fully construct.

23. A. NO CHANGE
    B. parts, pieces, sections, and segments
    C. parts, pieces and sections
    D. parts

24. F. NO CHANGE
    G. amphitheater, overall
    H. amphitheater overall
    J. amphitheater: overall,

world, and remarkably could hold as many as 50,000
　　25
spectators at one time. However, in the 6th century, instability in the Western Roman Empire forced an end to its events. |26|

Over time, the Colosseum became abandoned entirely. Large parts were removed to provide stone for other construction projects, much of the ornate
　　　　　　　　　　　　　27
construction—such as marble statues, was taken
　　　　　　　　　　　　　28
away or destroyed. Weather and natural erosion also played a role in its slow ruination as the once bustling amphitheater faded slowly into antiquity. While some form of conservation of the Colosseum technically began in the 18th century. Actual restoration did not
　　29
begin until the mid-1990s. |30|

25. A. NO CHANGE
　　B. world, but
　　C. world and
　　D. world;

26. The writer is considering deleting the preceding sentence. Should the sentence be kept or deleted?

　　F. Kept, because it gives the reader deeper insight into world events.
　　G. Kept, because it fittingly describes how the Colosseum's flourishing activity was halted.
　　H. Deleted, because it shifts the focus of the essay away from the Colosseum.
　　J. Deleted, because it makes no mention of the Roman Emperor Titus and whether or not he attended the Colosseum regularly.

27. A. NO CHANGE
　　B. projects; much
　　C. projects much,
　　D. projects: much,

28. F. NO CHANGE
　　G. statues
　　H. statues:
　　J. statues—

29. A. NO CHANGE
　　B. began. In the 18th century, actual
　　C. began in the 18th century, actual
　　D. began, in the 18th century, actual

Question 30 asks about the preceding passage as a whole.

30. Given that all of the following statements are true, which one, if added here, would best conclude the paragraph and the essay by referring back to the opening paragraph?

　　F. Although repair is ongoing, the Colosseum continues to be one of history's most recognizable landmarks.
　　G. It is true, however, that weather continues to affect landmarks worldwide.
　　H. Ultimately, the Roman Empire would fall, although the city of Rome carries on.
　　J. It is up to all of us to pitch in, donate, and be a part of restoration projects worldwide

## PASSAGE III

**Stunt Kite**

I used to think kites were boring or childish, but that changed when my uncle brought over a peculiar kind of kite for us to fly together. When he began to
     31

set it up I noticed something odd: instead of one
         32
string for height, this kite was controlled by two. As a

heavy wind blew over the field, we launched the kite,
            33
but unlike the lazy drifting of most I had flown, this

kite shot into the air like a very fast, rapid bullet. I
                    34
knew then that something different was at hand.

    I watched on in amazement and wide eyed as my uncle deftly controlled not only the height, but also knew how to cause the kite to fly higher. This was
                35

done by controlling the balance I could now see why
                36
he needed two strings: pulling on one string caused the kite to bank right, and pulling on the other string caused it to bank left. But that was not all, for he
                                37
could also do flips, dives, stalls, and other tricks.

    Suddenly as I was watching, the kite
          38
started to dive towards the ground. I shouted to

**31.**
- **A.** NO CHANGE
- **B.** kind
- **C.** type that was not that boring
- **D.** variety of my uncle's

**32.**
- **F.** NO CHANGE
- **G.** up, I noticed something: odd,
- **H.** up I noticed: something odd
- **J.** up, I noticed something odd:

**33.**
- **A.** NO CHANGE
- **B.** blew, over the field, we
- **C.** blew over, the field
- **D.** DELETE the underlined portion.

**34.**
- **F.** NO CHANGE
- **G.** bullet.
- **H.** very fast rapid bullet.
- **J.** bullet, quickly.

**35.** Which choice best emphasizes that the uncle possesses a control over the kite that is not limited merely to its distance from the ground?
- **A.** NO CHANGE
- **B.** where and in which direction the kite flew.
- **C.** watched on in amazement by my side.
- **D.** just how high the kite could fly.

**36.**
- **F.** NO CHANGE
- **G.** balance and
- **H.** balance, and
- **J.** balance,

**37.**
- **A.** NO CHANGE
- **B.** for, he
- **C.** for, my uncle,
- **D.** for he, my uncle,

**38.**
- **F.** NO CHANGE
- **G.** Suddenly as I was watching
- **H.** Suddenly, as I was watching,
- **J.** Suddenly,

my uncle thinking, for a moment, he had lost control; he smiled, and when the kite was just a few feet from a crash landing, he pulled back hard. |40|

Soon my uncle put the strings in my hands, and with patience he spent the rest of the day teaching me how it is to fly the stunt kite. Within a few hours I could do amazing figure eights and dive bombs!

Whenever I crashed, which happened more than a few times—my uncle used it as a teaching opportunity, encouraging me to pull with more or less force on one string or the other in a certain direction. Since that day I, though still a bit of an amateur, have gotten my own stunt kite and have had plenty of opportunities to hone my kite-flying skills. After years of stunt kite flying, it is hard to believe that I

39. A. NO CHANGE
    B. uncle thinking for a moment, he
    C. uncle, thinking, for a moment, he
    D. uncle, thinking for, a moment, he

40. At this point, the writer is considering adding the following true statement:

    The kite banked almost instantly and rocketed into the sky, averting disaster.

    Should the statement be added here?

    F. Yes, because the phrase "rocketed into the sky" pairs well with the rocket mentioned earlier in the paragraph.
    G. Yes, because it fittingly closes the paragraph by stating that the kite did not crash.
    H. No, because the reader can answer the question of whether or not the kite crashes for himself or herself.
    J. No, because this paragraph's concluding sentence ought to create anticipation that leads into the next paragraph.

41. A. NO CHANGE
    B. how it were to fly
    C. how to fly
    D. how flying it were

42. F. NO CHANGE
    G. figure, amazing eights
    H. amazing, figure eights
    J. amazing-figure-eights

43. A. NO CHANGE
    B. I crashed, that
    C. I crashed which
    D. I crashed—which

44. F. NO CHANGE
    G. Since that day, I, though
    H. Since that day, though
    J. Since that day, I though

once thought the hobby to be a boring one. |45|

> Question 45 asks about the preceding passage as a whole.

45. Suppose the author's main purpose had been to share how he came to acquire a new hobby. Would this essay accomplish that purpose?

   A. Yes, because the essay details how the author's uncle introduced him to stunt kite flying, a hobby he continued to learn.
   B. Yes, because the essay compares and contrasts the various hobbies the author has tried over the course of many years.
   C. No, because the essay never mentions that the author himself ever flies a stunt kite.
   D. No, because the main focus of the essay is the author's uncle and his difficulty learning to fly a stunt kite.

# Step 3 Correct Answers

| Passage I | Passage II | Passage III |
|---|---|---|
| 1: B | 16: H | 31: B |
| 2: F | 17: D | 32: J |
| 3: C | 18: J | 33: A |
| 4: J | 19: A | 34: G |
| 5: C | 20: F | 35: B |
| 6: J | 21: D | 36: H |
| 7: B | 22: H | 37: A |
| 8: H | 23: D | 38: J |
| 9: A | 24: F | 39: C |
| 10: G | 25: C | 40: G |
| 11: D | 26: G | 41: C |
| 12: G | 27: B | 42: F |
| 13: A | 28: J | 43: D |
| 14: H | 29: C | 44: G |
| 15: D | 30: F | 45: A |

Stumped on any? You will find the explanations for each answer beginning on page 139.

# STEP 4

*Verbs*

We will break this Step down into two parts regarding verbs: subject/verb agreement and proper verb tense.

## Subject/Verb Agreement

The ACT wants you to recognize which verb to properly match with a given subject, and which subject to properly match with a given verb. This is called "subject verb agreement" and is best illustrated with a few examples (see if you can correctly choose of the two choices in bold):

    a) My dog's food, made of only the finest ingredients, **is/are** pretty expensive.

    b) The pack of deer, made up of bucks, does, and fawns, **was/were** eating my grass.

    c) The **snake/snakes**, which, if my wife would have known, would have scared her to death, was slithering through the front yard.

    d) **Women/A woman** are more likely to buy a pair of shoes online.

Can you see in A/B which verb is correct, and in C/D which subject is correct? If you can't, it is helpful to strip away all nonessential material, prepositions, dependent clauses, etc. and simplify the sentence as much as you possibly can. The ACT will often put a distance between the subject and the verb to make it more difficult for you to find the correct answer.

    a) My dog's food (*singular noun*)…**is** pretty expensive.

    - *Here, "ingredients" isn't what is expensive, but the singular "food"*

    b) The **pack** (*singular!*) of deer…**was** eating my grass.

    c) The **snake**…**was slithering** (*singular verb*).

    d) **Women are** (*plural verb*) more likely…

## Verb Tense

Similarly, the ACT will test your ability to recognize the proper verb tense (for simplicity's sake, past, present, or future) that ought to be used in a sentence. For example:

    a) All through the baseball game, Jacob would jump up and **drop/drops** his popcorn.

    b) I am determined that, when I turn 16, I **will get/got** my driver's license.

c) My sister will drive to the store and, if they have fresh blueberries, **bought/will buy** me some.

d) My cat was walking along the fence until a stupid, aggressive terrier named "Chuck" ran up to her and **had been barking/barked**, causing her to jump down.

a) All through the baseball game, Jacob **would jump up** and **drop** his popcorn.

-*Here, we are dealing with past tense (specifically past perfect); "drops" is present tense!*

b) I **am determined** that, when I turn 16, **I will get** my driver's license.

c) My sister **will drive (*future tense*)** to the store and, if they have fresh blueberries, **will buy (*also future tense, thus correct*)** me some.

d) My cat **was walking (*past progressive*)** along the fence until a stupid, aggressive terrier named "Chuck" ran up to her and **barked**, causing her to jump down.

- *"had been barking" (which is the past perfect progressive tense) would only work if it said, "My cat had been walking."*

Think you can identify these and properly choose the correct verb or subject? I hope so, because that is the fourth most tested skill on the ACT.

*Step 4*

# *Step 4 Mini-Lesson: Correct Vocabulary and Idioms*

## Vocabulary

On occasion, the ACT will ask a question that requires you to choose the correct word based on its actual meaning (vocabulary). You should be able to spot these based on the context of the sentence. However, the options are usually pretty similar sounding, which are designed to confuse you. Here is an example:

> The magician created an **illustration/allusion/elution/illusion** when he pretended to saw my little sister in half.

Here, we need the word of the four that means "something that appears one way but is in fact another." In this case, it is *illusion*.

This kind of thing (as we've touched on a bit) is also seen with (and within) *phrases*. In other words, some phrases sound very similar, but only one is correct based on the sentence's context. For example:

> The professional is **better then/more better than/more better then/better than** the amateur.

Here the ACT would be playing on the similar sounding nature of two different words (than/then) but also adding on your ability to identify the proper adjective or adjective phrase. Here, the correct choice would be: The professional is **better than** the amateur. This is because "more better" makes no sense and "then" implies time moving along (like, one thing happened, *then* another).

## Idioms

In any language, there are groups of words that always go together. These are called idioms. The ACT may test your ability to be confident enough to choose words that always go together. Here is an example:

> **Once upon the time/Once on a time/Once upon a time/At one point upon a time** there was a princess who was kidnapped by a dragon.

Is there really anything grammatically better about "Once upon a time" compared to any of these other choices? Not really, but that is the phrase that is used to introduce fairy tales, so it is the correct option.

*The following practice passages are heavy on Step 4, but include Steps 3, 2, and 1.*

## PASSAGE I

### Norman Rockwell, American Artist

Some artists have chased trends or relied upon over-the-top details, colors, or gimmicks to garner attention. Norman Rockwell was not an artist of this sort. <u>Rather</u> Rockwell acquired fame for his art due to
<sub>1</sub>

his ability to create realistic pieces <u>as to depicting</u>
<sub>2</sub>
simple truths and situations in profound, yet

straightforward, ways. |3|

1. **A.** NO CHANGE
   **B.** He rather
   **C.** He, rather,
   **D.** Rather,

2. **F.** NO CHANGE
   **G.** then depict
   **H.** that depicted
   **J.** of depicting

3. At this point, the author is considering adding the following true statement:

   > As is quoted in Beowulf, "Fame after death is the noblest of goals," and artists of all sorts have sought after this goal.

   Should the writer make this addition here?

   **A.** Yes, because the topic of the paragraph is how Rockwell carries on the traditions of various works.
   **B.** Yes, because the preceding sentence speaks about the fame the Rockwell was able to gain.
   **C.** No, because the sentence shifts the focus away from Rockwell and his art.
   **D.** No, because Rockwell was not famous after his death, which has previously been stated.

In 1913, Rockwell was only 18 when he earned <u>his paying, first job</u> as an artist. He was hired by the
<sub>4</sub>
Boy Scouts of America and was paid $50 per month

to produce a cover for their magazine <u>*Boy's Life* and a
<sub>5</sub>
set of illustrations for a story within it.</u> His first cover,
<sub>5</sub>

*Scout at Ship's Wheel,* <u>remains today</u> as one of his
<sub>6</sub>
most valuable works.

4. **F.** NO CHANGE
   **G.** his first paying job
   **H.** was paid
   **J.** he was being paid

5. **A.** NO CHANGE
   **B.** *Boy's Life*, all of which happened when Rockwell was only 18 years of age!
   **C.** *Boy's Life* and was only paid $50.
   **D.** *Boy's Life* for the Boy Scouts of America.

6. **F.** NO CHANGE
   **G.** still remains
   **H.** remains to this day
   **J.** remains

Amazingly, he was promoted to art editor for the
                    7
magazine prior to his 20th birthday. This was a role that he maintained for more than three years, and the Boy Scouts, even though he eventually stepped away, was featured often in his work. For the following 47
        8
years, Rockwell produced covers for *The Saturday Evening Post, and was* frequently hired to do the
                       9
same for various publications throughout his career.

Rockwell attempted to enlist with the U.S. Navy
                         10
during the first World War, but he turned away for
                                11
being underweight. That evening, he gorged himself on food and drink, returned to the recruiting office again the next day, and was deemed fit to join. Though he served as an artist who drew for the
                            12
military and never participated in combat, he was willing to serve in any capacity to help the cause. It was this same spirit that, coupled with a speech by President Roosevelt, inspired and motivated him to
                       13
to paint his now famous collection titled *Four Freedoms*.

Norman Rockwell would produce over 4,000 original pieces of art in his lifetime. Many of them depict aspects of American culture, but some (such as *The Problem We All Live With* and *Murder in Mississippi*) intend to awaken the consciences of
              14
everyday Americans. Many of these pieces are held in Stockbridge, Massachusetts at the Norman

7. **A.** NO CHANGE
   **B.** was being promoted
   **C.** is promoted
   **D.** was receiving a promotion

8. **F.** NO CHANGE
   **G.** to be featured often
   **H.** was often featured
   **J.** were often featured

9. **A.** NO CHANGE
   **B.** *Post*, he was
   **C.** *Post* and was
   **D.** *Post* and he was

10. **F.** NO CHANGE
    **G.** exist
    **H.** insist
    **J.** in list

11. **A.** NO CHANGE
    **B.** he was turned away
    **C.** he turned them away
    **D.** they, being turned away,

12. **F.** NO CHANGE
    **G.** artist who draws
    **H.** artist
    **J.** artist drawing

13. **A.** NO CHANGE
    **B.** was an absolute inspiration for
    **C.** pushed him inwardly
    **D.** moved

14. **F.** NO CHANGE
    **G.** intend
    **H.** intends to
    **J.** intends

Rockwell Museum, which houses the largest collection of his work.

> Question 15 asks about the preceding passage as a whole.

15. Suppose the author's main purpose had been to write a brief essay focusing on the history of American art. Would this essay accomplish that purpose?

    A. Yes, because Norman Rockwell was an American artist, and the museum that safeguards much of his work is in America as well.
    B. Yes, because although the essay focuses mostly on one artist, the essay is written chronologically.
    C. No, because Norman Rockwell, while having lived most of his life in America, was born in Toronto, Canada.
    D. No, because the essay focuses on the life and art of one artist alone.

---

## PASSAGE II

### The Challenger Deep

It has been said that there is only one place on planet earth that is yet to be thoroughly explored, and that were its oceans. This is certainly true of the
                                    16

deepest and farthest down area of the ocean: the
              17
Mariana Trench, which is over a mile deeper than Mount Everest is tall. The deepest part of this trench is called *Challenger Deep; but only* a handful of
                                        18
brave souls have descended to the bottom of *Challenger Deep* in protective research submarines.

16. F. NO CHANGE
    G. that is
    H. that being
    J. which are

17. A. NO CHANGE
    B. deepest area
    C. more deeper and farther down area
    D. area

18. F. NO CHANGE
    G. *Deep,* only
    H. *Deep*; and only
    J. *Deep*; only

The first manned visit to the bottom of the Mariana Trench occurred in 1960 by Don Walsh of the United States and Jacques Piccard of Switzerland. They descended over 10,900 meters into the *Challenger Deep*; despite hearing a loud *crack* on the way down, they decided to carry on. At the bottom,

Walsh and Piccard claimed to have observe a flatfish, which scientists dispute, and other marine life as well. When the pair discovered cracks in the windows of the vessel, they cut their voyage shortly and ascended to the surface.

Incredibly the next explorer to reach the bottom of the *Challenger Deep* did not do so until over 50 years after Walsh and Picard. This happened in 2012 when filmmaker James Cameron, known for directing movies such as *The Terminator* and *Avatar*, descended alone by himself in a submarine he designed himself. Despite the failure of a few instruments on the way down due to the extreme pressure—the dive was a success. Cameron spent a

19. A. NO CHANGE
    B. Trench, having occurred
    C. Trench is sure to occur
    D. Trench is hoping to be occurring

20. Given that all of the choices are true, which of the following phrases most effectively communicates not only the danger of the voyage, but the courage of the two explorers?
    F. NO CHANGE
    G. this is nearly seven miles below the surface of the ocean.
    H. there are numerable dangerous creatures in the ocean, such as sharks, rays, and jellyfish.
    J. as the pair descended—which took a few hours—they busied themselves by monitoring equipment and gauges.

21. A. NO CHANGE
    B. have observed
    C. claiming to observe
    D. claimed to have observed

22. F. NO CHANGE
    G. cut their voyage short
    H. were cutting their voyage shortly
    J. cut their voyage low

23. A. NO CHANGE
    B. The incredible Cameron
    C. Incredibly,
    D. In an incredible way

24. F. NO CHANGE
    G. solo
    H. without anyone else
    J. solitarily and companionless

25. A. NO CHANGE
    B. pressure: the
    C. pressure, the
    D. pressure, and the

total of three hours, on the ocean floor.
                    26

As of 2021, these are the only three people to have reached the deepest, darkest point in the ocean, which is nine less than the number of people to have
27

walked on the moon! [28] Needless to say, the age of exploration is far from over. What creatures and other

wonders of nature waited to be discovered in the
                          29
depths of the Mariana Trench? It will be up to a new generation of explorers to find out.

26. F. NO CHANGE
    G. hours—on the ocean floor.
    H. hours on the ocean floor.
    J. down there.

27. A. NO CHANGE
    B. which were
    C. which will be
    D. which was to be

28. At this point, the writer is considering adding the following true statement:

    Neil Armstrong was the first man to walk on the moon; perhaps he was an inspiration to Walsh and Piccard.

    Should the statement be added here?

    F. Yes, because it helps the reader make connections between various explorers.
    G. Yes, because the paragraph questions the identities of those who have landed on the moon.
    H. No, because the information is irrelevant and distracts from the essay's primary focus.
    J. No, because the essay makes no mention of if Walsh, Piccard, and Cameron ever had aspirations to explore the moon.

29. A. NO CHANGE
    B. have waited
    C. are waiting
    D. is

Question 30 asks about the preceding passage as a whole.

30. Suppose the author's main purpose had been to explain in depth the technology behind and the purposes of various instruments aboard protective submarines. Would this essay accomplish that purpose?

    F. Yes, because to reach the *Challenger Deep*, precision instruments are necessary.
    G. Yes, because the author mentions how Cameron's submarine lost instruments as it descended.
    H. No, because although the essay mentions such instruments, it fails to describe them in detail.
    J. No, because the essay proved that such instruments are unnecessary and a burden to explorers.

## PASSAGE III

### The Pont du Gard

[1]

Visitors, to France, are likely to see the Eiffel Tower, the Louvre Museum, or Notre Dame Cathedral. However, there is a site in Southern France that deserves recognition from both visitors and natives alike: the Pont du Gard, having to be an aqueduct bridge estimated to be over 2,000 years old.

[A] The bridge crosses the Gardon River, and today is listed as a UNESCO World Heritage Site.

[2]

Aqueducts were constructed by the Romans throughout their empire. Their primary purpose was to carry water from one location to another using gravity alone. [B] The Pont du Gard aqueduct is a supreme example of the brilliance of Roman engineering. The bridge, though over 900 feet in length, can descend merely 1 inch from one side to the other!

[3]

Another architectural, noteworthy feature of the bridge worthy of note is its arches, of which there are

**31.**
- A. NO CHANGE
- B. Visitors to France are
- C. Visitors, to France are
- D. Visitors to France,

**32.**
- F. NO CHANGE
- G. Gard, which will be
- H. Gard, which was
- J. Gard, which is

**33.**
- A. NO CHANGE
- B. River and
- C. River—
- D. River, but

**34.**
- F. NO CHANGE
- G. all of their occupied land.
- H. the regions of Europe, West Asia, and Northern Africa that they had conquered.
- J. the places that they could claim as their territory.

**35.** Which of the following alternatives to the underlined portion would NOT be acceptable?

- A. the delivery of
- B. delivering
- C. to deliver
- D. having delivered

**36.**
- F. NO CHANGE
- G. descend
- H. is descending
- J. descends

**37.**
- A. NO CHANGE
- B. noteworthy, architectural feature
- C. noteworthy feature
- D. architectural feature

three tires. The lowest and middle rows contain 6 and
38

11 arches, respectively, all of which are over 65 feet
                39
in height. The top layer contains 35 smaller arches, each of which reaches a height of 23 feet. Due to its ability to undoubtedly distribute weight and force, it
              40
is the arch that has contributed to the longevity of the Pont du Gard. [C]

[4]

The actual composition of the bridge is also astonishing. The stones that make up the Pont du Gard were precisely cut into blocks designed to perfectly stack up one on top of the other really high.
              41
These limestone bricks were immensely heavy, weighing up to six tons apiece. [D] However, the Romans had mastered the ability to lift such blocks by a system of cranes and pulleys.

[5]

With the fall of the Roman Empire came the end of the Pont du Gard as an aqueduct; maintenance proved too difficult for peoples and governments
42
throughout history. Its use as a toll bridge throughout

38. F. NO CHANGE
    G. tiers.
    H. tears.
    J. tries.

39. A. NO CHANGE
    B. arches respectively, all of which
    C. arches, respectively all of which,
    D. arches respectively all of which

40. Which of the following placements for the underlined portion makes it clear that the timeless nature of the aqueduct can be attributed primarily to the arch?

    F. Where it is now
    G. After the word *has*
    H. After the word *distribute*
    J. After the word *longevity*

41. Which choice most effectively provides further evidence for the notion that Roman engineering was brilliant and ahead of its time?

    A. NO CHANGE
    B. and imprecisely fit together.
    C. fit together without the use of mortar.
    D. withstand rain and wind but not the test of time.

42. F. NO CHANGE
    G. proves
    H. continues to prove
    J. will have proved

Step 4   61

the centuries, on the other hand, has guaranteed some
                                    43

level of maintenance. |44|

43. A. NO CHANGE
    B. will guarantee
    C. guaranteeing
    D. to guarantee

44. Given that all of the following statements are true, which one, if added here, would best conclude the paragraph and the essay?

    F. Toll bridges are found all over the world.
    G. It is not too difficult to imagine that maintaining bridges takes skilled engineers.
    H. Ultimately, it is up to each one of us to remember all of the reasons for the fall of Rome.
    J. Today, the Pont du Gard is legally protected, and will hopefully survive for the enjoyment of future generations.

Question 45 asks about the preceding passage as a whole.

45. The writer is considering adding the following sentence to the essay:

    Aqueducts were thus meticulously constructed to run at a slight incline from the point of water to a populated end point.

    If the writer were to add this sentence, it would most logically be placed at:

    A. Point A in Paragraph 1.
    B. Point B in Paragraph 2.
    C. Point C in Paragraph 3.
    D. Point D in Paragraph 4.

# Step 4 Correct Answers

| **Passage I** | **Passage II** | **Passage III** |
|---|---|---|
| 1: D | 16: G | 31: B |
| 2: H | 17: B | 32: J |
| 3: C | 18: J | 33: B |
| 4: G | 19: A | 34: F |
| 5: A | 20: F | 35: D |
| 6: J | 21: D | 36: J |
| 7: A | 22: G | 37: D |
| 8: J | 23: C | 38: G |
| 9: C | 24: G | 39: A |
| 10: F | 25: C | 40: G |
| 11: B | 26: H | 41: C |
| 12: H | 27: A | 42: F |
| 13: D | 28: H | 43: A |
| 14: F | 29: C | 44: J |
| 15: D | 30: H | 45: B |

Stumped on any? You will find the explanations for each answer beginning on page 147.

# STEP 5

*Sentence Structure and Meaning*

Here, the phrase "sentence structure and meaning" is being used broadly. Yes, anything that affects a sentence could probably be grouped under this umbrella. However, I am referring to a couple of specific problems the ACT wants you to identify: a) Punctuation and word use that makes something a non-sentence, and b) identifying words and phrases that actually give a sentence the meaning that is intended or needed.

## Sentence Structure

Let's keep this simple. Sometimes, the wording of a sentence renders it not a sentence at all, but rather some kind of sentence fragment, run on, or nonsense. For example:

> When the Beatles, who had built up an overseas audience, famously landed in America, they brought <u>a nation along with</u> its knees.

Read that sentence again; remember the skill to *listen*? Does that "sound" like a sentence that functions to you? Did they bring a nation to America, as well as bring along some knees on the plane? That doesn't make sense. It is nonsense. The sentence of course should say, "…they brought <u>a nation to</u> its knees." Here's another example:

> Although they never found the treasure they were looking for, the pirates discovered <u>caves. Previously unknown</u> to man; today they are known as "Blackbeard's Caverns."

This is the kind of questions in which students are quick to put "NO CHANGE" because the period that comes after "caves" forms a complete sentence. However, the second sentence beginning with "Previously unknown" makes no sense at all. The semi-colon in the second sentence is unchangeable, so something about the underlined portion has to be changed. That is why the sentence should say, "Although they never found the treasure they were looking for, the pirates discovered <u>caves previously unknown</u> to man; today they are known as Blackbeard's Caverns."

You see? The main skill you need is the ability to *listen* to the sentence and spy out nonsense.

## Sentence Meaning

The skill that helps you determine whether or not a sentence belongs, or whether or not a phrase is the right phrase, or where a certain word belongs in a sentence (Step 1) is the same skill that is necessary here: *identifying the BEST answer based on context.* In other words, a sentence or a group of sentences *need* to say one thing *based on context*, but say something different. The ACT is testing here your ability to identify the *best* answer, but on a smaller scale, or sometimes the only possible correct answer. Let's break this into three smaller categories: a) Correct transitions ("connector words") between sentences or clauses, b) Correct pronoun use, and c) Correct prepositional phrase use.

### a) Correct transitions - words or phrases to connect sentences or clauses

Transitions are words or phrases like "However," "Because," "For this reason," "Instead," etc. These phrases *transition* thoughts and create a relationship between sentences. You need to be able to identify which one is the *best* based on context. Here is an example:

> The pirate was going to sail the Seven Seas. Because of this, he went to the mall.

Nothing grammatically incorrect here; the problem is one of context. What is needed is a word or phrase to begin the second sentence that implies contrast between the two sentences. As it is written, it makes it sound like the pirate's initial plan to sail *caused him* to go to the mall. But surely that's not what is being implied; what we need instead is a word or phrase to start the second sentence that tells the reader that there was a change of plan. Thus, it should say something like this: "The pirate was going to sail the Seven Seas. Instead, he went to the mall."

### b) Correct pronoun use

A pronoun is a word (like he, she, them, those, etc.) that refers to a person or persons or thing or things. A singular pronoun (like "it") can only refer to a singular thing (like "the watermelon"), and of course a plural pronoun (like "them") can only refer to plural things (like "the seeds in the watermelon"). Sometimes, it is a choice between the proper use of singular pronouns (it, he, etc.) or plural ones (them, those, they, etc.). Here is an example:

> The way you know if you've stumbled across a pirate treasure chest filled with gold coins and silver goblets is to examine them closely.

At first it seems like there is nothing wrong here. "Them" is a plural pronoun, and we have plural nouns like "coins" and "goblets." However, what needs to be examined closely? Not the coins and goblets, but the chest itself, thus the appropriate choice would be "it," not "them."

This can also come up with the essay's "POV", or Point of View. For example, look at these two sentences:

> I am going to the concert; I don't care what Mom says. She thinks I'm too young, but I have something to say to that: "She's a teenager now!"

Nothing grammatical here, but does the pronoun *she* really work there? No; the essay and sentence are in first person ("I"), and I don't think the daughter is telling her Mom that *she* (the mother) is a teenager now. Thus, what is need there is this: "I'm a teenager now!"

### c) Correct prepositional phrase use

Just like identifying the proper phrase in a sentence earlier, we can apply that same thinking to a smaller kind of phrase, a prepositional phrase. Prepositions are things like "at," "to," "under," etc., and they specify something's action or location. Thus, you might say, "I looked under the bed for a monster," or, "My sister plays solitaire in the house in her room by the window. All of those phrases work, but check out this example:

> Scurvy, which results from Vitamin C deficiency, is a common problem among pirates, who forget to pack oranges at their suitcases.

Well, do you pack something "at" a suitcase? No, of course this should read, "...who forget to pack oranges *in* their suitcases."

# *Step 5 Mini-Lesson: Modifying Clauses*

You know that adjectives can describe a noun (the <u>green</u> ball), and adverbs can describe a verb or how something is done (she kicked the ball <u>aggressively</u>). However, there is a clause that does this: a modifying clause. Look at the following example, which is written correctly:

<u>Watching television in the evenings,</u> Dad relaxes in the chair.

What is underlined here is called a "modifying clause," and it *modifies* (or you could say, describes) what comes immediately after the comma: "Dad." It is clear from the sentence that *Dad* relaxes in his chair *by watching television*. What would happen, however, if we rewrote it like this?

<u>Watching television in the evenings</u>, the chair is where Dad relaxes.

Do you see what's wrong? The way that it is written, it sounds like *the chair* (which comes immediately after the comma) is *watching television in the evenings*. Unless your chair is alive and has eyeballs, I doubt it is watching television. Can you see what is wrong, then, with these three examples?

    a) Admiring the clouds, the sky seemed different that day.

    b) After winning The Masters for the first time, the success of Tiger Woods seemed inevitable.

    c) Leaning over to touch my toes, my fitness needed some work.

All three of them make the same mistake: what comes after the comma in each is incapable of the *modifying clause* that comes before the comma. In a), the problem is that "the sky" can't admire the clouds. In b) the problem is that "the success of Tiger Woods" didn't win The Masters. In c), "my fitness" didn't lean over to touch my toes. They should look like this (keeping the modifying clauses the same):

    a) Admiring the clouds, he noticed that the sky seemed different that day.

    b) After winning The Masters for the first time, Tiger Woods seemed destined for success.

    c) Leaning over to touch my toes, I noticed that my fitness needed some work.

*The following practice passages are heavier on Step 5, but includes of course Steps 4, 3, 2, and 1.*

## PASSAGE I

### Steve Irwin, Crocodile Hunter

*Crikey!* is an exclamation you've probably heard, but <u>does he</u> know who popularized the word? His
      1
name was Steve Irwin, and he gained international fame through his television series *The Crocodile Hunter.* <u>Which</u> aired worldwide for over a decade.
        2
Steve was a native Australian whose fun-loving and addictive personality gained and raptured the attention <u>of the world.</u>
         3

Steve never enjoyed the spotlight or sought after <u>attention from other people</u>, but he was happy if it
        4
was a means to promote his conservation efforts. His philosophy <u>was: simple,</u> if you show people how
              5
wonderful nature is, you won't have to preach environmentalism to them. <u>Thus,</u> Steve was willing
                          6
to flash his trademark smile and confront wild (and sometimes dangerous) animals for the cameras.

Steve learned to work with all kinds of animals, even crocodiles, as a young boy. <u>Because, his parents</u>
                                               7
<u>were the owners</u> of the Australia Zoo, a 700 acre
        7

1. A. NO CHANGE
   B. do he
   C. do you
   D. does you

2. F. NO CHANGE
   G. *Hunter*, which
   H. *Hunter*, this
   J. *Hunter*; which

3. A. NO CHANGE
   B. in the world.
   C. at the entire world.
   D. of the whole world.

4. F. NO CHANGE
   G. them
   H. it
   J. attention

5. A. NO CHANGE
   B. was; simple,
   C. was simple,
   D. was simple:

6. Which of the following alternatives to the underlined portion would NOT be acceptable?

   F. Rather,
   G. Because of this,
   H. Hence,
   J. For this reason,

7. A. NO CHANGE
   B. Because his parents were the owners
   C. Because, his parents, were the owners
   D. Because they owned

facility in Queensland, he had access to them all. [8]

Eventually, Steve gained ownership of the zoo and

shares it with his wife, Terri. The couple was so
9

unwaveringly committed to the cause of
10

environmentalism that all of the dollars generated by
11

television and other media funneled were they back
12
into the zoo.

  Irwin was also a man of great courage and love

of people. In 2003 he was filming a documentary on

sea lions in Mexico. Upon hearing a message come
13
through the radio saying that two scuba divers were
13
missing in the area, the search was on, and the crew
13
got to work. They were able to assist one of the
13
missing divers, who was found perched on a rock.

8. At this point, the author is considering adding the following true statement:

> This included crocodiles, which are some of the most dangerous and fear-inducing animals on the planet.

Should the writer make this addition here?

 F. Yes, because it foreshadows Steve's future work with crocodiles.
 G. Yes, because it helps to further induce fear in the reader, which is the primary purpose of the paragraph as a whole.
 H. No, because, as is stated earlier in the essay, the Australia Zoo never held crocodiles because they were too dangerous.
 J. No, because the sentence is redundant and distracts the reader from the paragraph's purpose.

9. A. NO CHANGE
 B. shared
 C. share
 D. to share

10. F. NO CHANGE
 G. at a cause for
 H. for the cause at
 J. from a cause to

11. A. NO CHANGE
 B. the entire sum of all the money
 C. the funds
 D. DELETE the underlined portion

12. F. NO CHANGE
 G. were funneled
 H. funneled are
 J. will be funneled

13. A. NO CHANGE
 B. A message hearing came through the radio, two scuba divers were missing, and the search was on in the area by the crew.
 C. The crew heard a message, it came through the radio, saying that two scuba divers were missing in the area, and they stopped production to help in the search.
 D. A message came through the radio saying that two scuba divers were missing in the area, and immediately the crew aided in the search.

Tragically, Steve lost his life at the young age of

54 in 2006 filming around the Great Barrier Reef,
          14

and while snorkeling in shallow waters, he was

pierced by a stingray barb. The world mourned the

loss of the man who many saw as the face of

worldwide conservation efforts. |15|

14. F. NO CHANGE
    G. 54 in 2006, filming
    H. 54. In 2006 filming,
    J. 54. In 2006, he was filming

15. Given that all of the following statements are true, which one, if added here, would best conclude the paragraph and the essay?

    A. You can still carry on Steve's legacy by visiting the Australia Zoo, which, to this day, is owned and operated by Terri and their two children.
    B. Conservation has grown in popularity over the last few decades.
    C. To this day, crocodiles remain popular with children across the world, and any zoo that has them is sure to draw a crowd (and maybe a camera as well)!
    D. The Great Barrier Reef, located off of the coast of Australia, is under legal protection, and is home to countless animal species.

## PASSAGE II

### The Theory of Beauty

I don't see sunsets in the same way others do.

This is within the forest, a stream, a sunrise, or the
         16

night sky as well. What most people see when they

look at any of these beautiful sights is just that: one

sight. I on the other hand, have trained myself to first
     17

breakdown a scene into colors and shapes, then to

find the contrasts, then finally to see the bigger

picture. I have had this innate ability since a young

16. F. NO CHANGE
    G. true of
    H. to become
    J. only about

17. A. NO CHANGE
    B. I on the other hand have
    C. I, on the other hand, have
    D. I, on the other hand have

Step 5   73

age, and it has led me to study the theory of art.
                    18
One topic in art of all forms that has long

fascinated me is the question of beauty and its
                 ―――――――――――――――――――――
                              19
relationship with color. There are colors and
―――――――――――――――
       19
combinations of colors that, when isolated, appear

very beautiful indeed, but others however, appear
               ―――――――――――――
                    20
ugly or detestable. Most people would rather stare at

a gradient of blue morphing into yellow than at a

swirl of grey and black that intermixes, for example.
                  ―――――――――――――――――――――
                             21
However, if one adds a pattern of pink into the grey/

black image, the beholder's inclinations change

dramatically; all of a sudden, they find it to be
                                ―――――――
                                   22
beautiful.

   Interesting: preferences in aesthetics go far
   ――――――――――――――――――
              23
beyond colors and appear to be universal. For

example, architecture that displays skill, curves,

arches, and both acute and obtuse angles are

preferred by most when compared to a simple

building that is built in its entirety in right angles. I
                                       ―――――――――――――
                                             24
find this fascinating because right angles are not only

common, but is both efficient and simple in the
        ――――――
          25
construction of a building.

   I have studied the world of color and art. With
                                    ―――――――――――
                                          26
intensity and interest over the course of a lifetime. I
―――――――
   26

18. F. NO CHANGE
    G. has lead me
    H. will lead me
    J. have led me

19. Which choice best introduces the subject of the paragraph and the rest of the essay?
    A. NO CHANGE
    B. is whether or not people recognize the true beauty in others.
    C. is the theme of piercing light in the history of film.
    D. is how people, like myself, have come to be interested in this topic in the first place.

20. F. NO CHANGE
    G. indeed, but, others,
    H. indeed but others
    J. indeed, but others,

21. A. NO CHANGE
    B. black,
    C. black which intermixes
    D. mixing up black

22. F. NO CHANGE
    G. they found
    H. he or she found
    J. he or she finds

23. A. NO CHANGE
    B. Interesting preferences,
    C. Preferences interestingly
    D. Interestingly, preferences

24. F. NO CHANGE
    G. of right angles.
    H. at right angles.
    J. for right angles.

25. A. NO CHANGE
    B. but they are
    C. for is
    D. for they are

26. F. NO CHANGE
    G. and art with intensity
    H. and art, with intensity
    J. and intense art

Step 5   74

have designed the interiors of some of the world's most magnificent and grandiose homes. I have consulted <u>over the construction</u> of magnificent
27
galleries and headquarters for Fortune 500 companies. I have given lectures on the topic on every continent <u>except for the Southernmost, really</u>
28
<u>icy landmass.</u> In short, I have a lot of experience in
28
the world of art. I have, therefore, concluded that beauty is not just something in the eye of the beholder, nor is it merely a matter of opinion. Beauty *exists*, <u>and we</u> human beings are hardwired not only
29
to see it, notice it, or create it, but to experience it.

27. A. NO CHANGE
    B. on top of the construction
    C. in the construction
    D. under construction

28. F. NO CHANGE
    G. but Antarctica.
    H. apart from the continent down there.
    J. except for Antarctica, which is at the Southernmost tip of the globe.

29. A. NO CHANGE
    B. but all the
    C. although every
    D. and, in total, the

Question 30 asks about the preceding passage as a whole.

30. Suppose the author's main purpose had been to explain to a friend why she found the study of the theories of art and beauty to be both fascinating and worthwhile. Would this essay accomplish that purpose?

    F. Yes, because the essay is written from a first person point of view and uses color and architecture as examples of topics in these fields.
    G. Yes, because the essay is not written in the form of an essay, but rather it takes the form of a letter addressed to a friend.
    H. No, because the author insists that beauty is not in the "eye of the beholder," thus other people have to experience beauty in their own time.
    J. No, because the author clearly states that the intermixing of various colors can be both "ugly and detestable."

## PASSAGE III

### An Inventor's Childhood

Alexander Graham Bell is best known for his invention of the telephone. |31| There were three aspects of his childhood that all came together to make his future breakthrough possible. There was his mother's hearing disability and his father's work. Second, his parents and neighbors supported his curiosities and inventing spirit inside of him. Lastly, he possessed a natural genius that he refused to squander, rather, he used it for good.

Alexander's mother was nearly deaf. This more than anything awakened his curiosity about human speaking and hearing. Even so, as a boy, he developed a talent for voice throwing and ventriloquism that happily entertained family and friends in addition. His father, uncle, and grandfather were all specialists in elocution and teaching communication to the deaf. It seemed that the future

31. At this point, the author is considering adding the following true statement:

   In many respects, it was his upbringing that prepared him for this triumphant invention.

   Should the writer make this addition here?

   A. Yes, because Alexander Graham Bell invented the telephone as a child, as is stated later in the paragraph.
   B. Yes, because it transitions the subject of the essay to Bell's childhood.
   C. No, because the sentence implies that the invention of the telephone was "triumphant," an opinion not yet established in the essay.
   D. No, because the sentences that follow make no mention of his upbringing.

32. F. NO CHANGE
    G. Although, there
    H. First, there
    J. Except, there

33. A. NO CHANGE
    B. inventing spirit.
    C. the inventing spirit inside of him.
    D. a spirit of invention that had taken root in his spirit.

34. F. NO CHANGE
    G. squander rather:
    H. squander—rather
    J. squander; rather,

35. A. NO CHANGE
    B. very close to being unable to hear at all.
    C. almost unable to listen to everything.
    D. practically finding it impossible to hear.

36. F. NO CHANGE
    G. On the other hand,
    H. In fact,
    J. Be that as it may,

37. A. NO CHANGE
    B. friends, in addition, his
    C. friends in addition his
    D. friends. In addition, his

inventor of the telephone was one way or another destined of working over the realm of hearing.
                                        38

Alexander's parents also encouraged him to invent, to tinker, and he finds solutions to problems
                                                          39
from an early age. His curiosity about the natural world was tremendous, by commonly gathering plant
                                                      40
species and use them in science experiments.

Growing up in Scotland, a flour mill was run by
                              41
Alexander's neighbors, the Herdman family. Ben
                              41
Herdman was his best friend, and Alexander spent a lot of time around their operation. At the age of 12, young Alexander invented a dehusking device that was used by the family for a number of years in their
          42
mill. As a sort of reward or payment, Mr. Herdman created a space in which the two boys could invent and run science experiments.

It was clear to all that young Alexander had a brilliant mind. In fact with no training he mastered
                    43
the piano when he was but a child. Alexander was the type of boy who had the intelligence to do whatever he wanted, as long as he worked hard. Because of his mother's hearing issues, Alexander was naturally fascinated with acoustics, and thus applied her genius
                                              44

38. F. NO CHANGE
    G. to work within
    H. within to work inside of
    J. to be working all in

39. A. NO CHANGE
    B. he found
    C. he was finding
    D. to find

40. F. NO CHANGE
    G. tremendous, and by commonly gathering
    H. tremendous; he would commonly gather
    J. tremendous, for to be commonly gather

41. A. NO CHANGE
    B. Running a flour mill, Alexander grew up next to the family in Scotland that did so: the Herdman family.
    C. Growing up in Scotland, Alexander was neighbors with the Herdman family, who ran a flour mill.
    D. Being neighbors with Alexander, the flour mill was run by the Herdman family in Scotland.

42. F. NO CHANGE
    G. were used by the family
    H. to be in use with the family
    J. was using the family

43. A. NO CHANGE
    B. In fact, with no training,
    C. As a matter of fact: with no training,
    D. With no, in fact, training,

44. F. NO CHANGE
    G. their
    H. his or her
    J. his

Step 5  77

to that particular field. |45|

**45.** Given that all of the statements are true, which one, if added here, would best conclude the paragraph and the essay by referring back to the opening paragraph?

- **A.** Children are capable of more than society gives them credit for.
- **B.** As they say, "The family that plays together, stays together," and as Alexander became better at the piano, the closer his family became.
- **C.** If Alexander had never invented the dehusking device for his neighbors, it is unlikely the telephone would have ever been invented.
- **D.** As a consequence, everyone benefits from Alexander Graham Bell's breakthrough invention.

# Step 5 Correct Answers

| **Passage I** | **Passage II** | **Passage III** |
|---|---|---|
| 1: C | 16: G | 31: B |
| 2: G | 17: C | 32: H |
| 3: A | 18: F | 33: B |
| 4: H | 19: A | 34: J |
| 5: D | 20: J | 35: A |
| 6: F | 21: B | 36: H |
| 7: B | 22: J | 37: D |
| 8: J | 23: D | 38: G |
| 9: B | 24: H | 39: D |
| 10: F | 25: B | 40: H |
| 11: C | 26: G | 41: C |
| 12: G | 27: C | 42: F |
| 13: D | 28: G | 43: B |
| 14: J | 29: A | 44: J |
| 15: A | 30: F | 45: D |

Stumped on any? You will find the explanations for each answer beginning on page 155.

# STEP 6

*The Rest - All of the Little Things*

If you've made it to this point, you have come very far. What is left to learn represents 4-6% of questions on recent ACT English tests. This is also why I wrote this book: to put this stuff last to show how little it is asked. Why would you, as a student, spend an hour memorizing the difference between "less" and "fewer" when, odds are, you won't even have one question on ACT test day that tests your knowledge of this? It makes no sense, unless you've made it to this point.

This Step does not have a mini-lesson at the end of it because, well, the entire Step is made up of mini-lessons.

## Apostrophes

### a) Possessives (to show possession or ownership)

Apostrophes are used to show possession; here are the different situations that could come up with this.

i) Add an apostrophe and 's' to singular nouns and plural nouns that do not end in 's'

    ex) The **cat's** paws were white.         ex) This store sells **women's** shoes.

ii) Add an apostrophe to a plural noun that already ends in 's'

    ex) The **kids'** toys are there. (This refers to the toys that belong to multiple kids)

    ex) The **hyenas'** prey was eaten (This refers to the prey that was eaten by multiple hyenas)

iii) Make both nouns possessive for individual possession; make the final noun possessive for joint possession.

    ex) **Ben's** and **Bob's** hats are red. (This says that Ben has a red hat and Bob also has a red hat)

    ex) Kim and **Carla's** birthday party is today. (This says that Kim and Carla are having a joint party)

### b) Contractions (combining words)

Add an apostrophe to represent missing letters when words are joined (like do + not = **don't**).

*Special Case* - Its vs It's vs Its'

i) **Its** is the possessive for of "it."   ex) **Its** leg was injured.

ii) **It's** is the contraction for "it is" or "it has."   ex) **It's** time for bed.   ex) **It's** been a long day.

iii) **Its'** is not a word in English. Don't use it. Ever.

## They're vs Their vs There

i) **They're** is a contraction. If it can be replaced with "they are," then this is correct.

   ex) **They're** trying to escape from jail.

ii) **Their** is possessive. Plural subjects own something; if possession is being implied, this is correct.

   ex) Are you going to **their** house for dinner?

iii) **There** has a couple of uses. It can denote a location, for example (it is synonymous with "that place"). It is also used as a pronoun to place a conjugation of the verb "to be" (is/are/were/will be/etc.) before a subject.

   ex) The fox lives over **there**.

   ex) **There** will be no reason to go out tonight.

## Who vs Whom

Here is how the rule is stated: *who* goes where *he* goes, and *whom* goes where *him* goes. In other words if you can rephrase the sentence to put in the pronoun *he* or *him*, or if you can rephrase the sentence as a question in which the answer is either *he* or *him*, then you can be sure as to which to use.

   ex) Remember **who/whom** you are speaking to.

   Rephrase: Are you speaking to ***he, or are you speaking to him***? You would say, " I am speaking to **him**", which is why the answer is **whom**. (Remember whom you are speaking to).

   ex) **Who/whom** stole the cookie?

   Rephrase: Did ***he*** steal the cookie, or did ***him*** steal the cookie? You would say, "**He** stole the cookie", which is why the answer is **who**. (Who stole the cookie?).

## To vs Too

To is a preposition; too means "very" or "also" or "as well".

    ex) It is **too** wet outside, so I will not be walking **to** the store.

## Good vs Well

Good is an adjective (it describes a noun), and well is an adverb (it describes how something is done).

    ex) This is a **good** snack. There's a **good** chance I'll get a 36 on the ACT.

    ex) I did **well** on the ACT. How are you? I'm **well**, how are you?

## Than vs Then

I believe we covered this, but just to review. Than is used to compare things; then is used to show the passage of time.

    ex) I am older **than** my twin brother. I was born, and **then** he was born.

## Between vs Among

Between is used when referring to being between only 2 things or persons; among is used when there are more than 2 things or persons.

    ex) The policeman, though **among** a large crowd, stood **between** the bad guy and the victim.

## Lie vs Lay

Lie is something a subject does to itself; lay is something done to something else.

    ex) I'm going to **lie** down. (It is *lie* because I am doing it to myself).

    ex) He is going to **lay** the book on the table. (It is *lay* because he is doing it to something else).

## Less vs Fewer

Use fewer for things that can be numbered or counted; use less for something that can't be numbered.

ex) Because I had 2 gallons of milk to buy, I used the "Ten Items or **Fewer**" checkout line.

ex) There are **fewer** cars in my garage than my neighbor's.

ex) There is **less** Vitamin C in a banana than an orange. (You can't count the number of Vitamin C's).

ex) The Gulf of Mexico has **less** water than the Atlantic Ocean.

## Affect vs Effect

For ACT purposes, remember affect is a verb and effect is a noun. To remember this, think of the phrase "cause and effect," which is about 2 nouns.

ex) The previous mayor had a negative **effect** on the city because he **affected** it in the wrong way.

## Further vs Farther

Farther is a word that is always used to identify a distance. Further is used to indicate an additional amount of something that was done, is being done, must be done, etc.

ex) New York City is **farther** from my house than Atlanta.

ex) Scientists need to research **further** into the COVID pandemic.

ex) The athlete needs **further** training if she is to finish in first place.

## Last Semi-colon Use

Up to this point I've been saying there's a prime way to use a semi-colon: to combine independent clauses. Guaranteed, you will have to know *that* on ACT day! However, a semi-colon can also be used to set off items in a list, like commas can. All you could ever need to know is that if a sentence is setting off items in a list with semi-colons, you can't switch punctuation to commas or something else.

ex) The writers on my bookshelf include Flannery O'Connor, a National Book Award winner**;** Walker Percy, who won the same award**;** and C.S. Lewis, British author who preceded the other two.

That's a lot of little things. Like I said, you will have 3-5 questions that test your knowledge of the above material, but if mastery of these small rules is all that's left for you, then get to work on the following practice passages!

*While heavy on Step 6, each of the following 2 passages contains at least one question type from Steps 1-5 to keep you on top of it!*

# PASSAGE I

**Mammoth Cave**

[1]

Mammoth Cave located in Kentucky is the longest cave system in the world. No other surveyed cave matches its massive size. Researchers who have explored the cave have mapped out a total of around 360 miles, but estimates the total length of the cave to be roughly 3 times longer! [A] To put that into perspective, that is just about 40 miles further than the distance between Boston and Atlanta.

[2]

The limestone rock beds that make up Mammoth Cave have existed for about 350 million years. However, the caves' passages did not begin to form until 10-15 million years ago. [B] Over the passage of millions of years, water gradually widened those small cracks, which become less in number as they widened into passageways. The limestone walls actually accelerated the erosion: as the water moved through. The limestone, it actively dissolved minerals in the rock, speeding the process. Eventually, the cracks became passages large enough for humans to enter into, because they were now big enough.

1.  A. NO CHANGE
    B. Cave in Kentucky where it is located
    C. Cave, located in Kentucky,
    D. Cave located, in Kentucky,

2.  F. NO CHANGE
    G. can match it's massive
    H. matches it's massive
    J. is able to matches its massive

3.  A. NO CHANGE
    B. estimate, the total length,
    C. estimates, the total length,
    D. estimate the total length

4.  F. NO CHANGE
    G. further then
    H. farther than
    J. farther then

5.  A. NO CHANGE
    B. distances between
    C. distance among
    D. distances among

6.  F. NO CHANGE
    G. However the caves'
    H. However, the cave's
    J. However, the cave's,

7.  A. NO CHANGE
    B. become fewer
    C. became less
    D. became fewer

8.  F. NO CHANGE
    G. through the limestone,
    H. through, the limestone,
    J. through. The limestone

9.  A. NO CHANGE
    B. into the large caves.
    C. into.
    D. into over time.

[3]

Apart from its unique, massive size, Mammoth Cave also has a unique history. Early Native Americans, whom were truly the first to actually discover the cave, used it as shelter during certain times of the year as a way to escape the elements. These tribes also used it as a primitive mine as early as 3000 years ago, extracting mirabilite, epsomite, and gypsum. [C] How these minerals were used by the Native Americans is still unclear, but they did leave behind some of they're possessions that, today, are considered rare and valuable artifacts. There is also evidence that Mammoth Cave may also have had a more solemn use; members of the tribe will lay the body of a deceased companion within the cave to protect it from predators while it was prepared for burial.

10. F. NO CHANGE
G. who are
H. whom are
J. who were

11. A. NO CHANGE
B. to use them
C. used them
D. using it

12. F. NO CHANGE
G. of them
H. of there
J. of their

13. A. NO CHANGE
B. will lie
C. would lay
D. would lie

[4]

Mammoth Cave officially became a National Park in 1941. At that time, only 40 miles of passageway had been mapped. |14| In the time since, however, surveyors have made huge leaps in understanding the cave system. [D] Although researchers now comprehend the massive scope of the cave in much greater detail, archaeologists and other scientists continue to study Mammoth Cave, hoping to gain further insight into both how it was

14. The writer is considering deleting the preceding sentence. Should the sentence be kept or deleted?

F. Kept, because otherwise the reader is unable to infer that Mammoth Cave is now believed to be the largest cave system in the world.
G. Kept, because it gives the reader a benchmark for understanding just how far research has come since 1941.
H. Deleted, because it portrays the researchers working within the cave system prior to 1941 as incapable.
J. Deleted, because it shifts the focus of the paragraph away from a broad understanding of the cave's history to one that focuses on detail.

formed and how it has been used since.

> Question 15 asks about the preceding passage as a whole.

15. The writer is considering adding the following sentence to the essay:

    > At that time, flowing water entered the rock bed through small cracks and eroded the stone.

    If the writer were to add this sentence, it would most logically be placed at:

    A. Point A in Paragraph 1.
    B. Point B in Paragraph 2.
    C. Point C in Paragraph 3.
    D. Point D in Paragraph 4.

---

**PASSAGE II**

### Nikola Tesla

Few inventors have gained the type of notoriety as if Nikola Tesla. He was a brilliant and capable inventor who pioneered many of the technological concepts society relies on today. Though Tesla may have been misunderstood in his own time, history indicates that the overall more work and inventions of Nikola Tesla deserve respect and admiration.

Throughout his life, Tesla dedicated himself to science and technological pursuits.

16. F. NO CHANGE
    G. as Nikola Tesla have.
    H. that Nikola Tesla has.
    J. being like Nikola Tesla.

17. A. NO CHANGE
    B. overall work well
    C. overall well work
    D. overall good work

18. F. NO CHANGE
    G. Being dedicated, science and technological pursuits were the lifelong focus of Tesla.
    H. As a scientist, technological pursuits were Tesla's dedication throughout his life.
    J. From the beginning of his career in science, pursuits of a kind of technological type of focus of Tesla were what he was dedicated in pursuit of.

Step 6  90

Nikola Tesla was born in Croatia in 1856. He had humble beginnings, so his mother ran the family farm, and his father worked for the church. However, his early years were indicative of the future he would have: he was a bright student; he studied at the Technical University of Graz, and he flourished at the University of Prague. In 1884 Tesla emigrated to the United States and took a job as an engineer at Thomas Edison's electric company. During his employment under Edison, Tesla was often undervalued. Edison once promised to pay Tesla $50,000 for an improved invention design. [21]

19. A. NO CHANGE
    B. beginnings; his mother
    C. beginnings, which explains why she
    D. beginnings and his mother

20. F. NO CHANGE
    G. Graz, but
    H. Graz, however,
    J. Graz; and

21. At this point, the writer is considering adding the following true statement:

    When Tesla delivered, Edison refused to pay, telling Tesla that he "did not understand our American humor."

    Should the statement be added here?

    A. Yes, because, without it, readers will not understand what the author meant when he wrote that "Tesla was often undervalued."
    B. Yes, because it gives the reader insight into the nature of American humor, which is understandably different than that Tesla would have been used to.
    C. No, because the preceding sentence fittingly ends the paragraph and transitions to the following paragraph.
    D. No, because the sentence shifts the focus of the essay away from Nicola Tesla and to economics.

Unfortunately, Tesla's and Edison's lifelong rivalry against each other was established by this slight. Tesla moved on, and would go on to partner

22. F. NO CHANGE
    G. Tesla and Edison's
    H. Teslas' and Edisons'
    J. Teslas and Edisons

23. A. NO CHANGE
    B. rivalry
    C. rivalry, one being rivals with the other,
    D. competition between one another

with another electricity magnate, George
                        24

Westinghouse, whom he saw Tesla's potential. With
                25
the backing of Westinghouse's company, Tesla was able to experiment and develop some of his best inventions. It was while working for Westinghouse that Tesla created designs for oscillators, meters, and transformers; derivatives of these creations were first
                                                26
attributed to Edison, though they were Tesla's.
                    26

Tesla's most significant contribution to society may have been the development of his Alternating Current method of generating electricity, which is

still used to deliver power to homes and businesses
                             27
today. Despite his enormous contributions, Tesla's unconventional eccentricities became overwhelming, and they found it difficult to find funding. He
       28
continued to work on inventions until he died in 1943. It was not until after Tesla's death that the value of many of his discoveries came to light. One thing is for sure: Nikola Tesla was one of the
         29

foremost brilliant people of his day and age.
         30

24. F. NO CHANGE
    G. magnet,
    H. manage,
    J. magenta,

25. A. NO CHANGE
    B. whom saw
    C. who he saw
    D. who saw

26. Given that all of the choices are accurate, which one most clearly communicates that Tesla's inventions have had a lasting effect within the realm of technology?

    F. NO CHANGE
    G. were used for a brief time before, ultimately, they were phased out.
    H. are still used in many electronic devices produced today.
    J. were also created while Tesla was with Westinghouse.

27. A. NO CHANGE
    B. too homes
    C. too, homes
    D. to the homes

28. F. NO CHANGE
    G. he found it
    H. they were finding it
    J. he having found it

29. A. NO CHANGE
    B. to be for sure, and Nikola
    C. for sure, is that Nikola
    D. for sure, Nikola

30. F. NO CHANGE
    G. intellectual individuals of the early twentieth century.
    H. smart inventors to have lived when he did.
    J. geniuses of his time.

# Step 6 Correct Answers

**Passage I**

1: C
2: F
3: D
4: H
5: A
6: H
7: D
8: G
9: C
10: J
11: A
12: J
13: C
14: G
15: B

**Passage II**

16: H
17: D
18: F
19: B
20: J
21: A
22: G
23: B
24: F
25: D
26: H
27: A
28: G
29: A
30: J

Stumped on any? You will find the explanations for each answer beginning on page 162.

# STEP 7

*Full Length Practice Tests*

I hope you have found this book to be valuable. My goal was to root your ACT English preparation in just that: *preparation*, meaning specifically ordered preparation that puts first things first and last things last.

What follows now is two complete, full-length ACT English practice tests. Let's quickly review strategies (not content) before you set that timer and dive in.

## 1) "Listen"

Unless English is your second language, you have been listening to English your entire life. That means that you probably have good instincts. Even if you don't read a lot (which you should; want to improve on all aspects of the ACT? READ! I don't mean read classic novels, but anything written professionally: sports articles, fashion magazines, horror stories, etc.), every advertisement you've ever encountered on the radio, the internet, or live TV was written by people who know the English language, and this is especially true of anything your teachers have ever made you read in school. What I'm trying to say is this: *trust your gut; if something "sounds" weird, it probably is*. Just reading all four examples in context can often help you identify the correct or best answer, even if you can't pinpoint the exact reason why.

## 2) Answer questions as you go, but in context

By now you should know that you can't skip sentences or paragraphs that have no questions tied to them. This is, of course, true because there are always *context* questions waiting around the corner. Maybe you will need to identify the correct sentence to go at the end of the paragraph, maybe you will need to know the greater purpose of the entire essay, maybe you will need to choose the correct transition ("connector" word or phrase, like "Because of this" or "On the other hand"), or maybe you will need to identify the correct verb tense. Whatever the case is, context is key. Even when only one or two words are underlined, like this, it is still important for you to read the underlined portion within the entirety of the sentence.

## 3) Circle and return

Especially in ACT English and Math, there are questions that fall into the category of "maybe later." This simply means that you will probably be able to identify a question that will require a bit more time than normal; if you foresee that you will have to spend 1, 2, or 3 minutes on a question to get it right (like having to reread an essay to figure out the author's purpose, having to arrange sentences in a paragraph, etc.), then you should circle it, skip it (or temporarily guess), and come back at the end of the test with your spare time.

# Closing Notes

a) You have 45 minutes to complete 5 passages and 75 questions. That gives you 9 minutes per passage. Get a watch and keep time *on your own*. Make this a habit; don't count on there being a clock in front of you on ACT day. Make sure you're finishing Passage I prior to 9 minutes having passed, Passage II prior to 18 minutes having passed, etc.

b) There is nothing in the directions you need to know. Read them, if you like, before you start the 45 minute timer. However, certainly don't read them on test day. They never change.

c) Of course, guess on every question; there is no penalty for guessing.

**DIRECTIONS:** In the five passages that follow, certain words and phrases are underlined and numbered. In the right-hand column, you will find alternatives for the underlined part. In most cases, you are to choose the one that best expresses the idea, makes the statement appropriate for standard written English, or is worded most consistently with the style and tone of the passage as a whole. If you think the original version is best, choose "NO CHANGE." In some cases, you will find in the right-hand column a question about the underlined part. You are to choose the best answer to the question.

You will also find questions about a section of the passage, or about the passage as a whole. These questions do not refer to an underlined portion of the passage, but rather are identified by a number or numbers in a box.

For each question, choose the alternative you consider best and fill in the corresponding oval on your answer document. Read each passage through once before you begin to answer the questions that accompany it. For many of the questions, you must read several sentences beyond the question to determine the answer. Be sure that you have read far enough ahead each time you choose an alternative.

---

## PASSAGE I

**Fallingwater**

[1]

Most would agree that a boulder bulging through the living room floor are considered a waste of valuable space. After all, there is very little practical use, save for sitting on it or covering it up with some kind of blanket or other throw, for a large rock in the home. [A] However, for the famous American architect Frank Lloyd Wright, and his client Edgar Kauffman, such a feature was the perfect way to demonstrate the affect that the natural world can have on the structures built by man. [B]

1. **A.** NO CHANGE
   **B.** were
   **C.** is
   **D.** do appear to be

2. **F.** NO CHANGE
   **G.** use save for sitting on it
   **H.** use, save for sitting on it,
   **J.** use save for sitting on it,

3. **A.** NO CHANGE
   **B.** architect, Frank Lloyd Wright, and
   **C.** architect Frank Lloyd Wright; and
   **D.** architect Frank Lloyd Wright and

4. **F.** NO CHANGE
   **G.** effecting
   **H.** affecting
   **J.** effect

[2]

[1] Built over a waterfall in Southwestern Pennsylvania, Fallingwater draws over 100,000 visitors annually and has been praised by numerous institutions of American public life as a site with a view like few homes in America. [2] Fallingwater is the name of this home, and yes, any guest will easily see the purposeful unity of nature and architecture. [3] Thus, most students of the home are stunned to learn that Wright drew the initial plans in less than two hours. [7]

[3]

A first draft of the plans, which called for a home above the falls, did not suit the desires of Kauffman, who had wanted a home below the waterfall so that he could enjoy the view. [C] As a result, he came around to the bird's-eye view idea, but he continued to butt heads with Wright throughout the process of construction. At one point, Kauffman, thought the space set out for his personal desk, a tiny plot in the corner of his bedroom, that was too small. [D] On another occasion, Kauffman sought an engineer's opinions of one of Wright's designs. When the latter threatened to quit the job over this, Kauffman relented, apologized, and had the report permanently

5. 
   A. NO CHANGE
   B. Falling water is constructed over a
   C. The home is constructed over a
   D. It will be over a

6. Which choice best stresses the extensive recognition of the importance of Fallingwater?
   F. NO CHANGE
   G. that the original owners cherished.
   H. with historic and cultural significance.
   J. with unprecedented access to an unending supply of fresh water.

7. Which sequence of sentences makes this paragraph most logical?
   A. NO CHANGE
   B. 3, 1, 2
   C. 1, 3, 2
   D. 2, 1, 3

8. 
   F. NO CHANGE
   G. Kauffman was not thrilled with these initial plans, for they
   H. The plans first drafted cost Kauffman his view; thus, they
   J. These initial plans

9. 
   A. NO CHANGE
   B. However,
   C. Because of this,
   D. Otherwise,

10. 
    F. NO CHANGE
    G. Kauffman point,
    H. point, Kauffman
    J. point—Kauffman

11. 
    A. NO CHANGE
    B. to be
    C. it was
    D. DELETE the underlined portion

sealed up in an unknown wall of the house, which he
                                                    12

read again. |13|

[4]

Having been used for more than 25 years by the
           14
Kauffman family as a weekend getaway. When this time of personal use came to an end, the home was donated to the Western Pennsylvania Conservancy so that it could be maintained and appreciated by all. Fallingwater is not only a masterpiece of American architecture, but is proof that, sometimes, the struggle for beauty is just that: a struggle.

12. F. NO CHANGE
    G. by being
    H. he
    J. never to be

13. At this point, the writer is considering adding the following true statement:

    Not only the walls of the home, but the foundation and roof are sturdily built.

    Should the writer make this addition here?

    A. Yes, because it supports the idea already stated that it is unlikely that the plans will be accessed ever again.
    B. Yes, because it provides further evidence that Wright was not only a skilled architect, but also hired the best builders.
    C. No, because it provides information about Fallingwater's construction that is not relevant at this point in the essay.
    D. No, because it contradicts facts about the construction of the home presented earlier in the essay.

14. F. NO CHANGE
    G. Fallingwater was used for over 25 years
    H. While its use only lasted 25 years
    J. Though its using only spanned 25 years

Question 15 asks about the preceding passage as a whole.

15. The writer is considering adding the following sentence to the essay:

    This prompted Kauffman to contact Wright and ask if there was even enough room to write his architect a check!

    If the writer were to add this sentence, it would most logically be placed at:

    A. Point A in Paragraph 1.
    B. Point B in Paragraph 1.
    C. Point C in Paragraph 3.
    D. Point D in Paragraph 3.

## PASSAGE II

### Turn Out the Lights!

[1]

We saw the men sprinting from the beach in the direction of the restaurant where my siblings and I were dining. They shouted, "Turn off the lights!"
16
Needless to say, I was confused. How was I to finish my dessert if I couldn't see it? [A] How could a restaurant operate, with waitstaff crashing into walls
17
and drinks spilling across tables? Thankfully the out-of-breath men clarify what they meant for the
18
restaurant staff: sea turtles were hatching and would be confused by the restaurant's lights.

[2]

Sea turtle eggs hatch most often at nighttime when the air is cooler, which had the added benefit of
19
shielding them from many predators, such as birds.

Once the turtle is triggered by the temperature
20
change, it breaks free of sand and shell and follows its instinct to find the ocean. [B] When a beach is completely darkened, such as they were before the
21
invention of electricity, the turtles are drawn by the moon's reflection shimmering off of the water. This is why, when a turtle hatches, it can be led in the wrong direction by bright lights further inland.
22

16. F. NO CHANGE
    G. dining, shouted,
    H. dining shouting
    J. dining, they were shouting,

17. A. NO CHANGE
    B. restaurant operate with waitstaff crashing
    C. restaurant operate with waitstaff crashing,
    D. restaurant operate, with waitstaff crashing,

18. F. NO CHANGE
    G. were to clarify
    H. are clarifying
    J. clarified

19. A. NO CHANGE
    B. cooler, which, having
    C. cooler, which has
    D. cooler, had

20. F. NO CHANGE
    G. All at once,
    H. This is beneficial because
    J. Because of instinct, the turtle is ready for it,

21. A. NO CHANGE
    B. finally enveloped entirely and completely in darkness,
    C. in a situation in which the sun is no longer shining upon it,
    D. dark, like at nighttime when the air is cooler, and

22. F. NO CHANGE
    G. those lights further
    H. lights farther
    J. lights that went farther

[3]

Thankfully, everyone in the restaurant understood what had to be done. The diner quickly darkened and dozens of curious and eager patrons
23

(including ourselves) laid down enough cash to
24
cover the bill and the tip onto the tabletop. [C] We rushed from the restaurant down to the beach to catch a glimpse of a wonderful spectacle few ever get to witness. [25]

[4]

We arrived just in the time. [D] More and more
26
lights were turned off in all directions. Some on-the-spot volunteers even used black garbage bags on nearby piers that did not have a simple on-off switch to darken bait lights. I felt transported to a different
27
time, one free of light pollution in which humans and animals lived in complete harmony. I witnessed the fluorescent moon glaring off of the soft waves and, like the baby turtles, felt drawn, to it myself.
28

23. A. NO CHANGE
    B. comprehended in their minds the steps that had to be taken.
    C. had a knowledgable sense to do certain things and avoid others.
    D. succumbed to their intuition as to the things to do and the things not to do.

24. F. NO CHANGE
    G. lied down
    H. lay with
    J. lied within

25. If the writer were to delete the preceding sentence, the paragraph would primarily lose a statement that:

    A. emphasizes the tremendous effort people take all over the world to care for animals.
    B. restates why sea turtle eggs hatch most of the time during the night.
    C. provides a crucial detail in the flow of the story being told.
    D. helps to overcome prejudice against animal life that burdens human beings.

26. F. NO CHANGE
    G. just in time.
    H. in the time.
    J. just within time.

27. The best placement for the underlined portion (adjusting for capitalization as necessary) would be:

    A. where it is now.
    B. before the word *Some*.
    C. after the word *bags*.
    D. after the word *nearby*.

28. F. NO CHANGE
    G. turtles felt drawn,
    H. turtles, felt drawn
    J. turtles felt drawn

Step 7 - Practice Test 1   104

Questions 29 and 30 ask about the preceding passage as a whole.

29. The writer is considering adding the following sentence to the essay:

    Hundreds of baby turtles were waddling towards the ocean.

    If the writer were to add this sentence, it would most logically be placed at:

    A. Point A in Paragraph 1.
    B. Point B in Paragraph 2.
    C. Point C in Paragraph 3.
    D. Point D in Paragraph 4.

30. Suppose the author's main purpose had been to record the details and scientific background of a rare and meaningful personal experience. Would this essay accomplish that purpose?

    F. Yes, because the essay describes the author's interest in studying marine biology, and how that interest led her to study sea turtles.
    G. Yes, because the essay bolsters an encounter with sea turtles with facts about the animal's instincts, particularly when hatching.
    H. No, because the essay focuses too little on sea turtles and their habitat and too much on the author's feelings about the animal.
    J. No, because the essay indicates that a person can be dismissive of the sea turtle when, in reality, all have an obligation to vulnerable animal species.

## PASSAGE III

### Jefferson and Lewis

Thomas Jefferson is a former American president known for many things, and rightly so. The man who

authored the words that make up, the Declaration of Independence, became America's first vice-president

and second president, during which time he radically expanded the territory of the United States. This included the Louisiana Purchase from France, this acquisition nearly doubled the size of the nation. The purchase bolstered Jefferson's ambitions to catalogue

31. A. NO CHANGE
    B. president, which is known for
    C. president that known
    D. president knowing for

32. F. NO CHANGE
    G. the words, that make up the Declaration of Independence became America's first
    H. the words that make up the Declaration of Independence, became America's first
    J. the words that make up the Declaration of Independence became America's first

33. A. NO CHANGE
    B. France
    C. France:
    D. France; because

a route from the East Coast to the Pacific Ocean. |34|

Jefferson acquired funds from Congress in the amount of $2,324 to pay for the expedition, and he tapped Army Captain Meriwether Lewis as its leader. Lewis then chose Willam Clark to help him lead the now famous Lewis and Clark Expedition. Because Lewis boasted many of the qualities necessary to traverse the continent, there was much he did not know. Because of this, President Jefferson sent him to various experts to acquire skills that could prove important or even life-saving.

Lewis was first sent to study medicine |39| . Soon

34. Which of the following statements, if added here, would provide the best transition to the discussion of how Jefferson tapped Lewis to lead this expedition?

    F. Much of the West Coast, however, was not under American control.
    G. Jefferson was a busy man.
    H. The Pacific Ocean was on the West Coast.
    J. What he needed most was the right man for the job.

35. A. NO CHANGE
    B. which he
    C. it
    D. Jefferson having been

36. F. NO CHANGE
    G. Having to explain many
    H. Although Lewis possessed many
    J. Lewis, needing a change, still had many

37. A. NO CHANGE
    B. Because of this, experts were needed, and
    C. Because of, and having been caused by, this,
    D. Because of this (that there were many things Lewis did not know),

38. Which choice best stresses the seriousness of the training Lewis would receive?

    F. NO CHANGE
    G. to his friends he was a Renaissance man.
    H. his critics wrong.
    J. a fun entry into knowledge of all kinds.

39. At this point, the writer is considering adding the following true phrase:

    as a student of the physician Benjamin Rush in Philadelphia

Should the writer make this addition?

    A. Yes, because the reader needs to know that Lewis studied medicine.
    B. Yes, because it gives credibility to his study and follows the pattern of the paragraph.
    C. No, because it makes Lewis seem unqualified for his expedition.
    D. No, because it is too specific of a detail for this point in the essay.

after, Lewis tutored Andrew Ellicot, under an expert
                                         ―――
                                          40
in astronomy and navigation. Then, he learned the science of cataloguing plant and animal specimens from Benjamin Barton, latitude and longitude computations from Robert Patterson, and the science of fossils from Caspar Wistar. Though capable of learning such a vast array of knowledge, Lewis's
                                                ―――――――
                                                  41
intellect also showed that he was both willing and
――――――――――――――――
       41
eager. This explains the additional hours that he sat
                                                  ―――
                                                   42
studying in the vast library of Monticello, Jefferson's personal home. ⌊43⌋

The expedition set out from St. Charles, Missouri on May 21, 1804 with as many as 45 members in their party. The journey, however adventurous, proved difficult for obvious reasons, and the group faced challenges beyond the modern imagination. Conversely, only one brave explorer,
               ――――――――
                  44
Sergeant Charles Floyd, lost his life. In November of 1805, due in no small part to Lewis' vast training and knowledge, Jefferson got his wish: Lewis, Clark, and
                                       ―――――――――――――――
                                              45
the men under their command finally reached the
―――――――――――――――――――――――――――――――――――――――――
                        45
Pacific Ocean.
―――――――――――――
     45

40. The best placement for the underlined portion would be:
   F. where it is now.
   G. after the word *Soon*.
   H. after the word *and*.
   J. after the word *tutored*.

41. A. NO CHANGE
    B. Lewis's willingness to learn displayed
    C. Lewis, in addition, demonstrated
    D. multiple subjects were learned to show

42. F. NO CHANGE
    G. used up
    H. spent
    J. blew through

43. If the writer were to delete the preceding sentence, the essay would primarily lose a statement that:
    A. highlights the jealousy Jefferson must have had for Lewis.
    B. argues for the addition of libraries to most, if not all, homes.
    C. shows that Lewis was willing to go above and beyond the minimum requirements.
    D. demonstrates Jefferson's love of learning.

44. F. NO CHANGE
    G. Miraculously,
    H. Suspiciously,
    J. Uniquely,

45. Given that all the choices are true, which one best concludes this sentence and the essay as a whole?
    A. NO CHANGE
    B. the Louisiana Purchase was worth the cost.
    C. his library would need a new book to catalogue the adventures.
    D. adventure, like learning, is the work of a lifetime.

# PASSAGE IV

## The Eastern Indigo Snake

[1]

Though my friends are <u>timid around</u> snakes, I
<sub>46</sub>
find them fascinating. This is probably because my

father <u>is a biologist and professor at the local
<sub>47</sub>
university.</u> I grew up visiting him in his office and
<sub>47</sub>
spending hours among the reptiles housed in a nearby

building on campus. This is why, when finally

allowed as a teenager to be his <u>intern; I was</u> honored
<sub>48</sub>
to be asked to be a part of the Eastern Indigo Snake

Reintroduction Project and <u>I'm eager</u> to help in any
<sub>49</sub>
way I could. [A]

[2]

The Eastern Indigo Snake is not only the longest

<u>species of snake, native</u> to the United States, but in
<sub>50</sub>
all of North America. [B] It is also non-venomous

and plays an important role in the balance of life in

<u>those</u> across Florida, Southern Georgia, Alabama, and
<sub>51</sub>

Mississippi. However, <u>they have never been found in
<sub>52</sub>
Arkansas.</u> Decades have gone by between sightings
<sub>52</sub>
in areas they once inhabited in large numbers.

46. Which choice most clearly contrasts the author's feelings towards snakes with that of her friends?

F. NO CHANGE
G. terrified of
H. not the biggest fans of
J. enamored by

47. Given that all the choices are accurate, which one best connects this sentence to the information that follows in the next sentence?

A. NO CHANGE
B. took me camping all throughout childhood.
C. had a book of snakes that he kept on the bookshelf in his office.
D. told me many stories growing up that featured snakes, in both good and evil ways.

48. F. NO CHANGE
G. intern, I was
H. intern. I was
J. intern, then I was

49. A. NO CHANGE
B. eager
C. eagerly
D. eager in my desire

50. F. NO CHANGE
G. species of snake native
H. species, of snake native,
J. species, of snake, native

51. A. NO CHANGE
B. forests
C. them
D. all of them

52. Given that all the choices are accurate, which one best provides information about the Eastern Indigo Snake that is most clearly relevant at this point in the essay?

F. NO CHANGE
G. they eat small mammals and reptiles.
H. they are not the longest snakes in the world.
J. the species is critically endangered.

[3]

This new endeavor, a collaborative effort
     ―――――
       53
between biologists representing various organizations

(such as zoos, government agencies, and universities)

throughout the Southeastern United States whom
                                           ――――
                                             54
shared the urgency to protect this endangered species.

Longleaf, Pine forests that had been restored over
―――――――――――――――――――――――――――――――――――――
                   55
time to meet the particular needs of the Eastern

Indigo, such as habitat, prey, and isolation from

human interference, were preferable. Finally, a forest
                                      ――――――――――――――
                                            56
in Southern Alabama was selected. [C] When the day
―――――――――――――――――――――――――――――――
              56

of release finally came, I was beyond excited. |57|

[4]

The team, including myself, hiked miles deep

into the forest carrying a dozen of the endangered

reptiles that had been carefully chosen for

reintroduction. When we arrived to the preselected

location, my father lifted a beautiful snake from its

cage, but instead of letting it slither away, he handed

it to me. "You do the honor," he said. [D] I would

never see this snake again, but as it got away, since
                                       ――――――――――――
                                            58
that is why we were there, from my loving hands, I
――――――――――――――――――――――――
          58
knew we had done the best we could for this

endangered species.

53. A. NO CHANGE
    B. endeavor, having been
    C. endeavor had been
    D. endeavor was

54. F. NO CHANGE
    G. they that
    H. who
    J. which

55. A. NO CHANGE
    B. Longleaf Pine forests that had been restored
    C. Longleaf Pine forests, that had been restored
    D. Longleaf Pine forests, that had been restored,

56. Given that all the choices are accurate, which one most effectively transitions the essay from a focus on research to a focus on the actual release of the snakes back into the wild?

    F. NO CHANGE
    G. Eastern Indigo Snakes need the right habitat.
    H. The researchers needed time to select the correct forest.
    J. The Longleaf Pine is a tree found in many different states, especially in the Southeast.

57. At this point, the writer is considering adding the following sentence:

    My father teaches biology at a local university, and he and I spent a lot of time together around reptiles.

    Given that the information is true, should the writer make this addition here?

    A. Yes, because it gives the reader necessary background information about the writer.
    B. Yes, because it clarifies why the writer is personally involved in the project.
    C. No, because it repeats information about the writer that is provided earlier in the essay.
    D. No, because it suggests that the writer was a part of the project.

58. F. NO CHANGE
    G. slithered off, the snaked I mean,
    H. escaped
    J. wriggled, slithered, and went out

> Questions 59 and 60 ask about the preceding passage as a whole.

59. The writer is considering adding the following sentence to the essay:

    It is black but boasts a beautiful blue or purple sheen that flashes as it slithers through the sunlight.

    If the writer were to add this sentence, it would most logically be placed at:

    A. Point A in Paragraph 1.
    B. Point B in Paragraph 2.
    C. Point C in Paragraph 3.
    D. Point D in Paragraph 4.

60. Suppose the author's main purpose had been to recount a meaningful participation in an important project. Would this essay accomplish that purpose?

    F. Yes, because it recalls how the author personally organized a serious and enduring effort to restore Longleaf Pine forests.
    G. Yes, because it describes how the author helped to begin the restoration of an endangered species.
    H. No, because the author is writing about an effort that involved only her father and not her personally.
    J. No, because the essay provides plenty of evidence to show that the author was forced to participate, making it less meaningful.

## PASSAGE V

### Fred "Nall" Hollis

When Fred <u>Hollis nicknamed Nall,</u> graduated
                    61
from high school in a small town with a population of less than 10,000 people, it would have been nearly impossible for him to <u>foresee</u> the international
                                    62
acclaim that would one day be his. Nall's artwork has been featured across Europe, particularly in Italy, and is famous for elevating the frame of a piece to a new <u>level of artistic genius</u> by incorporating it into the art
       63

61. A. NO CHANGE
    B. Hollis, nicknamed Nall,
    C. Hollis nicknamed Nall
    D. Hollis, nicknamed Nall

62. F. NO CHANGE
    G. foresee into the future
    H. foresee—having grown up in an area with a very low population—
    J. foresee back then

63. Given that all the choices are accurate, which one most strongly suggests that Nall's art is both unique and beautiful?

    A. NO CHANGE
    B. area
    C. status that is really good
    D. group to be recognized

itself. It's almost impossible to pass by one of Nall's
breathtaking pieces without stopping to contemplate the beauty and purpose in every detail.

After graduating from college, Nall was admitted to the School of Fine Arts in Paris, here he learned to further harness his natural artistic ability. He spent a great deal of time traveling as well in these early days, visiting a variety of cultures being as Mexico, India, and North Africa. After having a number of pieces incorporated in both America and Europe, he trained under artistic legend Salvador Dalí.

Any observer of Nall's most famous pieces can see the influence of Dalí's surrealism. However, Nall seems to tamper the absurdity in his own images with the beauty of mosaics, color, and order. For example, a human character may be depicted in black and white—with lovely hints of color to highlight their

64. F. NO CHANGE
    G. Its
    H. Its'
    J. They're

65. If the writer were to delete the underlined portion (adjusting the punctuation as needed), the essay would primarily lose:

    A. a reason to pass by one of Nall's pieces without stopping.
    B. the idea that Nall creates beautiful art.
    C. details that create irony given that he is from a small town.
    D. the reasons why a person would stop to think and wonder about a Nall piece.

66. F. NO CHANGE
    G. Paris and
    H. Paris; here
    J. Paris

67. A. NO CHANGE
    B. those being
    C. much
    D. such

68. F. NO CHANGE
    G. featured
    H. seasoned
    J. underwhelmed

69. Given that all of the choices are true, which one most effectively leads the reader from the first sentence of this paragraph to the information that follows in the paragraph?

    A. NO CHANGE
    B. As a matter of fact, there is speculation that Dalí is actually the artist who created many of Nall's early pieces.
    C. Many of these pieces of art ended up on public display in Europe.
    D. On the other hand, maybe Dalí had no influence on Nall after all.

70. F. NO CHANGE
    G. white with
    H. white:
    J. white with,

features. Oftentimes, these human features are out of proportion, creating in the distorted observer a sense of wonder. However, the absurdity and distortion are
71
further transformed as they are framed in by a beautiful array of wood, tile, or some other combination of bright materials, some of which make their way into and become a part of the art itself.

His art has undoubtedly become famous, Nall
72

has not forgotten his small town roots. In fact, they
73
still owns and operates a studio in his home state,

from which he creates pieces for local museums and
74
hotels featuring and inspired by the beauty of the area. All in all, Fred Hollis is living proof that artistic ability can be found anywhere and, as long as it is nurtured, can blossom into something truly inspiring.

71. Which choice provides the clearest indication that the person discerning Nall's contorted art is often in awe?

A. NO CHANGE
B. These distorted human features often create in the observer a sense of wonder out of proportion.
C. Oftentimes, these human features are out of proportion or distorted, creating in the observer a sense of wonder.
D. The observer, out of proportion and distorted, is often in wonder at these human features.

72. F. NO CHANGE
G. Without a doubt, Nall's art is famous throughout the world,
H. He became famous,
J. Although his art has become famous,

73. A. NO CHANGE
B. there
C. he or she
D. he

74. F. NO CHANGE
G. artfully crafts works of art
H. brings art into existence
J. designs and produces examples of his art

Question 75 asks about the preceding passage as a whole.

75. Suppose the writer's main purpose had been to explain the reasons why, how, and when various art galleries around the world displayed Nall's work. Would this essay accomplish that purpose?

A. Yes, because the essay clearly states that Nall's work was shown in Europe.
B. Yes, because the author traveled extensively around the world to countries like Mexico and India.
C. No, because although the writer mentions Nall's art being shown in Europe, the writer does not elaborate on when or how any specific gallery did so.
D. No, because the writer never mentions any international attention that Nall's art was able to garner.

## PASSAGE I

### Goodall and the Chimps

[1]

When Jane Goodall entered the Gombe Stream National Reserve in Tanzania, she was determined to make history, and that she did. While she is known today as a woman who made headway in a scientific field dominated mostly by men; she would prefer to be known by the body of knowledge she produced and cultivated during her time. Much of what we know about chimpanzees is the direct result of Goodall's efforts.

[2]

One groundbreaking observation of it was tool use among the primates. She watched as one chimp, inserting repetitively into the mounds of termites grass that was tall, for example. The termites would climb the stalk, which the chimpanzee would remove from the mound. The insects that came up with the

1. **A.** NO CHANGE
   **B.** did earn a spot in history.
   **C.** did do when she entered the reserve.
   **D.** did, her name being Jane Goodall.

2. **F.** NO CHANGE
   **G.** men, preferring
   **H.** men, but she would prefer
   **J.** men, she would prefer

3. Which choice best portrays Goodall's work as the result of years of difficulty and strife?
   **A.** NO CHANGE
   **B.** by her blood, sweat, and tears.
   **C.** by working.
   **D.** through hard work.

4. **F.** NO CHANGE
   **G.** hers
   **H.** theirs
   **J.** ours

5. **A.** NO CHANGE
   **B.** over and over insert, for example, stalks of tall grass into where the termites lived.
   **C.** with tall stalks inserted in there, where termites are living.
   **D.** for example, repeatedly inserted tall stalks of grass into termite mounds.

6. The writer is considering deleting the underlined portion (adjusting the punctuation as needed). Should the underlined portion be kept or deleted?
   **F.** Kept, because otherwise we would not know the type of ape she saw hunting termites.
   **G.** Kept, because it provides a necessary step in the tool use observed by Goodall.
   **H.** Deleted, because it repeats a detail provided earlier in the paragraph.
   **J.** Deleted, because it shifts the focus of the paragraph away from what Goodall observed.

stalk got eaten.
      7

[3]

Another discovery of Goodall's was that chimpanzees eat meat. Up to that time, it was believed that chimps ate a mostly vegetarian diet supplemented by the consumption of some insects.
                                8
However, on one occasion, Goodall witnessed a hunting group climb a tree, and surround a colobus
                      9
monkey, with which they shared a habitat. [A] The aggressive apes blocked off all possible exits for the colobus while one among the group singlehandedly killed the monkey. The chimps then shared the
                                          10
carcass with one another.

[4]

One probable reason that Goodall was able to make such strides, with the chimpanzees is because
      11
she named them. At the time, it was customary to number animals. Goodall, on the other hand, found joy in assigning names to them, *David Greybeard*, *Fifi*, and *Mr. McGregor* being a few examples. [B] This helped her to bond with them, and thus to live
                    12
among the troupe for so long a time.

[5]

When Goodall first arrived, a chimp titled
                                        13
Goliath was the alpha male. [C] Sadly, Goodall was attacked on a regular basis by a very aggressive male chimpanzee named Frodo. When Frodo became the

7. Given that all the choices are accurate, which one best emphasizes the chimpanzee's nature as hunter?
   A. NO CHANGE
   B. didn't live for much longer.
   C. were swallowed.
   D. fell victim to the hungry predator.

8. Which of the following alternatives to the underlined portion would NOT be acceptable?
   F. the eating of
   G. the combustion of
   H. the ingestion of
   J. DELETE the underlined portion.

9. A. NO CHANGE
   B. climb a tree, and surround,
   C. climb, a tree, and surround
   D. climb a tree and surround

10. F. NO CHANGE
    G. having a share of
    H. in sharing with
    J. share

11. A. NO CHANGE
    B. make such strides, with the chimpanzees,
    C. make such strides with the chimpanzees,
    D. make such strides with the chimpanzees

12. F. NO CHANGE
    G. form a deep, heartfelt connection
    H. grow really close
    J. share a bond

13. A. NO CHANGE
    B. named
    C. known by
    D. designated

alpha male, Goodall knew that it was time for her to

step away from the troupe. [D]

> Questions 14 and 15 ask about the preceding passage as a whole.

14. Upon reviewing the essay and finding that some information has been left out, the writer composes the following sentence incorporating that information:

    > He was succeeded by Mike, a cunning primate with a thirst for power.

    If the writer were to add this sentence, it would most logically be placed at:

    F. Point A in Paragraph 3.
    G. Point B in Paragraph 4.
    H. Point C in Paragraph 5.
    J. Point D in Paragraph 5.

15. Suppose the writer's main purpose had been to highlight the contributions to the knowledge of animals by a scientist. Would this essay accomplish that purpose?

    A. Yes, because the essay centers on Jane Goodall, and details her comprehensive study of the chimpanzees.
    B. Yes, because the essay compares and contrasts the scientific achievements of various researchers over time.
    C. No, because Jane Goodall, though a scientist, did not conduct research among the chimpanzees, but merely observed them.
    D. No, because the writer focuses more on the emotional reactions of chimpanzees to stimuli as opposed to the scientist behind it.

---

## PASSAGE II

### A Fishing Memory

When my grandfather woke me on those early mornings, he always did so in a <u>gentle, yet urgent,</u> fashion. I would take a deep breath, roll out of the

bed, and stare <u>from</u> the dark morning that awaited

outside my window. <u>I always had a sense that the fish knew that we were coming.</u>
    Every evening before one of our fishing trips he would rig each fishing pole from scratch. He checked the drag, the strength of the line, the knots that held

16. F. NO CHANGE
    G. gentle yet urgent
    H. gentle yet urgent,
    J. gentle, yet urgent

17. A. NO CHANGE
    B. behind
    C. into
    D. above

18. Given that all of the choices are true, which one best concludes this paragraph and transitions to the following paragraph?

    F. NO CHANGE
    G. Then, I got back into bed.
    H. We were ready to go, our tackle and poles having been prepared in advance.
    J. The darkness was thick and intimidating.

the treble hooks, and the weights. "Can I help, Grandpa?" I'd ask, and even though he never needed
19
it, he'd let me be his assistant.

After all that work, we would be well on our way
20

in the boat. Grandpa's favorite spot was a large oil rig
21
about a mile off the coast of the island. There was

never need for an anchor: he was simply tying a rope
22

to the structure and we were ready to fish. Carefully,
23
he would hook my line up with a shrimp, and because we would arrive before the changing of the tides, we always set ourselves up for the greatest possibility of success. |24|

[1] In other words, it was a thrill every time no matter how big or small the catch might be. [2] It

19. A. NO CHANGE
    B. therefore,
    C. as a matter of fact,
    D. DELETE the underlined portion.

20. Given that all of the choices are accurate, which one most effectively introduces the paragraph by returning to the topic of the essay's opening paragraph?

    F. NO CHANGE
    G. Due to unforeseen weather,
    H. Before first light,
    J. With the fishing poles ready,

21. A. NO CHANGE
    B. large oil rig,
    C. large oil, rig,
    D. large, oil rig

22. F. NO CHANGE
    G. to tie simply he would
    H. he would simply tie
    J. tying he did simply

23. Which choice best emphasizes the grandfather's delight in fishing with his grandson?

    A. NO CHANGE
    B. Unexpectedly,
    C. Excitedly,
    D. Dutifully,

24. At this point, the writer is considering adding the following true statement:

    Shrimp are decapod crustaceans, and because there are thousands of species around the world, they are commonly eaten by a vast variety of fish.

    Should the writer make this addition here?

    F. Yes, because it answers a rhetorical question raised earlier in the paragraph.
    G. Yes, because it transitions the preceding paragraph to the paragraph that follows.
    H. No, because the sentence implies that the pair are going to successfully catch fish.
    J. No, because it detracts from the story that is being told as the essay progresses.

seemed the fish were always biting, for we would fill our ice chest with Speckled Trout, White Trout, Sheepshead, Mangrove Snapper, Redfish, Flounder, and a kind of other delicious fish. [3] Though I enjoyed the taste of a deep-fried fillet from any one of these, my favorite part, quality time not included, was never knowing what we would pull from the water. |28|

I remember fighting a large fish for what seemed like hours as the sun was rising. Workers on the rig gathered above us to see what a visiting kid from the Midwest might pull in after such a battle. |29| When the fish was just below the surface, the line snapped and the pole recoiled; I tried to keep calm under the watchful gaze of the workers. Though I missed the big one, which I had on the line for a very long time, Grandpa was able to cheer me up by speculating as to what kind of fish it might have been.

25. A. NO CHANGE
    B. they filled
    C. we were to be filling
    D. we would filling

26. F. NO CHANGE
    G. lack
    H. type
    J. variety

27. A. NO CHANGE
    B. part quality time not included,
    C. part, quality time not included
    D. part quality time not included

28. Which of the following sequences of sentences makes this paragraph most logical?

    F. NO CHANGE
    G. 2, 3, 1
    H. 1, 3, 2
    J. 3, 2, 1

29. If the writer were to replace the word *battle* with the word *try* in the preceding sentence, the sentence would primarily lose a word that:

    A. emphasizes the difficulty and length of time it took to reel in the fish.
    B. restates a theme introduced in the first paragraph.
    C. understates how tiresome it was to get the fish into the boat.
    D. fails to transition the sentence to the one that follows.

30. The writer is considering deleting the underlined portion (adjusting the punctuation as needed). Should the underlined portion be kept or deleted?

    F. Kept, because it adds a dramatic detail that makes the story more relatable.
    G. Kept, because without it the reader would assume that the fish got away quickly.
    H. Deleted, because it restates a fact that has been stated elsewhere in the paragraph.
    J. Deleted, because it fails to mention the reaction of the group of workers who were watching.

## PASSAGE III

### The Sailing Stones

Visitors to the American West have no shortage of potential sites to visit, from lively cities like Portland, OR and Las Vegas, NV to the Redwood forests of California, any vacation to the area is sure to be, as one may experience, too short. One rarity,

however, has been on the receiving end of growing interest in recent years: sailing stones.

Sailing stones are a natural phenomenon in which, from the point of view of the casual observer, stones appear to have been walking or sailing across the desert. This movement, trails that sometimes swerve smoothly or, on occasion, cut at sharp angles. These trails eventually end at the base of a large stone, thus giving the allusion that the stone has been moving of its own accord. To the untrained eye, it looks as if the stones have been moving by themselves through the sand.

The stones are indeed moving across the desert, but there is a scientific explanation. During cold

31. A. NO CHANGE
    B. visit from,
    C. visit. From
    D. visit from

32. F. NO CHANGE
    G. be, most definitely,
    H. be, though it may be obvious,
    J. be

33. A. NO CHANGE
    B. changing
    C. illuminating
    D. taking

34. Which choice best suggests that the sailing stones are difficult to explain because they are not man-made?
    F. NO CHANGE
    G. thing that happens
    H. logically consistent happening
    J. neat event

35. A. NO CHANGE
    B. movement, which creates
    C. movement creates
    D. movement to create

36. F. NO CHANGE
    G. giving the elusion
    H. giving the illusion
    J. giving the effusion

37. A. NO CHANGE
    B. More recently, these stones have been getting a lot of attention.
    C. All of this happens naturally.
    D. DELETE the underlined portion.

38. F. NO CHANGE
    G. moving
    H. moves about
    J. moved around

nights, sheets of ice form on the desert floor. |39| The sheets are broken up on sunny days. When this breakup is accompanied, the ice is pushed across the
                                   40
desert floor and against the base of the stone, thus pushing the stone itself.

   This process is known as ice shove. Although ice shove is a buildup of ice in areas one might expect, such as the arctic—scientists have
   41
shown that even if there is very little ice involved, and even if it is occurring in the desert, ice buildup combined with gusts of wind still though technically
                                                 42
qualifies as an example of ice shove.

   Throughout the 20th century there was much speculation as to the cause of the stones' movements. Some hypothesized that movement of mud was to blame the others theorized that something more
   43
supernatural or extraterrestrial was at work. Thankfully a handful of serious scientists sought a more accurate explanation. Now, all whom travel far
                                               44
to catch a glimpse of the sailing stones benefit from the scientists' thorough research. |45|

39. If the writer were to delete the preceding sentence, the essay would primarily lose a sentence that:
   A. describes every detail in the water cycle.
   B. distracts from the paragraph's purpose.
   C. rightly contrasts cold nights with hot days.
   D. explains how ice comes to be in the desert.

40. F. NO CHANGE
    G. accompanied through wind, the
    H. accompanied with the
    J. accompanied by high wind speeds, the

41. A. NO CHANGE
    B. expect—
    C. expect:
    D. expect

42. F. NO CHANGE
    G. on the contrary, though technically,
    H. though technically altogether
    J. technically

43. A. NO CHANGE
    B. blame, and though others
    C. blame, while others
    D. blame

44. F. NO CHANGE
    G. themselves whom
    H. who
    J. they

45. The writer is considering deleting the preceding sentence. Should this sentence be kept or deleted?

   A. Kept, because it reinforces that scientists must do their research wholeheartedly.
   B. Kept, because it fittingly ends the essay by linking with the first paragraph.
   C. Deleted, because it shifts the focus from the stones to tourists who visit the stones.
   D. Deleted, because it presumes that everyone will eventually see the stones firsthand.

## PASSAGE IV

### The Moai of Easter Island

Easter Island sits in the Pacific Ocean off the coast of Chile; of which it is a special territory. Its name stems from the first European visit to the island, which occurred, on Easter Sunday in 1722. Though its history and isolation from the mainland are of interest to many, the most academically appealing aspect of the island, not to mention its most mysterious: is its Moai.

Moai are large human figures carved from stone and are thought to represent ancestors of natives. The average stone's and its height and weight is about 13 feet and 12 tonnes, respectively; though they vary in size. Characteristic of each statue is an oversized head, nose, and chin. They carve from a quarry called Rano Raraku, which is an inactive volcanic crater on the Western side of the island.

While nearly half of all Moai remain at the site of the quarry, hundreds of statues were transported around the island between the years 1250 and 1500. This has led to an immense amount of pillow talk as to the means of the transportation, a mystery deepened by the fact that the island was nearly

46. F. NO CHANGE
    G. Chile of which
    H. Chile, and which
    J. Chile, of which

47. A. NO CHANGE
    B. island, which occurred on Easter Sunday,
    C. island, which occurred on Easter Sunday
    D. island which occurred on Easter Sunday

48. F. NO CHANGE
    G. mysterious, is its,
    H. mysterious, is its
    J. mysterious is its

49. A. NO CHANGE
    B. stones' and its
    C. stone's
    D. stones

50. F. NO CHANGE
    G. respectively,
    H. respectively
    J. respectively, and

51. A. NO CHANGE
    B. are carving
    C. do the carving
    D. were carved

52. F. NO CHANGE
    G. inactive, volcanic, crater
    H. inactive, volcanic crater
    J. inactive volcanic crater,

53. A. NO CHANGE
    B. quarry—hundreds
    C. quarry. Hundreds
    D. quarry hundreds

54. F. NO CHANGE
    G. conjecturing of guesses
    H. people talking and chatting
    J. speculation

treeless when Europeans first arrived in the 18th
century.

One hypothesis is that the stones were rolled across lubricated logs. Although men pulled on the stones by rope, others lifted logs from the back of the line to the front so that the stone could continue rolling in the direction of its final destination. A scientific analysis has shown that at one time, the island was very wooded indeed |57| .

A second hypothesis about the transportation of the Moai, however, has been gaining a steady following among many anthropologists. This theory postulates that ropes were tied to the carved statues by the natives while they were upright. As men pulled on the enormous statues, others would rock the statue back and forth to the rhythm of a chant or song. Slowly, the statues would "walk" across the island. No matter how them were transported from Rano Raraku across the island, all can appreciate their beauty, mystery, and history.

55. Which of the following alternatives to the underlined portion would NOT be acceptable?
   A. landed
   B. came
   C. reached the shore
   D. glanced

56. F. NO CHANGE
    G. While
    H. However
    J. Contrary to popular belief

57. At this point, the writer is considering adding the following information:

   which would lend credence to this theory

   Should the writer make this addition here?
   A. Yes, because otherwise the reader would not know that the island was once wooded.
   B. Yes, because it connects the fact of the island's wooded past to the hypothesis put forward by the paragraph.
   C. No, because the paragraph has nothing to do with historical theory.
   D. No, because it fails to provide a credible source for the scientific analysis already mentioned in the sentence.

58. F. NO CHANGE
    G. have been gaining
    H. have gained
    J. gains

59. A. NO CHANGE
    B. statues
    C. previously carved statues
    D. statues, previously carved,

60. F. NO CHANGE
    G. the Moai
    H. it
    J. all they

## PASSAGE V

### John Hart, Unsung Hero

[1]

Stories of that long ago American war and the heroism of many of the nation's founders abound.

On the contrary, most are familiar with Thomas Jefferson, George Washington, Benjamin Franklin, John Adams, and John Hancock, to name a few, but they are not the only ones who took risks instead of so great a nation. [A] There were 56 total signers of the Declaration of Independence—many of whom fly under the radar—including some person from New Jersey. |65|

[2]

John Hart was the son of a farmer and owned hundreds of acres of farmland himself in Hunterdon County, a rural area north of Trenton. [B] As a politician who had penned his name to the parchment that declared the sovereignty of the American colonies; Hart was a wanted man when the British army closed in on his home in December of the same year.

61. 
   A. NO CHANGE
   B. the American Revolution
   C. all of the fighting that started in 1776
   D. all the shots fired and battles waged over the states

62. 
   F. NO CHANGE
   G. As a result, most
   H. In conclusion, most
   J. Most

63. 
   A. NO CHANGE
   B. on behalf of
   C. to the detriment of
   D. rather

64. Which choice best fits the tone of the essay and most strongly introduces the subject of the essay as a man whose story is worthy of being told?
   F. NO CHANGE
   G. a man
   H. an unsung hero
   J. a great citizen

65. At this point, the writer is considering adding the following true statement:

   George Washington embarked on his famous crossing of the Delaware into New Jersey in the winter of 1777.

   Should the writer make this addition here?
   A. Yes, because it ties in well with the more famous signers of the Declaration mentioned earlier in the paragraph.
   B. Yes, because it provides historical evidence for the important role New Jersey played in the American Revolution.
   C. No, because it is only loosely related to the information provided in the first paragraph.
   D. No, because the first paragraph makes no mention of George Washington.

66. 
   F. NO CHANGE
   G. colonies, Hart
   H. colonies, but Hart
   J. colonies. Hart

[3]

After entrusting the safety of his children to a family that lived near him, Hart was forced into the
                                    67

Sourland Mountains, where he hid among the rocks
                                              68
and in caves for over a month. [C] His empty farm was raided and damaged by troops. Not finding Hart at home, the British hunted him like an animal
                            69
throughout the surrounding area, but to no avail: Hart, though in his 60's, was able to elude their efforts to track him down. [D]

[4]

[1] Finally, American troops retook Trenton; after living in terrible conditions for such a long time, the relief of returning home was incredible. [2] For
                                              70
example, prior to the Battle of Monmouth, Hart's abundant farmland was used as camping grounds for Washington's patriot army. [3] Its even said that
                                                71
Washington himself dined one night with his cosigner of the Declaration. [4] Over a year later the war was ongoing, and Hart was still doing his part. |72|

[5]

Sadly, Hart would not live to see the end of the Revolutionary War. He passed away peacefully in 1779 there and was buried in the local churchyard.
          73

67. **A.** NO CHANGE
    **B.** group of people under one roof nearby
    **C.** family in the general vicinity
    **D.** local family

68. **F.** NO CHANGE
    **G.** to hide
    **H.** be hiding
    **J.** were to hide

69. Given that all of the choices are accurate, which one most effectively dramatizes the situation at hand and stresses the urgency of Hart's circumstances?

    **A.** NO CHANGE
    **B.** the troops searched far and wide
    **C.** enemy forces took a good look
    **D.** soldiers in red uniforms checked out some places

70. **F.** NO CHANGE
    **G.** Hart was relieved and able to return to his home.
    **H.** home was waiting for Hart, who was relieved.
    **J.** the caves were traded for the home Hart was used to, which explains just how relieved he truly was.

71. **A.** NO CHANGE
    **B.** They
    **C.** It's
    **D.** Its'

72. For the sake of logic and cohesion, Sentence 4 should be placed:

    **F.** where it is now.
    **G.** before Sentence 1.
    **H.** after Sentence 1.
    **J.** after Sentence 2.

73. **A.** NO CHANGE
    **B.** there is hope that Hart will be remembered
    **C.** under his own roof and in his own bed
    **D.** at his home

Since Hart had donated the land to build the church
                              74
in the first place, it was a fitting burial for a generous and courageous man.

74. F. NO CHANGE
    G. the land, to build the church,
    H. the land to build the church,
    J. the land to build, the church,

> Question 75 asks about the preceding passage as a whole.

75. At this point, the writer is considering adding the following information:

    > He had thirteen children, but sadly his wife passed away in October of 1776, relatively soon after Independence Day earlier that summer.

    If the writer were to add this sentence, it would most logically be placed at:

    A. Point A in Paragraph 1.
    B. Point B in Paragraph 2.
    C. Point C in Paragraph 3.
    D. Point D in Paragraph 3.

# Step 7 Correct Answers

## Practice Test 1

| **Passage I** | **Passage II** | **Passage III** | **Passage IV** | **Passage V** |
|---|---|---|---|---|
| 1: C | 16: F | 31: A | 46: G | 61: B |
| 2: F | 17: B | 32: J | 47: A | 62: F |
| 3: D | 18: J | 33: C | 48: G | 63: A |
| 4: J | 19: C | 34: J | 49: B | 64: F |
| 5: A | 20: F | 35: A | 50: G | 65: D |
| 6: H | 21: A | 36: H | 51: B | 66: H |
| 7: D | 22: H | 37: A | 52: J | 67: D |
| 8: J | 23: A | 38: F | 53: D | 68: G |
| 9: B | 24: F | 39: B | 54: H | 69: A |
| 10: H | 25: C | 40: J | 55: B | 70: G |
| 11: B | 26: G | 41: C | 56: F | 71: C |
| 12: J | 27: C | 42: H | 57: C | 72: J |
| 13: C | 28: H | 43: C | 58: H | 73: D |
| 14: G | 29: D | 44: G | 59: B | 74: F |
| 15: D | 30: G | 45: A | 60: G | 75: C |

## Practice Test 2

| **Passage I** | **Passage II** | **Passage III** | **Passage IV** | **Passage V** |
|---|---|---|---|---|
| 1: A | 16: F | 31: C | 46: J | 61: B |
| 2: J | 17: C | 32: J | 47: C | 62: J |
| 3: B | 18: H | 33: A | 48: H | 63: B |
| 4: G | 19: A | 34: F | 49: C | 64: H |
| 5: D | 20: H | 35: C | 50: G | 65: C |
| 6: G | 21: A | 36: H | 51: D | 66: G |
| 7: D | 22: H | 37: D | 52: F | 67: D |
| 8: G | 23: C | 38: F | 53: A | 68: F |
| 9: D | 24: J | 39: D | 54: J | 69: A |
| 10: F | 25: A | 40: J | 55: D | 70: G |
| 11: D | 26: J | 41: B | 56: G | 71: C |
| 12: F | 27: A | 42: J | 57: B | 72: H |
| 13: B | 28: G | 43: C | 58: F | 73: D |
| 14: H | 29: A | 44: H | 59: B | 74: F |
| 15: A | 30: H | 45: B | 60: G | 75: B |

Stumped on any? You will find the explanations for each answer beginning on page 167 (Practice Test 1) and 178 (Practice Test 2).

# In Conclusion

Congratulations! If you have completed this entire workbook, I must say, I am impressed. Rest assured that you have not wasted your time with out of order prep. You have systematized your preparation, and in doing so you've put first-things-first, and I hope you have seen which areas of content and skill need more work.

If you are still in need of practice, I recommend doing an internet search for the terms "Preparing for the ACT" followed by the current year (like: "Preparing for the ACT 2022"). This will bring up a PDF document of an authentic, recent, and publicly available ACT test that you are free to use and practice with. There are, of course, also dozens of ACT prep books of all kinds.

The ACT also has a program called **Test Information Release** (or TIR). If you take the ACT exam in December, April, or June, you are eligible. Essentially, you can pay an extra fee to get back from the ACT your original answers to the test, the correct answers, and the questions themselves. This can help you see what is actually bringing your score down or up from the ACT's point of view.

What follows is the explanations to every practice question in this book. Thanks for using The ACT English System!

# Answer Explanations - Step 1 - Passages I and II

**Correct Answers:**

| Passage I | Passage II |
|---|---|
| 1: C | 9: B |
| 2: J | 10: G |
| 3: A | 11: D |
| 4: G | 12: F |
| 5: B | 13: A |
| 6: J | 14: H |
| 7: A | 15: C |
| 8: J | 16: F |

**Passage I: Flannery's Childhood Home**

**#1** The correct answer is **C**. It might seem like the answer should be "Yes,..." because the previous sentence mentions peacocks. However, stay focused: the **subject** of the paragraph is the writer Flannery O'Connor, not the peacocks. Thus, an additional sentence about them derails from the focus, which is why **A** and **B** are incorrect. **D** is incorrect because the information has not already been provided.

**#2** The correct answer is **J**. These types of questions are among the most missed on ACT English. I believe this is true because the question itself is simply kind of *l o n g*. However, the question says we need a sentence that tells us two things: a) The house is still standing, and b) The house is open to the public. **J** tells us that the home is "preserved to this day" (still standing) and has been converted into "a museum" (open to the public). **F** may be about homes, **G** may be about Flannery O'Connor, and **H** may be a bout Savannah, GA, but none of those three options fulfill the basic two requirements of the question itself.

**#3** The correct answer is **A**. The remainder of this paragraph is about Flannery as a child, thus **A** works as it says it "gives us a window into the everyday childhood environment" of her. In addition, only **A** makes sense when you read the next sentence, which says, "Flannery was **one of these children**." Without the sentence in question, that phrase makes no sense, and should leave you asking, "What children?" **B**, though it says the sentence should be kept, has a subject matter that is irrelevant; this essay and this paragraph are not about trees and their value. **C** and **D** of course are incorrect because they say the sentence should be deleted.

**#4** The correct answer is **G**. There are clues in the sentence that tell us where it should be located. One of these clues is "all girls." All of a sudden, we are talking about multiple girls, not just Flannery O'Connor, thus a sentence before must change the subject matter to a multiple girls; this is what the first sentence of the paragraph does. As written, the second sentence in the paragraph mentions "these activities." That is another clue as to the location; the sentence to be added mentions activities: drawing and playing make-believe. This is why the sentence belongs at point B sandwiched between the sentence that mentions her "friends" and the sentence that mentions "these activities." Thus, answer choices **F, H,** and **J** make no logical sense.

**#5** First of all, the question asks you which phrase introduces the subject of a paragraph. Thus, you need to read the paragraph first to understand the subject of it (how else is there to do it?). Well, after a reading, hopefully you see that the subject of the paragraph is a physical space where the family raised chickens and where Flannery trained a chicken. **A** fails to define a space, so it is incorrect. The answer can't be **C** because chickens aren't raised in a car. **D** is a tempting wrong choice because the word "coop" is a space where chickens are raised, but later in the paragraph it speaks of the space being a place to grow plants, which is of course more fitting for a garden than a coop. That's why the answer is **B**; that is a space where chickens can be raised, that borders an alley, where plants are grown, and where a girl can spend time.

**#6** This question is extremely similar to #1. It seems like a relevant sentence. It's about the O'Connor family, and it's about chickens, so what's not to like? Well, there is something about it that is unlikeable: *it's obviously true*. Is there some other reason that a family would raise chickens? Additionally, it shifts the subject matter away from Flannery and the garden to the family as a whole. This is why the answer can't be **F** or **G**. The answer can't be **H** either; this is because we do need more information about her childhood home because that is the subject of the essay as a whole. Thus, the correct answer is **J**; we should assume that information to be true.

**#7** Oh boy…if you see those sentences numbered as they are in this paragraph, you know what's coming! Either you're going to be asked about the location of a sentence or their proper order. In this case, it's the former. You might be surprised at a reread of the paragraph because all seems well. The first sentence mentions that there was no air conditioning, and then the second sentence (the sentence in question) mentions a reprieve from the heat, and then the third sentence mentions hearing voices below the home (presumably, while the windows are open). Well, if this was your thinking, your instincts were correct. The answer for those reasons is **A**; no other ordering of the sentences makes logical sense.

**#8** This "Yes or No" question represents the mini-lesson I slipped in. This question (a classic ACT example) asks about the author's **main purpose**. In this case, is the main purpose of the essay Flannery O'Connor's characters? You should think, "No, that's not the main purpose, though I do remember some mention or mentions of her characters." If you don't know whether or not at this point the answer is yes or no, circle the question and move on; you shouldn't waste valuable time and reread the essay at this point. In other words, come back to it at the end of the test if you have time. Now, the purpose of the essay is to speak on her childhood home, not her characters. That eliminates **F** and **G**. Of our two "No" options, **H** is incorrect because the history of Savannah, though mentioned in the essay, is not its primary purpose. Thus, the answer must again be **J** because, as it says, the purpose of the essay is to describe her home.

**Passage II: The Texas State Fair**

**#9** Context is key. Context is key. If you haven't learned this by now let me say it again: context is key. Sentences belong (or don't) in paragraphs if they move it along from one sentence to the next. Imagine this paragraph without the sentence: how could we understand what the last sentence says ("what he meant") without the sentence being kept there? Who is "he" and what did he say? Thus, the sentence should be kept, so that eliminates **C** and **D**. However, reading the other answer choices don't make immediate sense. Do we need to know the father's desires (Answer **A**)? If this is an essay about the father's desires, then yes. Do we need anticipation to be built (Answer **B**). Well, the writer of the essay (the daughter) and her little brothers don't understand what he's talking about. Then, in paragraph 2, they begin to get excited. All of this points to two things: first, this is not an essay about the father's desires, and second, this essay is building anticipation. Thus, the answer is **B**.

**#10** We need a phrase that explains their excitement (the first part of the sentence) and makes it clear that they are going to the fair (following sentence). Thus, **H** does not work because it doesn't explain their excitement (how can you begin to get excited while you sleep?). **J** is simply a redundancy; we already know excitement is building. **F** fails because the father's rumbling stomach could not possibly cause the children to believe they are going to the fair. This is why the answer is **G**; the giant carousel explains the excitement and causes them to understand that they are going to the fair.

**#11** Smell that funnel cake (also called an "elephant ear" in some places)? It evokes lots of feelings of being at a fair or carnival of some kind. This feeling may be enough for some people to choose **A** or **B**. However, this sentence is a complete disruption. Without it, we have a good connection between "packs of little tickets" mentioned in the first sentence and "almost all of theirs" in the third. "Almost all of theirs" makes little or no sense if the sentence is inserted. It's not **C** because people are mostly familiar with that food, but even if not, that's not the main reason why it doesn't belong. This is why **D** is the correct answer: the details interrupt the paragraph's logical flow.

**#12** This time, the question isn't asking you outright if the sentence belongs. Rather, we need to ask the following: what does the sentence do for the paragraph? We go from spotting the ride (sentence 1) to paying tickets (sentence 3). This is why **F** is correct. Let's eliminate the other choices as well. **G** is probably the most tempting option of the four because "an eternity" is an exaggeration, but it is a necessary or fitting one. This is because the sentence provides context for our understanding of the word "finally" in the third sentence. **H** doesn't work because there's no mention anywhere else of the fear that is referred to in this option. **J** doesn't work because the time waiting in line isn't mentioned to let the reader know that it takes time to count tickets, but rather is mentioned to bridge sentences, continue the logical flow the paragraph, and build anticipation.

**#13** One clue to getting this question correct is the pronoun "it" after the colon that refers to something spinning. That pronoun doesn't work with choice **D** because "stars" is plural, so that option is out. It doesn't work with **C** either because you would never refer to the father as "it." Lastly, **B** does not work either because, while the stomach could be "it," it isn't the stomach that is spinning so as to pin the father and daughter to the walls. Thus, **A** makes sense: when the room ("it") spins, they are pinned to the walls.

**#14** The clue here is that we need a choice that not only works, but refers back to the opening paragraph. Let's go one option at a time. **F** has a consistent tone with the rest of the essay, but it: a) Doesn't refer back to the opening paragraph, and b) Contradicts the father's smiling in the sentence before. Thus, A is out. **G** does not work because the books of tickets aren't mentioned in the first paragraph. **J** doesn't work for the same reason; no mention of dragon coasters in paragraph 1! Thus, the answer is **H**; it mentions the father, who is grinning in the previous sentence. Most importantly however, it mentions the turkey leg that is referenced in the first paragraph.

**#15** In a way, you may have known this sentence was coming because of the letters A, B, C, and D sprinkled throughout the essay. We need a location in the essay that gives the reader an understanding of "them" and references a ride that goes at high speeds. This is why **C** has to be the correct answer. **A, B,** and **D** do not make any sense in context.

**#16** Again, you want to know if the answer is "Yes" or "No" before we get to the answer choices. If you don't know, then don't reread the essay at this point; circle this question, skip it in your answer booklet, and then come back with time at the end. The idea that this is a gift for her father is a bit irrelevant, the main question is this: is this essay a fun family memory? I hope it is pretty clear that the answer is "yes." That eliminates **H** and **J**. Answer choice **G** correctly says "yes," but it proposes that the essay is all about different kinds of family activities, but that isn't true: the essay focuses on one activity, which is going to the fair. That is why **F** is the correct answer: the essay focuses on the fun she shared with her father at the fair.

# Answer Explanations - Step 2 - Passages I and II

**Correct Answers:**

<u>Passage I</u>
1: D
2: G
3: D
4: J
5: C
6: G
7: A
8: H
9: B
10: F
11: D
12: H
13: B
14: J
15: B

<u>Passage II</u>
16: F
17: B
18: H
19: A
20: G
21: C
22: J
23: D
24: J
25: A
26: F
27: C
28: H
29: B
30: H

**Passage I: Uluru**

#1 As written, it is redundant; we already know this took place in July. Thus, **A** is out. This also eliminates answer choices **B** and **C**. These options also are redundant. You may be tempted by **C** because it provides the most information, but don't be fooled: we already know all of it. That is why the correct answer is **D**.

#2 Another classic "Kept" or "Deleted" question. In this case, the preceding sentence is about Gosse discovering the rock, and the sentence after the one in question is about the rock already having a name. This fact, "the rock already possessed a name," is contrasting. That contrast is highlighted if the sentence is included here. Thus, that eliminates **H** and **J**. Speaking of choice **H**, it was just shown that the details about Ayers are fitting, but the details are also in line with the paragraph's purpose, thus **H** is eliminated. As for **J**, it raises no questions. **F** is incorrect because Ayers is not the one who discovered the rock; that was Gosse. Thus, **G** must be correct. **G** also says exactly what we want the sentence to do: contrast with the rock's other name.

#3 At first glance, the commas in the answer choices are distracting. Are we setting off these phrases correctly with the commas? Well, it turns out, this isn't a question of comma usage. The first three words of the sentence are "This latter name," referring to *Uluru*; thus we don't need to again state that the name that is the subject of the paragraph that "was given to it by the Pitjantjatjara." This is why **A**, **B**, and **C** are all incorrect: they're all redundant (comma problems with B and C besides). Thus, the answer is **D**. When we delete the phrase altogether and the commas with it the sentence flows on perfectly well and links "This latter name" with the verb "was."

#4 Here we have our third question out of the first four that tested your ability to spot redundancy. Were you able to see why the phrase "like a mountain" does not belong at the end of this sentence, which provides a definition of an inselberg? We already heard that it is "a hill or mountain." **G** says "that surrounds it," referring to the landscape; however, before the word "landscape" is the word "surrounding," thus this option is incorrect as well. **H** mentions that an inselberg is made of rock; however this is information we already know as well (earlier it says an inselberg is "composed of rock").

That leaves **J**, which is, of course, correct. That an inselberg is isolated is a detail that has not yet been mentioned.

**#5** Hopefully you see now if you didn't at first that "closest" and "nearest" are synonyms; we don't need to say the same thing twice. This already eliminates **A** and **B**. As for **D**, "most in proximity" is overly wordy compared to **C**. You may think, "that's not fair, they mean the same thing!" That's correct, they do, but the "tie" so to speak goes to the answer choice that is less wordy; it is *best*. This is why **C** is the correct answer; it communicates that a formation is near without being redundant or too wordy.

**#6** While this question does not test redundancy or verbosity recognition, it harkens back to Step 1; one of these phrases is the *best*. However, in this case, you are given very specific instructions for the purpose of the phrase: you need one that illustrates a "precise distance." As written, "which is pretty close by" is not specific enough, so **F** is out. Letter choice **H** has the same problem; it is too vague. Letter choice **J** starts to be more specific by mentioning a mode of transportation, but it never says how long it would take to get there by car (or, while we're on it, how far away it is *precisely*). Thus, **G** is correct; it gives a precise distance: "16 miles to the West."

**#7** The word "remnant" means something leftover or remaining. Thus, **B** and **D** are redundant. As for **C**, it basically defines the word "remnant" in the place of the word itself, which means it is too wordy. This is why **A** is the correct answer.

**#8** In this case, **G** may be tempting at first glance. This is because it is a little less wordy than the phrase as written, choice **F**, and still makes sense. However, the phrase "the test of time" implies that time has gone by; we don't need, then, to say that time "has passed" or that it is "still passing." This is why **H** is correct. **F, G,** and **J** all redundantly and unnecessarily say that the time "has passed" or "is passing."

**#9** Notice a theme to these questions? "Species" and "types" of bats mean the same thing. This is why **A** can't be the correct or *best* answer. **D** adds the adjective "categorical" to "types," but even that is redundant; different types are by definition different categories of things. That leaves **B** and **C**; each of these choices is one simple word. In this case, although we haven't discussed the uses of colons, you might see that inserting one here is at a minimum disruptive to the sentence. **B** is correct for these reasons.

**#10** We are looking for an option that tells us that 70 or more species of reptiles have been found around Uluru. Well, all of the answer choices do that. This is a classic question of verbosity; which option gives us what we are looking for that is the least wordy? That is clearly not **G, H,** or **J**; all of them are too wordy. **F** is correct for this reason.

**#11** Here, we have a sentence giving an example of a reptile, and the question is whether or not it belongs. Notice that after bats are mentioned, we aren't given a type of bat. If the sentence said something like, "For example, the Black Fanged Slitherer was previously thought to be extinct until it was caught just off of Uluru," then we'd be on to something more relevant. In addition, a historic or scientific essay of this type isn't going to deal in categories that are, for the most part, presumed to be true: most people know that snakes are reptiles. These are all reasons why the sentence doesn't belong. If we examine the "Yes" options one by one, they also fall apart for other reasons. **A** can't be correct because it presupposes a question asked earlier in the essay, but no such question exists. **B** can't be correct because it does not deepen our understanding of the animal life because it is not specific enough. Examining the "No" answers, we see that **C** can't be correct because this information about snakes is not given elsewhere in the paragraph. That leaves **D**, which hits the nail on the head. The sentence adds nothing to our understanding about Uluru, as it says, which is why it is the correct answer.

**#12** This question combines your ability to see if sentences belong in context and to recognize redundancy. In this case, the sentence is about how bats make their home around Uluru. No big deal, except that has already been said in the second sentence of the paragraph. For this reason, it doesn't belong, and thus **F** and **G** are incorrect. **J** can not be correct because the sentence is on topic; this paragraph is about animal species in and around Uluru, and so is the sentence. **H** correctly recognizes that the information given in the sentence is redundant and doesn't belong, and thus it it the correct answer.

**#13** While the colon used in choice **D** is appropriate, the answer is incorrect for the same reason that **A** and **C** are incorrect: they are all too wordy! This is a classic question of verbosity, and thus the correct answer is **B**; it communicates the present name of the rock in the least amount of words possible, and thus it is *best*.

**#14** The sentence in question gives us a clear context clue. It says "This episode took place…" That is just about all we need to correctly place it; it will come after a sentence that mentions an event or episode. The details about the millions of years or technical names of the periods this episode took place in might look scary, but are really not necessary to perfectly comprehend to get this question correct. Starting with answer choice **F**, the sentence before Point A is about the name of the inselberg being Uluru; no event is mentioned. **F** therefore is incorrect. **G** does not work for the same reason; the sentence before point B is the definition of an inselberg, and there is no mention of an event in it. Now let's turn our attention to choice **H**. However, point C comes after a sentence about the rock being composed of arkose; putting a sentence here also would separate two sentences that logically flow from one to the other. That leaves **J**, which is correct; point D in paragraph 3 comes immediately after mention of "the Peterman Orogeny," an event that fits the description of the sentence!

**#15** This question asks whether or not the essay as a whole is about the history of an important Australian landmark. Because the entire essay is about one, Uluru, then yes, this essay certainly does just that. This eliminates answer choices **C** and **D**, both of which say "No." Let's look now at choice **A**. While this option begins with "Yes," it says that the essay is about the author's firsthand experience visiting the landmark. However, there is no evidence that the author has been there, and the entire essay is in the third person (as opposed to the first person, which would be written with the word "I", like "When *I* visited Uluru, it was really hot…"). This is why **B** is correct; this option syncs with the requirements of the question and accurately says that all of these requirements have been met by the essay.

**Passage II: The Palace of Versailles**

**#16** All four of these answer choices, essentially, say the same thing. However, three of them are overly wordy (verbose). These wrong answers are **G, H,** and **J**. As it is written, it is less wordy and communicates what needs to be. Thus, **F** is the correct answer.

**#17** As it is written, it seems like nothing is wrong. However, at a closer glance, you may notice that "wealth" and "money" are the same thing. That is redundant, so **A** has to be incorrect. **C** is also incorrect because "power" and "control" are the same thing. Lastly, choice **D** had a redundancy built in ("gold" and "money"); the wording is also strange and irregular. **B** is correct; the two words are not synonyms and communicate different ideas.

**#18** This is an example of a classic ACT question that tests your ability to recognize the proper ordering of words as well as when an option is too wordy. Here, what needs to be communicated is that some of the structures are still standing. The best and fastest way to get this question correct is to let your "ear" pick up on which choices sound wrong. By "ear," I simply mean your ability to read and hear in your head that something is off. This kind of intuition should eliminate choices **F** and **G**; in these examples, the ordering of words is out of whack. The remaining two choices are almost identical, and the ordering of their words is on par. Because they mean the same thing, and because both make sense, there must be a tiebreaker: verbosity. So, which has fewer words? That would be **H**, making it the correct answer, and making **J** incorrect.

**#19** We need a sentence that transitions. A good transition sentence will build on the topic of the first paragraph and tease or introduce the topic of the second paragraph. The first paragraph was about

European palaces and their general history and importance. The second paragraph is about the Palace of Versailles in particular. That is why the correct answer is **A**; the first, dependent clause of the sentence mentions the homes of Paragraph 1, and the second, independent clause of the sentence references the Palace of Versailles in particular. **B** references the plural homes or palaces of Paragraph 1, but Paragraph 2 has nothing to do with homes being destroyed. **C** references plural landmarks, which probably fulfills our first requirement about Paragraph 1, but although Paragraph 2 mentions gardens, that is certainly not the topic of the paragraph as a whole. Lastly, **D** also references plural homes, but Paragraph 2 has nothing to do with groups raising funds.

#20 Here, "uniquely" and "stands apart" are synonymous; they both indicate that there is something special about the Palace of Versailles relative to other palaces. As written, it is redundant, so **A** is incorrect. **H** is problematic because it places the adverb "uniquely" behind the verb "stands", which in the context of this particular sentence does not work. Based on everything that we've said, it would be most tempting to conclude that the least wordy choice would be correct. However, in this case, **J** is also incorrect because it does not indicate that the Palace of Versailles is unique or special; the use of the word "stands" here makes it sound like the Palace has political or moral views that it will never abandon. This is why **G** is correct; it says what the sentence requires without the redundancy.

#21 We already know that the Hall of Mirrors is large ("…a massive mirror-filled room…"), so **A** is incorrect because it is redundant. **D** is incorrect for the same reason; it is redundant. Like #20, it may be tempting to choose **B** because it is less wordy, but that changes the meaning of the sentence completely; the Hall of Mirrors isn't the Palace, but in it. This is why **C** is correct; we want to know that the Hall of Mirrors is the best-known feature within the Palace.

#22 Here you are asked what would happen if the preceding sentence about a couple of the Palace's other features was deleted. **F** is incorrect because the sentence has nothing to do with visitors and their ability to enter the Palace. **G** may be tempting because you may think, "If the Palace and these features were lost, that would be tragic". That's true, but there is nothing in the previous sentence that mentions what would happen if the Palace were destroyed. As for **H**, for all you know, visitors may very well be going East to West when they go from the Garden to the Royal Opera, but there is no indication of that in the sentence (or anywhere else in the essay for that matter). **J** then is correct because the sentence does just what choice **J** indicates: it continues a paragraph that was designed to point out some of its more beautiful and historic features.

#23 The dependent clause at the beginning of this sentence ("With ornate statues…") ends with the comma. It is called a *modifying clause* (more on that in a later Step). All you need to know for now is that it modifies or describes the noun after the comma. In this case, that's "the Palace." Thus, we do not need the word "Palace" in the clause itself. That would be like saying, "As I took a bite of my delicious hamburger, my hamburger tasted good!" So, we can eliminate answer choices **A** and **C**. Choice **B** can also be eliminated because: a) "each and every" is redundant, and b) the word "decorated" is redundant because the clause itself is saying there are decorations in every corner. For these reasons, **D** is correct; it is not verbose or redundant and tells simply where the statues and decorations are.

#24 This is a case of both verbosity and redundancy. Choice **F** is redundant; if something is aesthetically pleasing (at least in this case) it is beautiful. Same with **H**; we do not need the adverb "attractively" to describe "pretty" because that is redundant. As for the other two choices, **G** is not *wrong*, but it is certainly not the best choice between the two. A four-word three-hyphened word is, well, *wordy*. In addition, "easy-on-the-eye" has a connotation of slang, which makes it a bit informal for this kind of essay; it is also simply wordier than the correct answer. That is why the *best* answer, and the correct answer, is **J**; it says what is needed without verbosity or redundancy.

#25 This question is very similar to that of #18 in this same Step. The ACT is fond of this kind of question; what is the best ordering of words? Well, again, your best guide is your "ear" or instinct; which one sounds correct, and says what needs to be said in the fewest words possible? **B**, **C**, and **D** are all problematic; they jumble words and should sound "off." Only choice **A**, as it is written, says that the Palace is still popular without a jumbled mix of incorrectly ordered or oddly used words.

**#26** To get this question correct, we need to first read the sentence before, then the proposed sentence, and then the sentence after to determine if the proposed sentence fits the paragraph well. In this case, it does! It helps to transition from the idea that the palace has historical significance and gives context for the phrase "After the Revolution" in the following sentence. Thus, it does belong, so we can eliminate **H** and **J**. Letter choice **G** makes no sense at all because the Palace was not destroyed and is talked about as still standing in the present day. This is why **F** is correct, and in fact, this choice says what we concluded at the beginning of this explanation in that it gives evidence of the Palace's historical significance.

**#27 A** might be a very tempting choice here because it is a great way to start a sentence and tells us how long the Palace was used as a home for French royalty. However, we already know that based on the end of the sentence ("for about 100 years"). Thus, **A** is incorrect. The same is true for choice **B**; we know later in the sentence that the home was used for monarchs. That leaves **C** and **D**. **D** is incorrect because "Palace Versailles" is not the correct title of the palace. Thus, **C** is correct because it correctly titles the palace and adds no redundancies.

**#28** This is an example of the kind of question I proposed in mini-lesson 2. What you need to do is to re-read the sentence with the underlined portion in the various proposed places. We need a place that stresses that the Palace's condition has gotten better and gotten worse. Let's try **F**, "Where it is now." This position rightly says that the Palace was restored in many phases, but it fails to stress that the Palace also went through various spouts of disrepair or worsening. Choice **G** is incorrect because it then makes the sentence say, "In the many phases of years," which is a phrase with no meaning. Choice **H** makes the sentence say, "...the Palace went through many phases of disrepair and restoration." This is the correct answer; it correctly describes the many phases of ups and downs the Palace has had. **J** is incorrect because "many phases of Palace" is also a phrase that makes no sense.

**#29** Let's start with choice **D** this time. Ending the sentence with a period might not be grammatically incorrect, but it is certainly incomplete, meaning it creates an incomplete thought ("took place..." where?). That leaves **A, B,** and **C**. All three of these choices essentially say the same thing, so now we are in the territory of trying to identify the *best* answer. **C** is simply odd; who says that? No one. That leaves us with **B** and **A**. While **A** is acceptable, and is even heard of or said often, **B** says the same thing in a less-wordy way. This is why **B** is the *best* answer, and thus is correct.

**#30** It is one of the goals of these lesson plans to have you be able to answer these questions "Yes" or "No" before you read the answer choices. We are being asked if this essay compares and contrasts different buildings. However, almost the entirety of the essay is about the Palace of Versailles, and it is never compared to other European buildings. That is why the answer the to initial question is "No." Thus, **F** and **G** are incorrect. **H** says that the essay is only about the Palace of Versailles, which is true, which is why choice **H** is correct. Looking over choice **J**, it says that the essay has nothing to say about other buildings. That is not true; the first paragraph is a general overview of historic European palaces. Thus, **J** is incorrect.

# Answer Explanations - Step 3 - Passages I, II, and III

**Correct Answers:**

| Passage I | Passage II | Passage III |
|---|---|---|
| 1: B | 16: H | 31: B |
| 2: F | 17: D | 32: J |
| 3: C | 18: J | 33: A |
| 4: J | 19: A | 34: G |
| 5: C | 20: F | 35: B |
| 6: J | 21: D | 36: H |
| 7: B | 22: H | 37: A |
| 8: H | 23: D | 38: J |
| 9: A | 24: F | 39: C |
| 10: G | 25: C | 40: G |
| 11: D | 26: G | 41: C |
| 12: G | 27: B | 42: F |
| 13: A | 28: J | 43: D |
| 14: H | 29: C | 44: G |
| 15: D | 30: F | 45: A |

The three passages within this Step tested all three Steps so far. Of course, there was emphasis on Step 3, but it is important to continually refresh the subject matter of Steps 1 and 2 because, after all, they are the most frequently asked types of questions.

You were required to complete three passages this time, not merely two, because the amount of content is increasing.

**Passage I: Unity Through Tragedy**

**#1** Here, "Like many Americans" is a dependent clause; it introduces the sentence. The independent clause, "I remember where I was on September 11, 2001" can stand alone as a sentence, but the dependent clause can't. As an introductory phrase, it must be set off by a comma. If it were at the end of the sentence, we wouldn't need a comma, but because it's at the beginning, it must be. Answer choice **A** and **C** can be eliminated because they do not have a comma after "Americans." Choice **D** can also be rejected because it isolates "Americans" by commas as if the word were a nonessential phrase; in this sentence, that is not the case. That is why the answer is **B**; it separates the introductory phrase from the rest of the sentence by a comma.

**#2** Here we have a question of wordiness and context. "Awoke up" is not a grammatically proper phrase, so **H** is incorrect. **G** has the problem of being overly wordy; why say "rose up from my mattress" when there is a less-wordy option available? While **J** is not grammatically incorrect, it is something that is never said and makes no sense. Thus, **F** is the correct answer because it makes sense in context in the least words possible.

**#3** This question is one of those in which the words are jumbled up; we need the answer choice that simply makes the most sense. What is a "down the street good friend"? Don't try to convince yourself that this is a thing or somehow makes sense, just recognize that it is a meaningless phrase designed to distract you. Thus, we can eliminate answer choices **A** and **B**. **D** is incorrect because deleting the underlined portion makes the sentence a fragment and incomplete. **C** is the correct option because it correctly characterizes the friend as "good" (the adjective is placed before the noun) and then puts the propositional phrase after in a place that makes sense.

#4 We said that the number one most tested comma rule is the ability to recognize when nonessential phrases should be set off by commas. Think about the sentence when the phrase "unaware of what was happening in New York" is removed. Now we have, "I attended my high-school classes through mid-morning." That is a sentence that works, and that's why the phrase in the middle is nonessential. Choices **G** and **H** place commas in incorrect places, isolating the wrong phrases, and that's why they do not work. Choice **F** has no commas at all, thus is incorrect. Thus, choice **J** is correct because it sets off the nonessential phrase.

#5 Here we are revisiting our Step 1 skill: does this sentence belong? Is it relevant and does it move the paragraph along, or is it a detour, shifting the topic of the paragraph? In this case, it is a distraction. It may seem relevant since the sentence previous mentioned English class and so does the sentence in question, but that is not good enough. The paragraph is about what happened that day; the sentence in question is about English class, and that's a distraction. Thus, we can eliminate **A** and **B**, which both say yes. Letter **D** says that it doesn't belong because the paragraph is about Math class; that's not true, so it is incorrect. The correct answer is **C** because it says that the proposed sentence "shifts the focus;" that is true.

#6 As written, we have a comma followed by a FANBOYS conjunction, in this case "and." That would be correct if the clauses before and after were both independent clauses. "Horrifyingly, I watched as the second tower was struck" is such a clause, but "as the Twin Towers then collapsed one after another" is not; that can't stand alone as a sentence. So, **F** and **G** are both out for this reason. **H** removes the "and," but then that makes the sentence sound like all of the events happen at the exact same time (the second tower is struck <u>as</u> the Towers fall). Only **J** maintains the integrity of the sentence and proposes the events in the correct order as taking place one after another.

#7 Of course, there is no nation called "United America." That eliminates **A**. For that matter, it also eliminates **D**, which also has the problem of putting a comma after the adjective "United." As for **C**, there is nothing grammatically wrong with it, but it is overly wordy. That is why the answer is **B**: America.

#8 Here we have a nonessential clause ("but also those from a generation before me") inserted into the greater sentence. We learned that you can set off such a clause with commas, and that seems to be what is at play here, but **F** has a problem: the clause is finished with an em dash. That means it has to be started with an em dash as well, just like you would with parentheses. **J** and **F** properly set off the phrase in some way, but neither are an em dash, and thus are incorrect. **G** does not work because it does nothing to set off the nonessential clause, not to mention that it has no em dash. That is why the answer of course is **H**; it provides the first em dash that pairs with the other already in the sentence.

#9 Let's assume that we are unsure as to whether or not this is a proper way to use a colon. Where does that leave us? We know the answer can't be **B** because it puts a semi-colon in its place, but we know a semi-colon can only be used to separate independent clauses. **D** is the kind of option that makes you second guess what you know or recognize commas. The question is, if it kind of sounds like a "pause" works, can we throw a comma in there? No, remember, we can't just throw in commas to make pauses; commas are used deliberately. For a comma to belong here, we would need a complete, dependent clause to follow (something like, "forget, which is unity"). So **D** is incorrect. If you can get that far, you can know that the colon is being used correctly. As a reminder, a colon has many uses, but it always follows a complete clause/sentence. Here, the tiebreaker is wordiness. **C** is incorrect because it says what is needed but in too many words. Thus, the correct answer is **A**, no change.

#10 Here we have multiple adjectives in a series in front of a noun. Before we review the rule, let's eliminate choice **J** since it puts two adjectives between commas without any context and thus it is meaningless. The question is whether or not a comma is needed after the word "simpler." Or, looking at choice **H**, whether or not we need to reverse the adjectives. We would need to reverse the adjectives only if one of them absolutely belonged prior to the noun (in this case "identity"). Like we said in the lesson, there are lots of combinations like that; even with the word "identity" you could have a combination like

Step 3 Explanations   140

"stolen identity." However, there's no reason to have the word "simpler" or "truer" tied to "identity" in any specific order. Not only does this mean that **H** is incorrect, but it also means that we need a comma after "simpler." Thus, **F** is also incorrect because there is no comma. Only choice **G** puts the comma, and this is why it is correct.

**#11** All of the choices are grammatically correct, thus there is something else to look out for here. Because all of the answer choices have different meaning, we must have a question of redundancy here. Let's start with **A**, which says "at retail locations…" This is incorrect though because the sentence already says "at stores." Moving to **B**, this too is redundant; the sentence begins by letting us know that it is American flags that were in short supply, so it is redundant to put it at the end of the sentence again. Looking at **C**, we have a similar problem; **C** tells us that the flags were once easy to purchase, but this is also something we already know ("once readily available at stores"). Thus the answer is **D**; it is the only choice that is not redundant.

**#12** Here again we have adjectives in a series. This time, there is something else at play: do we need a comma after the introductory clause? Let's start with the adjectives rule. Can we reverse the adjectives "awful" and "terrorist" and still get the same meaning? "Because more than twenty years have passed since these terrorist, awful attacks…" Um, no, that changes the meaning; a "terrorist attack" is a particular kind of attack; this is an adjective/noun combo that can't be separated. This means that we DO NOT need the comma after "awful." That eliminates **F** and **H**. The question then becomes whether or not we need a comma after "attacks." In this case, the answer is yes. This is clearly an opening dependent clause, thus we need a comma to separate it from the main clause. That is why **J** is incorrect and why **G** is the correct answer.

**#13** The student who thinks that commas exist to create artificial pauses that sound good is likely to get this question wrong. Some answers have a comma after "pride." Let's examine that first. Letter **C** does this, and it makes "I've noticed that the pride" a dependent clause to open the sentence. But that's not a dependent clause, and it makes a mess of the rest of the sentence. So **C** is incorrect. **D** does a similar thing, but this time making the clause extend to after the word "unity." But look at what would then come after the comma: "that strengthened in the months following has slowly faded away." That is a sentence nothing short of interrupted by something! Turning our attention to **B**, we see that this option makes "and unity" into a nonessential clause. However, that is not a nonessential clause. "Unity," along with "pride" are what are strengthened; just because it kind of sounds nice to put in commas, that doesn't mean they belong. The answer then is **A** because the sentence is fine the way it is written.

**#14** We need to go back and simply insert this sentence into the different places and see where it fits; it's as simple as that. The correct answer on these kinds of questions is never going to kind of be an OK place for a sentence; rather, it is going to deliberately belong in that paragraph for a reason. **F** is incorrect because inserting the sentence as the last sentence of the first paragraph disrupts the flow of event's for the author's morning. **G** is an example of a place where you might be tempted to say, "Well that kind of sounds OK." But it is not. The sentence following is "This is particularly true…." What is particularly true? That changes if we insert the sentence there. Because the sentence is a positive statement about people coming together, **H** would work (and yes it is the correct answer). This works because it begins a list in the paragraph of all of the positive things Americans did after 9/11. **J** for what it's worth is not a good fit; the sentence before stresses a negative, thus to throw in a sentence about people coming together is contrary to the sentence before it.

**#15** Again, we need to know if the answer is "Yes" or "No" before diving in. The question asks if the essay is a history of the USA. Although it is an event from American history, it is certainly not a history of America. We can eliminate then **A** and **B**. **C** says that it's not a history of America because the essay says nothing about any event within American history. Well that's not true; the entire essay is about an event from American history. **D** says that the answer is no because the essay is not only about only 1 event, but it is also more of a personal perspective (as opposed to a historical text that is usually less personal). That is why **D** is the correct answer.

**Passage II: The Colosseum**

**#16** As written, I hope you can see that the sentence needs to offset some kind of introductory phrase with a comma. We need to think: what is the independent clause of this sentence, the piece that could stand alone as a sentence? Is it: "history the Colosseum was first constructed nearly 2000 years ago"? No; that doesn't make sense. This is why **G** is incorrect. Letter **F** has this same problem of failing to separate the dependent clause from the independent. The independent clause of the sentence is "the Colosseum was first constructed nearly 2,000 years ago," so we need an answer that separates that off. That's why the answer is **H** because it properly does this. **J** is incorrect because it incorrectly makes "history" a nonessential word or phrase, which it is not.

**#17** Here we have underlined a bridge between two clauses. What we need to know is if these two clauses are independent (can stand alone as a sentence) or if one is dependent. In this case, what comes before and after the semi-colon are both independent clauses. The question itself is worded a bit differently; it asks for which option is unacceptable. In other words, there will be three correct answer and one wrong one, which must be identified. Here, you are being tested as to whether or not you know the ways to combine these clauses. **A** is acceptable; it treats the clauses as independent sentences. **B** is also acceptable; we discussed that an em dash (—) is a way to combine independent clauses. **C** is also acceptable; it uses a comma and appropriately adds a FANBOYS (for, and, nor, but, or, yet, so) conjunction to bridge them. **D**, then, is not acceptable; you can't add a FANBOYS conjunction after a semi-colon, only after a comma. Thus **D** is our correct answer because it is the only incorrect option.

**#18** Nothing grammatically incorrect here with any of the options. What we need is the *best* option. All of them say essentially the same thing, but one of them says it in the most succinct or you might say "regular" way. That is why the answer is **J**. Other choices (**F, G, H**) are all incorrect because they are simply too wordy.

**#19** Let's eliminate choice **D** simply because it is too wordy. There has to be a way to line up these words properly. Hopefully your "ear" (your ability to "hear" that things are right or wrong) can tell you that **C** is also incorrect; not only because the words are out of order but because it artificially inserts commas between them. We said before that adjectives in front of nouns act like one big noun. "Terrorist attack" was an example from the previous test. Other examples are things like "bowling ball" or "sports car." In this case "Roman emperor Vespasian" acts like one big noun; we don't need commas to separate off any of those words. **B** then is also incorrect for this reason. **A** is correct because it rightly adds no commas and orders the words properly.

**#20** This is an example of a jumbled words kind of question. Read the sentence with each option in place. **H** doesn't work because it makes the sentence an incomplete sentence or dependent clause. **G** is also incorrect; it confuses various verb tenses into nonsense. **J** would be correct if what comes before or after "generated" were a dependent clause, but that is not the case; the comma artificially splits the sentence open. **F** is the correct answer then; the verb tense is correct and treats the sentence for what it is: one sentence or independent clause.

**#21** Word to the wise: unless it is used in a question, the word "which" usually comes after a comma. "Which" is one way to begin a dependent clause. Here you can see that "The Colosseum was fully constructed after ten years" is the independent clause. **B** is incorrect because we aren't linking two independent clauses. **C** is also incorrect because it artificially makes "ten years" into a nonessential series of words, but that is incorrect. **A** is incorrect because it fails to segregate off the dependent clause that starts with "which." This is why **D** is correct.

**#22** These kinds of questions are among the most missed in ACT English. The reason for this is that there's a lot to read, not because it is too difficult. The question tells you what the sentence must do: talk about "consecutive emperors." **F** speaks about Vespasian and his rise to power, but nothing about consecutive emperors. **G** speaks of the Roman Empire, but nothing about emperors or even the Colosseum for that matter. **J** speaks of the time it would take to build large structures, not emperors. **H** correctly speaks of Vespasian's death and his son's opening of the Colosseum as emperor. That is why **H** is correct.

**#23** Parts, pieces, sections, and segments are all synonyms. That is why **A, B,** and **C** are all incorrect; they are redundant. **D** is the correct answer because it says what the sentence requires without the redundancy.

**#24** Here we are dealing with the question of nonessential words and phrases, our #1 comma ability based on recent ACT's. Already let's eliminate **J** because it uses a colon, which must follow an independent clause, and in this case it does not. Let's also eliminate **G** because it sets off "The amphitheater" from the rest of the sentence, but that fractures the independent clause (there is no dependent clause in this sentence to set off at all; from start to finish it is independent). The question is whether or not "overall" is nonessential. The test for this is to remove it from the sentence and see if what is left works as an independent clause: "The amphitheater covers about 300,000 square feet." Yes, that clearly works. The word "overall" then is added for emphasis and is thus nonessential. That is why **H** is incorrect; it fails to set off "overall" with commas. The correct answer is **F** because it does separate "overall" off with commas.

**#25** This is a question again of linking clauses, or not. Are these two independent clauses? A quick check tells us no. The second clause in the sentence "remarkably could hold as many as 50,000 spectators at one time" looks like an independent clause, but it is missing a subject, like the word "it" or even "the Colosseum" or "the building." This is why **A, B,** and **D** are all incorrect; each would work if we were combining independent clauses. **C** is correct because what follows "world" isn't a dependent clause at all; remove the punctuation from the middle of the sentence and it flows from start to finish as one independent clause or complete thought.

**#26** At first read, the sentence in question does not seem irrelevant. Throughout the paragraph we have phrases like "For centuries" and "It once," which implies that at one day the Colosseum was bustling, and now it is not. The sentence in question begins to wind down, so to speak, the Colosseum as a center of bustling activity to an abandoned building. In fact, reading on to the second paragraph, we see this is what is happening. Thus, the sentence must be kept, which is why **H** and **J** are incorrect. As for why it should be kept, notice that **G** says what we just inferred: that the activity of the Colosseum was halted. That is why **G** is correct. As for **F**, getting "deeper insight into world events" is too broad; there are millions of sentences we could throw in here that would give us that kind of insight, but that wouldn't mean they would belong.

**#27** As written, we have one comma after the word "projects," which would turn something into a dependent clause. However, we are dealing here with combining independent clauses. Separate the two and ask, "Can these stand alone as sentences?" Let's look at them: "Large parts were removed to provide stone for other construction projects" and "Much of the ornate construction—such as marble statues—was taken away or destroyed." Those are both independent clauses; we need something more than a comma (a comma could work, but we'd also need a FANBOYS conjunction, but that's not here). Thus, **A** is incorrect. For that matter, **C** is out as well; it inserts a comma without purpose after "much." **D** uses a colon to separate the clauses; this is OK to do of course. The problem is that it puts a comma after "much," which disrupts the sentence; again, we can't just put in commas for no reason. That's why the answer is **B**; it properly unites the independent clauses with a semi-colon.

**#28** If you read the last answer explanation, I already gave this one away! One use for em dashes (—) is to set off clauses or words like parentheses. The phrase "such as marble statues" is set off in the beginning with an em dash, so it must be fully set off in the end with the same punctuation (this would also apply if it were commas or parentheses). That is why **J** is the correct answer. **F, G,** and **H** fail to finish the "setting off" with an em dash, and are thus incorrect. As a reminder, we could have a single em dash in a sentence if it is used to set off independent clauses, but that's not what is happening before the word "such."

**#29** Here, the phrase "While conservation of the Colosseum began in the 18th century" is the dependent clause, and "actual restoration did not begin until the mid-1990's" is the independent clause. To combine them into one complex sentence, all we need is one thing: a comma. Using a period implies two independent clauses, but we don't have that, so **A** and **B** are both incorrect. The preposition "in the 18th century" is not nonessential; prepositions generally "flow" with a sentence. Thus it does not need to be set off, which is why **D** is incorrect. **C** correctly sets off the opening phrase with a comma and is the right answer.

**#30** Here we have a clue: "by referring back to the opening paragraph." Starting with **F,** you may notice that not only does it close the preceding paragraph well ("Although repair is ongoing"), but also refers back to the opening paragraph by referring to how recognizable the Colosseum is (the first sentence of the essay says, "Few archetypes of ancient civilization are better known…"). That is why **F** is correct. **G** would work if the essay was about the effect of weather on landmarks worldwide, but it isn't. **H** fails because the purpose of the essay isn't the Roman Empire or its fall. **J** is the longest option, and it is probably good here to reject the myth that the longest option is always correct. That isn't true. Here, the sentence sounds really nice, but there is nothing in the opening paragraph about how landmarks around the world need help, so it too is incorrect.

**Passage III: Stunt Kite**

**#31** Here, there is nothing grammatically incorrect about any of the options, thus, this is a question of verbosity (overly wordy) reminiscent of Step 2. Thus, we need the least wordy option. Well, **A, C,** and **D** are all incorrect for that very reason; they all say what is needed for the sentence, but in too many words. That is why the answer is **B**. The word "kind" works because we know what that represents: a kind of kite, because "kites" is used in the first clause of the sentence.

**#32** This question is testing two things from Step 3. The first is how to set off a dependent clause with a comma. In other words, "When he set it up" is that clause, and must be set off from the rest of the sentence with a comma. This eliminates choices **F** and **H**. Every option (including **F** and **H**) uses a colon. Thus, we need to remember the colon rule: *it must follow a complete thought*. Of our remaining options, we can eliminate option **G** because, although "When he set it up, I noticed something" is a complete thought when set apart from the sentence, in this case, we can't separate "something" from "odd." What comes after the colon in that case is, well, also odd; the word "odd" being set off by a comma. That makes something that, hopefully, looks and "sounds" too off. Technically speaking, what must follow a colon is a list, a quote, a complete/independent clause, or a noun/noun phrase that emphasizes, completes, or dramatizes the first clause. None of these things occurs in this case. That's why the answer is **J**; we have a complete clause before and after the colon.

**#33 D** is always a tantalizing option for questions like this. At first when you delete the underlined portion, the sentence kind of flows and works. But doesn't it sound odd? It starts the sentence off with two dependent clauses back to back. Not only that, but we have ", but" (a comma followed by a FANBOYS) after "kite," which would work if what came before it were an independent clause. That's not the case; by deleting the underlined portion, we're left with "As a heavy wind launched the kite;" that's not independent, so **D** is incorrect. As we said, the ", but" means that what comes before is a complete thought that could stand alone, so let's deal with that. There we have "As a heavy wind blew over the field" and "We launched the kite." The first part is an introductory phrase that must be set off by a comma, the second is the complete thought it must be set off from. This is why **A** is correct. **B** and **C** have too many commas and are incorrect.

**#34** Since **J** is formatted a bit differently than the other options, let's start there. The adverb "quickly" is misplaced; if we were going to use that word, we would need to use it like this: "…this kite quickly shot into the air…" It simply makes no sense to end a sentence with an adverb set off by a comma. **J** is thus incorrect. The comma used in choice **F** is correct, so it may look tempting. But **F** and **H** are both incorrect for the same reason: they are redundant. **G** is right because it communicates that the kite went off quickly in only one word. We already know that bullets are fast and rapid; that's why the simile "like a bullet" works in the first place.

**#35** Here the question is asking for the best phrase. In this case, the best phrase is the one that attributes to the uncle the ability to control more than just the height. However, **A** and **D** both speak of the height, so they are wrong. **C** speaks nothing of the uncle's control (another necessity based on the question itself), so it is incorrect too. **B** speaks of the uncle's ability to direct the kite to a certain spot in which direction, and thus it is correct.

**#36** We are trying here to join two independent clauses. As written, there is no punctuation to denote the distinction between the two independent clauses, so **F** is incorrect. Same goes for **G**; although there's a FANBOYS (for, and, nor, but, or, yet, so) conjunction, there is no comma. **J** is wrong for the opposite reason: there's a comma, but no FANBOYS conjunction. Only choice **H** correctly separates the independent clauses with a comma and a FANBOYS conjunction, so it is correct.

**#37** After the word "for," the sentence's second independent clause begins. We don't need to separate off the subject of the sentence, "my uncle," which is why **C** is incorrect. **B** has the problem of putting a comma after the conjunction, which is purposeless; **B** is incorrect. **D** is grammatically correct, but we already know who the pronoun "he" refers to, so we don't need to restate that (it is redundant, in other words). That is why the answer is **A**; it allows the second independent clause to proceed as normal.

**#38** At first this seems like a straightforward question of how to use a comma: do we have an introductory phrase that is straightforward, or do we have a nonessential phrase in there that has to be set off by commas? However, the phrase "as I was watching" is redundant! The entire essay is from the author's point of view; of course he is watching! That is why the answer is **J**; it is the only option that deletes that phrase. **F, G,** and **H** are all redundant. You may think, "but that's not fair!" Well, the ACT mixes and matches question types; it isn't all straightforward.

**#39** This is a lot of commas to sort through, but let's do that by first identifying the independent clause here. It is: "I shouted to my uncle." That is enough for us to know that we will need a comma after the word "uncle." That eliminates **A** and **B** as incorrect. After that, the question is whether or not "for a moment" is a nonessential phrase. If we remove it, we are still left with a dependent clause: "thinking he had lost control." That signals that, indeed, "for a moment" is nonessential and must be set off by commas. That means we need three commas total: after "uncle," after "thinking," and after "moment." That is why **D** is incorrect; it sets off the wrong phrase ("a moment"). This is why **C** is correct. It has all three commas in the correct places.

**#40** The way the paragraph is written, without the proposed sentence, it ends on kind of a cliffhanger: what happened to the kite when he pulled back hard? The sentence that is being proposed answers that question: it rockets into the sky and disaster was avoided. So, yes, we want the sentence. That eliminates **H** and **J** as incorrect. **F** says "Yes," which is correct so far, but it mentions something about the word "rocketed" linking with a rocket mentioned earlier. However, there is no rocket mentioned earlier, so it is incorrect. **G**, then, is correct because it rightly says that the proposed sentence tells the reader that the kite did not crash, which is what we need to know (it is a fitting end to the sentence).

**#41** We have here four options all essentially saying the same thing in different words and very tenses. We need to read them all in the context of the sentence and find the shortest one that is also grammatically correct. Hopefully you noticed off the bat that "how it is to fly" is correct, but could be said in a shorter way: *how to fly*. That is why **C** is the correct answer; it says what is needed in the fewest words possible. Like we just said, as written is too wordy, which is why **A** is incorrect. **B** has a similar problem and is incorrect; "it were" is an unnecessary addition to the phrase. **D** simply makes no sense and is incorrect.

**#42** Here we have two adjectives describing the word "eights." But, we can't rearrange these adjectives; it makes no sense to say, "I could do figure amazing eights." So, "figure eights" is more like the noun with only one adjective, "amazing," describing it. We don't need a comma between them, in other words. For these reasons, we can eliminate **G** and **H** as incorrect. **J** is incorrect because it puts a hyphen between "amazing" and "figure-eights"; we don't do that with adjectives. That is why the answer is **F**; as written, it correctly describes the figure eights as "amazing."

**#43** There is an em dash later in the sentence, which can only mean two things. First, there are two independent clauses being linked, or second, em dashes are being used as parentheses. What comes before the em dash later in the sentence is NOT an independent clause, so it must be parentheses. Only **D** correctly opens the phrase with an em dash, so it is correct! **A, B,** and **C** fail to do so, so they are all incorrect.

**#44** This one is tricky, but common on the ACT. First, let's recognize that "Since that day" is an opening phrase and will need a comma to come after it to set it off. That eliminates **F**, which is an incorrect option. Looking at the rest, let's identify the independent clause: "I have gotten my own stunt kite…" So, "though still a bit of an amateur" is the nonessential phrase and must be set off by commas. **H** fails to include the pronoun "I," so it is incorrect. **J** fails to begin to set off the nonessential phrase by eliminating a comma, so it is out. That is why **G** is correct; it correctly sets off both the introductory phrase and the nonessential phrase.

**#45** Again, we want to know: is the answer Yes or No? Here, the question asks if the essay is about the author acquiring a new hobby, which it indeed is. So that eliminates **C** and **D**. **B** says that the answer is "Yes" because the essay compares and contrasts different hobbies. But that isn't true; the only hobby mentioned is flying stunt kites. So **B** is incorrect. **A** correctly says that the essay is about how the author came to acquire the hobby of flying stunt kites.

# Answer Explanations - Step 4 - Passages I, II, and III

**Correct Answers:**

| Passage I | Passage II | Passage III |
|---|---|---|
| 1: D | 16: G | 31: B |
| 2: H | 17: B | 32: J |
| 3: C | 18: J | 33: B |
| 4: G | 19: A | 34: F |
| 5: A | 20: F | 35: D |
| 6: J | 21: D | 36: J |
| 7: A | 22: G | 37: D |
| 8: J | 23: C | 38: G |
| 9: C | 24: G | 39: A |
| 10: F | 25: C | 40: G |
| 11: B | 26: H | 41: C |
| 12: H | 27: A | 42: F |
| 13: D | 28: H | 43: A |
| 14: F | 29: C | 44: J |
| 15: D | 30: H | 45: B |

**Passage I: Norman Rockwell, American Artist**

#1 Here we have an introductory phrase that must be set off by a comma. We know this because if we remove the word "Rather" from the beginning, what comes after is a complete, independent clause. That is why the correct answer here is **D**. Choice **A** has the problem of no comma. **B** and **C** both have a different problem: they introduce a pronoun ("He") into the sentence when it is not justified to do so; a pronoun isn't needed there because the name "Rockwell" immediately follows, thus we know who "acquired fame" apart from the pronoun.

#2 The verb tense of this sentence is past tense; we want a choice that matches up with "acquired fame." This would be **H**, which is the correct answer and continues the past tense. As written, it is nonsensical; nobody says "as to depicting." **G** doesn't work because the sentence has no use for the word "then" because the sentence isn't describing something chronological. **J** is also nonsensical; "of depicting" would have to follow a very specific noun, like: "I am conscious of depicting my brother as crazy in my new book," or something like that. That's not what this sentence does though.

#3 Although the sentence prior to the one in question mentions fame, that doesn't mean that a sentence about fame can be inserted here. In this case, the sentence quotes another text altogether to give us information about fame and how artists have achieved it. This can't work here; it shifts the focus away from Rockwell dramatically, and moves from specific to broad without any justification; that is why **A** and **B** are incorrect. **C** says exactly what we are looking for, that the focus of the paragraph and essay shift into something irrelevant if this sentence is inserted. **D**, while correct that the answer is "No," incorrectly says that Rockwell was not famous after his death. We may be able to guess that he was famous at death, but the last part ("which has been stated") makes us sure: so far in this little paragraph, there's been no mention that Rockwell is not famous after death.

#4 As far as commas go, the way it is written seems correct because we have two commas identifying one noun, and the comma comes after the first adjective. However, this is a case in which the adjectives ("paying" and "first") can't be reversed, which is why **F** is incorrect. A "paying job" is a noun all its own and is used often in plain speech to distinguish it from volunteer work or school work. And if that's the case, and "first" comes before "paying," we will not need a comma. That is why **G** is the correct answer. **H** seems the shortest, and it is, but it makes no sense when read in context. This is also true for **J**; when inserted, it makes the sentence into something else, as in not a sentence any more!

#5 Three of these options are redundant. Choice **D** is one of these redundant options; it has already been stated that this work was done for the Boy Scouts. Moving to **C**, we see this is incorrect as well; it was stated earlier in the sentence that this was done for $50, so this option is incorrect. Then there's **B**, which is also redundant; the opening sentence of the paragraph says he was 18. That is why **A** is the correct answer; it tells us something relevant that has not been stated.

#6 The word "remains" implies that something from the past is still true or relevant in the present time. This is why **F, G,** and **H** are all incorrect. Each of them is redundant; if his cover *remains* as one of his most valuable works, we already know that it is that way today. "Today," "still," and "to this day" are all redundant when combined with the word "remains." This is why **J** is the correct answer; all we need is the word "remains" to communicate the necessary idea that today this cover is still valuable.

#7 First, let us eliminate answer choice **C**. This option is in the present tense, but the paragraph is in the past tense. When put into the sentence, **A, B,** and **D** all seem to fit in a way. Let's look at **B** and **D**. You could easily say a person "was being promoted" or "was receiving a promotion" but the sentence itself doesn't call for this wording (called the *past progressive tense*). That wording would make more sense if: a) The rest of the paragraph was in this tense, or b) The use of it is a setup for another past event taking place (such as like this: "he was being promoted when his life took an unexpected turn…" or "he was receiving a promotion when he received a letter from his mother…"). For those reasons, let's eliminate answer choices **B** and **D**. As written, the sentence works, is not wordy, and is in the proper verb tense. That is why the correct answer is **A**.

#8 This kind of question is indicative of the way in which the ACT pairs verbs with subjects. The verb (as underlined, "was featured") comes after a nonessential clause is set off by commas. If we eliminate that nonessential clause, and only read the independent clause that comes after the comma, we have a sentence that says this: "The Boy Scouts was often featured in his work." That kind of splicing is what makes sense of the sentence if you fail to see it the first time. As written, "was" (singular) does not fit with "Scouts" (plural). That is why **F** is incorrect. **H** has the same problem, so it is out. As for **G**, it is incorrect because it creates a sentence fragment ("The Scouts to be…"?); the verb "to be" needs to be conjugated here. That is why the answer is **J**; it has a plural verb ("were") with a plural subject ("Scouts"). As for the ordering of "often" and "featured," it doesn't really matter which comes first.

#9 Here we have a comma and a FANBOYS conjunction (as a reminder: for, and, nor, but, or, yet, so) underlined. Again, this is only going to work if what comes after the "and" is an independent clause, so let's put that to the test: ", and *was frequently hired to do the same for various publications throughout his career.*" That's not a complete thought…what or who *was* frequently hired? There's no subject within the clause to fit with the verb *was*. thus, **A** is incorrect. **D** is incorrect for the completely opposite reason; in this option, the subject "he" is put before the verb "was," creating an independent clause. However, this clause needs to be set off with a comma, and it is not. **B** would work if it had a FANBOYS conjunction; just like **D**, choice **B** puts a subject to the verb, but it is missing the necessary conjunction to set it off properly. Only **C** works because it recognizes that what comes after *Post* is not an independent clause, but rather a continuation of the clause already at play (which begins with "Rockwell"). That is why **C** is correct.

#10 Here we have four options that all look similar. This was our mini-lesson in part 4. We need the one that means "to join." This is why **F** is correct; "enlist" means "to join." **G, H,** and **J**, though they look like "enlist" and are spelled similarly, are incorrect from a vocabulary point of view, which is why those three are incorrect.

#11 As written, we have a contradiction. If Rockwell tried to join the army, why would he turn away? In other words, when someone "turns away" they are *choosing* to turn away, to not be a part of something anymore. The context of the sentence, that he is underweight and that he wants to join the Navy, implies that the Navy turned him away, not that he did so voluntarily. Thus, **A** is out and is incorrect. **C** has the same problem; it implies that Rockwell somehow turned the Navy away, so it is incorrect. **D** creates a sentence fragment; it has no verb to fit with the subject "they." These are all reasons why **B** is correct; it rightly identifies that Rockwell was the one who was turned away from the Navy, the reason being that he was underweight.

**#12** Grammatically speaking, there is no problem with the way this is written. However, remember, the ACT expects sometimes the *best* answer, not any given grammatically correct one. It is redundant to add the description of him as an artist who draws; that is implied in the word "artist." **F, G,** and **J** all have this flaw. **H** is correct because it is the only choice that is not redundant.

**#13** This question is a good example of verbosity in that you need to identify which of the options is the least wordy while giving the sentence what it needs. Here, all four choices say the exact same thing and imply that Rockwell was inspired to paint the *Four Freedoms* because of a Roosevelt speech. **A, B,** and **C** all grammatically work, but are too wordy when compared to the correct answer: **D**.

**#14** First of all, the verb "intends" needs the word "to" if we are being told what is actually intended. "I intend to go to the store today" is an example. Because that is the case in this sentence, we can eliminate **G** and **J** because neither have the word "to" following it. This question reminds me of the *listen* rule. You don't need to memorize what I have said in this paragraph…doesn't it just sound funny to say, "I intend go to the store today"? It sounds like a caveman talking. Now, back to the question. We need proper subject/verb agreement. Thus which is correct: "Some intend to awaken…" or "Some intends to awaken…"? Of course, it is the first option; "Some" is plural, and needs the plural conjugation of the verb "to intend." That is why **F** is correct and why **H** (which conjugates the verb as if the subject were singular, as in "He intends to") is incorrect.

**#15** It is your goal to know if the answer is "Yes" or "No" before reading through the answer choices. The question asks if the essay is about the history of American art. While Rockwell is an American artist, the essay is only about him, so the answer is No. This eliminates **A** and **B**. Answer choice **C** (which is incorrect) says that Rockwell was born in Toronto. The essay never says if that is true or false (by the way, it is false), but even if it is true that's not the reason why the answer is no. **D** correctly says that the essay is only about one artist.

**Passage II: The Challenger Deep**

**#16** This sentence is in the present tense, but the underlined verb "were" is in the past tense, so **F** is incorrect. **H** and **J** could work if they came immediately after the comma and not after the word "and," but they don't, which is why they are incorrect. **G** is correct because it pairs the singular, present tense verb "is" to the subject, which is "one place."

**#17** "Deepest" and "farthest down" are synonyms. In other words, as written, this question is redundant. For this reason alone we can eliminate choices **A** and **C** as incorrect. In questions of redundancy the correct or *best* answer is usually the shortest, but in this case that is not right. If we simply put the word "area" into the sentence (which is what answer choice **D** suggests), we have a new problem: the sentence no longer expresses a complete thought. You wouldn't say, "This is certainly true of the area of the ocean: the Mariana Trench" because there are many areas of the ocean; it would be more proper to say "an area," but it doesn't. **B** is correct because it identifies the Mariana Trench as the *deepest* area of the ocean, not just an area.

**#18** As written, the underlined portion has a semi-colon, which is fine. However, that semi-colon is followed by a FANBOYS (for, and, nor, but, or, yet, so) conjunction, which is not fine. That is why **F** is incorrect. The same is true for **H**; you can't put a FANBOYS after a semi-colon. **G** has the problem of failing to put a FANBOYS after the comma, which is necessary because this part of the sentence is bridging two independent clauses. That is why the correct answer is **J**; it properly uses a semi-colon to combine two independent clauses without adding in a FANBOYS conjunction.

**#19** If you read the entire sentence before looking to all of the answer choices, the underlined portion should strike you as working just fine. That's because it does! **A** is correct; it is past tense and fits with the subject "visit" well. You are allowed to be confident about an answer, circle it, and move on. This sentence is one independent clause, containing no dependent clauses or nonessential words or phrases. This is why **B** is incorrect because it shows that a nonessential phrase is beginning, but that phrase is never set off later. **C** has the problem of being in the future tense; **D** is incorrect because it is in the present tense (and is too wordy and awkward) but somehow hopes that something will happen in the year 1960.

**#20** Here you are asked for a phrase that serves a dual purpose: a) It tells that the voyage was dangerous, and b) It shows the explorers were courageous. Let's start with **J** and go backwards. Although this choice talks about the two explorers, it neither reveals the danger nor speaks of their courage, so it is incorrect. **H** speaks of danger, but that probably isn't the kind of danger that two men in a submarine are worried about (not to mention, the phrase says nothing of their courage). **G** says how deep they had to go; just speaking of the depth might be enough for a reader to assume it was dangerous, but again, there is nothing here about their courage. **F** is the correct answer; the *crack* they hear on the way down reveals the danger, and their decision to carry on reveals their courage.

**#21** Here, "have observed" (choice **B**) is incorrect because that is the present perfect tense; we need something in past tense. **C** is incorrect because it creates an incomplete sentence by never fitting a verb with "Walsh and Piccard," the subject of the sentence. The only difference between **A** and **D** is that the last word is either "observe" or "observed." Think about this sentence: "They have observe a fish," or this one: "I have observe a shooting star." Do either of those make sense? No, which is why **A** is incorrect and why **D** is correct.

**#22** The problem with choice **F**, the way this is written (which is also one of the problems with choice **H** as well), is that it turns the word "short" into an adverb: "shortly." It makes no sense to perform the act of cutting in a "short" way, which is how the adverb "shortly" modifies the verb "cut." For those reasons alone, F and H are incorrect. To "cut something short" means to end something prematurely, and just because "low" and "short" are synonyms, that doesn't mean they are interchangeable. For this reason, J is incorrect and G is the correct answer.

**#23 B** might have you wondering: who is Cameron? This may prompt you to read on and see that James Cameron was the next to reach the *Challenger Deep*. However, he is introduced in the next sentence, and thus it is inappropriate to throw out his name here. Even so, **B** is also incorrect because it would need to be set off by a comma and then later would need a verb to create an independent clause. This question is merely a question of setting off introductory words or phrases. **D** is an introductory phrase, but is not set off by a comma. So then the question is: if a sentence is begun with an adverb like "Incredibly" does it need a comma? The answer is yes. *But wait!* you think, *I read articles and books all the time in which this isn't done!* That is true, but guess what? This isn't an article on some website, but ACT English. It's what *they want* that matters, and they want you to see when commas ought to have deliberate use. In this case, you need to set off the word with a comma. **A** is thus incorrect, and **C** is correct due to its comma.

**#24** When you are alone, you are by yourself. As written, then, this is redundant. **F** is thus incorrect. **J** has the same problem; "solitarily" and "companionless" are synonymous and thus redundant, so it is incorrect as well. The tiebreaker between **H** and **G** is verbosity, meaning (because neither is redundant, they are both grammatically correct, and they both mean the same thing) the less wordy one is *best*. This is of course G, the correct answer.

**#25** An em dash can be used to set off two independent clauses, so that's what we need to check here. Before the em dash we have, "Despite the failure of a few instruments on the way down due to extreme pressure." That is not an independent clause; it is a dependent one. Any option that tries to link this clause with the one that comes later ("The dive was a success") as if they are independent clauses will be incorrect. This is why **A** is incorrect. **D** does the same thing in that it tries to link the clauses using a comma and a FANBOYS conjunction. **B** uses a colon, but you have to remember the colon's number one rule: it always follows a complete thought, which is not the case here, so **B** is also incorrect. **C** correctly sets off the opening/dependent clause with a comma from the independent clause that follows.

#26 Here, the prepositional phrase "on the ocean floor" is set off from the rest of the sentence. Although prepositional phrases come up in the next Step, here it is important to know that they don't need to be set off by commas in the flow of a sentence. Think about this sentence: I went to the store on the hill in the rain under an umbrella next to my daughter. Lots of prepositional phrases there, but they don't need to be set off by commas. For this reason, both **F** and **G** are incorrect. **G** has the additional problem that "on the ocean floor" is not an independent clause, which is what is needed if only one em dash is going to be used in a sentence. **J**, grammatically speaking, is fine. However, it leaves the reader wondering...three "what" down there? Three days? Hours? Minutes? That is why **H** is the correct answer; it defines what "three" refers to and doesn't arbitrarily set off the prepositional phrase.

#27 This sentence moves back into the present tense, which you can tell by the phrase "these are" at the beginning. This question is entirely a question of verb tense because that is the only difference between all of the answer choices. **B** and **C** are incorrect because they are past and future tenses, respectively. **D** says it "was to be." This kind of wording would only make sense if the sentence went on to say something like, "which was to be the total number **until** three more people dove down there for fun." This is why **A** is correct; it simply keeps the verb tense present.

#28 The sentence that is being proposed is tricky and indicative of the kinds of sentences or phrases the ACT will propose to you on test day. It is tricky because the sentence *mentions* Walsh and Piccard, who you already know were two of the men to descend into the *Challenger Deep*. However, the subject of the sentence is not the *Challenger Deep* or the men who descended into it, but rather the two men to have landed on the moon. Just because the sentence prior mentions the moon landing, that does not mean any sentence about the moon is appropriate. This sentence is like a detour or pit stop and interrupts the flow of the paragraph, so it does not belong. **F** and **G** are thus incorrect. **H** is correct because it rightly identifies the sentence as a distraction from the focus of the essay. **J**, although it correctly says "No," is incorrect because the reason for that No (that the essay makes no mention of the explorers being inspired by the men who landed on the moon) is not correct; that's not *why* the sentence doesn't belong.

#29 As written, you might be tempted to put "NO CHANGE" because most of the essay was in the past tense; "waited" makes it sound like the explorers were going to the bottom and there waited new creatures to be discovered. But, we are out of that part of the essay and are now on to a new paragraph in the present tense. **A** and **B** are both incorrect for reasons of verb tense. **D**, while it is in the present tense, is singular, but we need a plural conjugation to fit with "creatures and other wonders." This is why **C** is the correct answer; the creatures are as of yet undiscovered, so they "are waiting."

#30 The question asks if the essay's purpose was to describe the instruments on board submarines. The answer to that question is "No"; the essay was about *The Challenger Deep*. That eliminates **F** and **G**. Choice **H** correctly says "No," but says the instruments are mentioned somewhere but not described. If you can't remember if they were mentioned or not, it is OK to go back and look. Spoiler alert: they are mentioned (remember a few of Cameron's failed?). This is why **H** is correct. However, if you can't figure that out, ask yourself if **J** is definitely true or false. **J** says that these instruments are unnecessary and a burden. Even if you don't remember reading anything about instruments, you can probably assume that instruments on board a protective submarine are important! Thus, **J** is incorrect.

**Passage III: The Pont du Gard**

#31 A prepositional phrase (like "to France") is not something that needs to be set off by commas, which is why **A** is incorrect. Because it is "visitors to France" who "are," we don't need to separate the former subject from the latter verb. In other words, "Visitors to France" isn't an introductory phrase, but is essential to the independent clause of the sentence. **C** incorrectly sets off the word "visitors" and **D** incorrectly sets off the whole phrase as some kind of introductory phrase. This is why **B** is the correct answer; it does not separate an essential part of the independent clause (the subject that pairs with the verb "are") from the rest of the sentence.

**#32** Are we trying to say that the Pont du Gard *has to be* an aqueduct bridge? No, we are simply trying to say that the Pont du Gard is an example of an aqueduct bridge. This is why **F** is incorrect. The other options test your ability to recognize verb tenses. Because the rest of the paragraph is in the present tense, we need an option in the present tense. This is option **J**, which is the correct answer. **G** is in the future tense, which is incorrect. **H** is in the past tense, which is also incorrect.

**#33** Again, what you need to be able to identify is the nature of the clauses that come before and after the comma. Before we have this: "The bridge crosses the Gardon River," which is an independent clause (it can stand alone as a sentence). After we have this: "today is listed as a UNESCO World Heritage Site," which is NOT an independent clause (it begs the question: *what* is listed as a UNESCO Site?). So, **A** is incorrect for this reason, **D** is incorrect for this reason, and **C** is also incorrect for this reason! All three of those options are ways of combining independent clauses into one sentence. That is why **B** is correct; it smoothly maintains the sentence as one long independent clause or thought uninterrupted by punctuation.

**#34** This is a question of verbosity, meaning wordiness. **G, H,** and **J** are all incorrect because, though they say the same thing and do so in a grammatically correct way, they are all too wordy. **F** is correct because the word "empire" is shortest and what the sentence is intending to communicate.

**#35** These kinds of questions are more often than not missed on ACT day. The reason? Many students read "the delivery of" (choice A) in the context of the sentence, see that it works, bubble it in, and move on. However, the question asks for a choice that does NOT work. **A**, then, is incorrect because it *is* an appropriate alternative. The same is true for both **B** and **C**; all three of those options work when substituted into the sentence. **D**, however, does *not* work, which in this instance actually makes it the correct answer. "Having delivered" is the kind of phrase that would begin a dependent clause, like in this sentence: "The delivery driver, having delivered all of the packages, went home."

**#36** The way this is written makes it sound like the steepness of the bridge is the bridge's decision, or that there are circumstances that change whether or not the bridge goes down by one inch from one side to the other. That isn't the case, which is why **F** is incorrect. The previous sentence shifts the verb tense from past tense to present tense (notice how the sentence says, "The Pont du Gard aqueduct *is…*" However, although choice **H** uses the word "is," this tense (called the present progressive) makes it sound like the bridge is in motion, descending an inch like someone "is descending" down a mountain. That is why **H** is incorrect. The difference between **G** and **J** is a matter of subject/verb agreement. "The bridge" is singular, so we need a singular conjugation, which is provided by choice **J**, which is why it is correct. "The bridge descend" does not have subject/verb agreement, which is why **G** is incorrect.

**#37** Choices **A** and **B** make it seem like this question is testing the ordering of adjectives before a noun. Sometimes that is important of course. Between those two options, **B** would be better, however, **A** and **B** are incorrect for a different reason: they have the word "noteworthy" in them. For that matter, **C** is incorrect for the same reason. If you keep reading, it says that the feature of the bridge is "worthy of note." Thus, **A, B,** and **C** are all incorrect because they are redundant! **D** is correct because it leaves out the word "noteworthy." Remember: *read all answer choices in the context of an entire sentence!!!*

**#38** This is another example of a vocabulary in context question. All of these options look similar, but we need an option that means "layers" or "rows" (which are words used in the next couple of sentences). The only answer then is **G**, because "tiers" means "layers," like the seven tiers on a wedding cake. **F, H,** and **J** are all words with incorrect meanings for this context.

**#39** The question here is one of nonessential words and phrases. Does the word "respectively" detour the sentence, or is it a part of the flow? Well, I'll just tell you: it is a detour; it must be set off by commas. Think of the sentence without it: "The lowest and middle rows contain 6 and 11 arches, all of which are over 65 feet in height." Clearly, when you throw the word "respectively" in there, it is a bit of a pit stop or detour. That is why **A** is the correct answer. **D** has no commas at all, even to set off the final dependent clause, which is why it is incorrect. **C** makes it seem like "respectively all of which" is its own nonessential phrase, but that disrupts the final clause of the sentence, which is why it is incorrect. **B** is probably the most tempting incorrect option, but it fails to completely set off the nonessential word "respectively." You may disagree and think, "but a pause isn't necessary there." It isn't about pauses in your mind, it's about a comma's deliberate use. That is why **B** is incorrect.

**#40** This is the second time you've seen such a question in the practice passages. Here, it is about the proper placement of the adverb "undoubtedly." Try out each of the choices. Because it is presented as a fact that arches distribute weight and force, the adverb "undoubtedly" before "distribute" is over the top, which is why **F** is incorrect. **H** is incorrect for the exact same reason; it simply places the adverb after distribute instead of before, but it has the same effect on the verb distribute and the sentence as a whole. **J** is incorrect for a bit of a different reason. Putting the adverb "undoubtedly" after "longevity" sounds OK, but it would have to be set off by commas. Thus, **J** is incorrect. **G** is correct because it places the adverb in a place that makes sense for the sentence ("undoubtedly contributed") and doesn't need to be set off by commas.

**#41** Here again you have to read the question precisely: which option gives evidence that Roman engineering was brilliant? **A** does not display the brilliance of Roman engineering; stacking blocks up on top of each other is not brilliant engineering. **B** says that the blocks fit together imprecisely; but if blocks are placed imprecisely, that is the opposite of brilliant engineering. **D** starts off well, saying that the blocks could withstand wind and rain "but not the test of time." How can the engineering be brilliant if it can't withstand the test of time? **C** is thus the correct answer; it says that the blocks did not need mortar, which displays a brilliance in engineering.

**#42** We need a verb here that is past tense because the action of the sentence is in the past (and the sentence says, "came the end," which is past tense. **G** is present tense, so it is incorrect. **H** is also present tense, so also incorrect. **J** is future tense, so it is incorrect. **F** is correct because it rightly uses the verb "to prove" in the past tense.

**#43** What is needed here is an option that helps the reader understand that the Pont du Gard has lasted because it was used as a toll bridge. **B** is incorrect because it implies that the bridge is being used as a toll bridge now; but that is not the case. **C** is incorrect because it does not create even a complete sentence; there is no subject/verb agreement. **D** has the exact same problem; if you read the sentence with "to guarantee" in place, the sentence will make no sense and will be begging for another clause to finish it out. Only choice **A** makes sense; it implies that the bridge was used as a toll bridge and from then to the present day the funds from that use has guaranteed that the bridge was maintained.

**#44** **F** is incorrect because, though it is about toll bridges, which are mentioned in the previous sentence, the essay isn't about toll bridges. **G** is incorrect for similar reasons; skilled engineers and maintaining bridges are mentioned in the essay, but that is not a fitting conclusion because that is not what the essay is about. **H** has the problem of shifting to the first person: it uses the pronoun "us," which is not used elsewhere in the entire essay. Not only that, but it posits that the point of the essay was to discuss the Fall of Rome, which it was not. **J** is the only sentence that is explicitly about the Pont du Gard, which is the focus of the essay; this is why **J** is correct.

**#45** Here we need to read the sentence and bring its general purpose to the 4 proposed points. The sentence is about the running of water on an aqueduct. Thus, it needs to be placed in a paragraph or among sentences that would be fitting. Choice **A** doesn't work; you might think it would be fine there, but the sentences around it are not about the function of an aqueduct generally. **B** is the correct answer because the sentence before is about how aqueducts carry water. **C** does not work because the sentence prior is about the function of the arch, which is the purpose of that paragraph as a whole. Lastly, **D** is incorrect as well because the paragraph it is in is about stacking blocks; this is also the focus of the sentence before and the sentence after as well.

# Answer Explanations - Step 5 - Passages I, II, and III

**Correct Answers:**

| Passage I | Passage II | Passage III |
|---|---|---|
| 1: C | 16: G | 31: B |
| 2: G | 17: C | 32: H |
| 3: A | 18: F | 33: B |
| 4: H | 19: A | 34: J |
| 5: D | 20: J | 35: A |
| 6: F | 21: B | 36: H |
| 7: B | 22: J | 37: D |
| 8: J | 23: D | 38: G |
| 9: B | 24: H | 39: D |
| 10: F | 25: B | 40: H |
| 11: C | 26: G | 41: C |
| 12: G | 27: C | 42: F |
| 13: D | 28: G | 43: B |
| 14: J | 29: A | 44: J |
| 15: A | 30: F | 45: D |

**Passage I: Steve Irwin, Crocodile Hunter**

**#1** As written, there is nothing grammatically incorrect. However, the sentence is directed to "you"; this is called "Second Person," and thus the pronoun "he" is wrong. This means that **A** and **B** are both incorrect. **D** is incorrect because "does you" does not have subject/verb agreement. This is why **C** is the correct answer; the pronoun is appropriate, and there is subject/verb agreement with "do you."

**#2** This is an example of "sentence structure" that was taught in Step 5. As written, there is no problem with the sentence ending with "*Hunter*." But, what comes next is a sentence fragment, in other words, not a sentence that can stand alone. In fact, "Which" is only going to begin a sentence that is a question. This is why **F** is incorrect. **J** is incorrect for the same reason; the semi-colon proposes that there are two complete thoughts (independent clauses) being combined, but the second one begins with "which" and is a fragment. **H** is tempting, but this creates two independent clauses, and we can't combine them into one complex sentence with only a comma; we would need a FANBOYS conjunction as well. This is why **G** is the correct answer; it correctly combines an independent clause with a dependent clause via a comma.

**#3** Here, you must choose the correct prepositional phrase as was taught in Step 5. This is also an idiom (as was mentioned in Step 4). Do you keep the attention...in the world? No, that is why **B** is incorrect. Do you keep the attention...at the entire world? No, that isn't a phrase either; that is why **C** is also incorrect. **D** works; you keep the attention *of* the world, but it is a bit wordier than choice **A**, which says the same thing. This is why **A** is correct.

**#4** Hopefully you can see that "attention from other people" is very wordy compared to "attention." So, let's go ahead and eliminate choice **F** as incorrect for this reason. **G** has a different problem: what is "them"? There is nothing plural in the sentence (or even the sentence prior) that could reasonably be referred to by the pronoun "them," thus **G** is incorrect. That leaves us with two choices: "attention" or "it." What could "it" possibly refer to? It would refer to "the spotlight," which is a synonym for "attention." Tricky? Yes. Subtle? Yes. However, this is why **H** is correct and **J** is incorrect; **J** is technically redundant.

**#5** As written, we have a colon after "His philosophy was", but that is not a complete thought. That is our #1 colon rule, so **A** is incorrect. **B** as the exact same problem; what comes before the semi-colon is not an independent clause, so it can't have semi-colon after it. This is why **B** is incorrect. **C** has the problem of failing to combine two independent clauses in a proper way; if there's a comma, a FANBOYS (for, and, nor, but, or, yet, so) is needed. **D** is the correct answer because there is an independent clause before, thus the colon is appropriate.

**#6** Here we need the correct transitional phrase (or "connector word/words") that bridges the two sentences. Actually, according to the question (which is NOT acceptable), we need to identify either three correct ones or the one incorrect one. We know that "Thus" works, because getting rid of it is not an option. "Thus" implies cause and effect, like this: "I'm old. Thus, my hair is turning grey." My hair is turning grey *because of* (cause and effect) being old. **G, H,** and **J** all do this, and are all synonymous with "Thus." This is why **F** is the correct answer (because it is incorrect); "Rather" implies contradiction, but that is not the relationship between the two sentences.

**#7** Isolating the word "because" with a comma makes it seem like an introductory word; this is tempting because "his parents were the owners of the Australia Zoo" is an independent clause. However, so is "he had access to them all" later in the sentence. So, we can't keep this sentence as is, and **A** is wrong. **D** turns the sentence into nonsense; "Because they owned of..." makes no sense, so **D** is incorrect. **C** separates the subject ("his parents") from the verb ("were"), and thus it is incorrect. **B** correctly has no commas, ensuring that "Because his parents were the owners of the Australia Zoo" is left as a dependent clause.

**#8** Like many sentences proposed by the ACT, this one detracts from the purpose of the paragraph by shifting the focus of the paragraph from Steve Irwin to crocodiles. That is why the answer is "No," and thus **F** and **G** are incorrect. **H** says that "the Australia Zoo never held crocodiles" was "stated earlier in the essay", but that is not true; it never said that. This is why **J** is correct; it rightly notes that the proposed sentence is redundant (it already said that he dealt with crocodiles in the zoo) and, like we said, it notes that the proposed sentence detracts from the paragraph's purpose.

**#9** This is a question of verb tense, as was taught in Step 4. It says that Steve "gained," so we need a past tense verb to match to that subject. This is why **B** is the correct answer. **A** is wrong because it is present tense; **C** is wrong because it is the plural conjugation (like, "They share"). **D** is incorrect because "Steve...and to share" is nonsensical.

**#10** Here you have to choose the correct prepositional phrase. Do you commit to, at, for, or from a cause? You commit *to* something, and even though the other answers have problems beyond this first word, that is why **G, H,** and **J** are all incorrect. **F** is correct because you commit *to* something.

**#11** First, let's deal with **D**. This is why underlined portions must be read in the context of the entire sentence. "...that generated..." is a phrase that could occur in many sentences. However, in this circumstance, if the underlined portion were eliminated, we would have no subject to link with the verb "generated"; in other words, we'd be left wondering, "What was generated?" Thus, **D** is incorrect. As for the other options, they are all grammatically correct and synonymous; the tiebreaker is the *best* answer, and the best answer here is the least wordy one: that is why **C** is the correct answer and by **B** and **A** are incorrect.

**#12** Because the sentence is in the past tense, we can eliminate options that are not. This includes option **H** (incorrect because it is in the present tense) and option **J** (incorrect because it is in the future tense). Does it make sense to say, "The funds funneled were they?" Unless you are Yoda, that doesn't make any sense; the ordering of the words is backwards (and the pronoun "they" is thrown in there). That is why **F** is incorrect. **G** is correct because it has subject/verb agreement in the proper tense (and it makes sense!).

**#13** As written, what is *trying* to be communicated is clear, which is why many will put **A** as the correct answer. However, remember the teaching about modifying clauses from Step 5: whatever comes after the comma is what is being modified. In this case (as written), the sentence says that "the search" (after the comma) is the one who heard "a message come through the radio." Searches can't hear messages, which is why **A** is incorrect. **B** is also incorrect; "A message hearing come through the radio" is nonsensical and ought to sound funny. **C** is tempting, but notice that the first two clauses in the sentence ("The crew heard a message" and "it came through the radio") are both independent clauses; the fact that they are separated by a comma makes the sentence grammatically incorrect; thus **C** is incorrect. That leaves **D**, which is correct because it properly combines two independent clauses (comma and "and," one of the FANBOYS conjunctions) and communicates the proper message as well.

**#14** If we strip away the punctuation, we are left with two independent clauses in this long sentence. They are: "Steve lost his life at the young age of 54" and "he was pierced by a stingray barb." As written, the punctuation does not account for this (there is no comma/FANBOYS, semi-colon, colon, em dash), so **F** is incorrect. While we are thinking like that, **G** is incorrect for the exact same reason. **H** and **J** both make two sentences of the material, but which is best? Choice **H** puts a comma after "filming," which makes "In 2006 filming" into an introductory phrase, but that doesn't work because it unnecessarily separates those three words from the prepositional phrase "around the Great Barrier Reef." That is why **J** is correct; this option actually creates two independent clauses in the second sentence, which works because there is a ", and" after "Barrier Reef."

**#15** At first, **A** seems like it could not be the correct answer because it begins with the word "You." However, that isn't a disqualifier because the entire essay is written to "You." In fact, the first paragraph proves this and contains "You" statements. The sentence for **A** mention's Steve's legacy and the Australia Zoo. This is the correct answer! **B** is about conservation, but that's not really the focus of the essay even though is it mentioned as important to Steve Irwin. **C** is incorrect because the essay isn't about crocodiles and their appeal to children. **D** is incorrect because, like the other choices, just because the sentence mentions something that is also mentioned in the essay (in this case, the Great Barrier Reef), that doesn't mean it is the best sentence.

**Passage II: The Theory of Beauty**

**#16** In the preceding sentence, the author mentions seeing sunsets in a unique way. She is trying to make the same point about "the forest, a stream, or the night sky" too. The choice that effectively makes this point is **G**, making the previous sentence "true of" those things as well. The other choices might not have grammatical problems all, but should *sound* strange. Is she seeing sunsets "within the forest", etc.? No, which is why **F** is incorrect. When she sees sunsets, does she "become the forest", etc.? No, which is why **H** is incorrect. Saying that this is "only about" the forest, etc. is a contradiction; we just said it's true about sunsets in the first sentence; that is shy **J** is incorrect.

**#17** Here, "on the other hand" is a nonessential phrase. If it was to be removed, the sentence would flow perfectly well: "I have trained myself...". This is why it has to be set off with commas. Only answer choice **C** does this. **B** ignores that it is nonessential by failing to have any commas. **A** makes "I on the other hand" into an introductory phrase, but that is problematic because it separates the subject "I" from "have" as part of its own dependent clause; that doesn't work here. **D** either makes "I" into an introductory phrase or begins to set off the entire middle of the sentence as nonessential; neither works.

**#18** This is a question of subject/verb agreement. In this case, the subject is "it", which is singular. **J** is incorrect because "have" is the plural conjugation. **H** is incorrect because it is in the future tense. This means that you have to determine if the correct spelling is "has led" or "has lead." "To lead" is a verb, but also "lead" is a heavy mineral. When conjugated in the past singular, you would say "led," like, "I led the team to victory." That is why the correct answer is **F**. **G** misspells the word "led."

**#19** In this case, you must have a grip on the general topic of the paragraph to ensure that you get the question correct. Reading on, you should see some sentences about colors intermixing and things like that (as a side note, it is also appropriate to leave this question for now and return after reading through the paragraph and answering any questions you encounter). This is why **A** is the correct answer; the phrase as written brings up the ideas of beauty and color. **B** is incorrect because the paragraph is not about recognizing beauty in other people; **C** is incorrect because the paragraph is not about the history of film or light use in those films; **D** is incorrect because the paragraph is not about how different people like herself have come to be interested in the topic of art (besides, we already learned that in the first paragraph, which makes this choice a bit redundant as well).

**#20** Here we have another instance of setting off nonessential words or phrases which, again, is the #1 tested comma usage on recent ACT's. Here, we have an independent clause that is ended with a comma, then a FANBOYS conjunction is present ("but"). This signals the beginning of another independent clause. Looking, we see that "Others appear ugly or detestable" is also an independent clause. Off the bat we can thus eliminate **H** as incorrect because there is no comma before the "but," which would be necessary since we are combining multiple independent clauses. The key to the question is recognizing that the word "however" is nonessential. **F** fails to set off this word with commas, so it is incorrect. **G** sets off "however," but it also sets off the word "others," but "others" is not a nonessential word. That is why **J** is correct; it sets off "however" as nonessential and has the comma+FANBOYS to separate the two independent clauses.

**#21** **C** is incorrect because the word "which" must be set off by a comma. Even if you couldn't see that, however, there is another reason why **C, D,** and **A** are all incorrect: they are redundant. The sentence just said that grey and black are in a *swirl*, which means already that the two colors are intermixing or mixed up. This is why the correct answer is **B**.

**#22** This is a question that tests your ability to use the correct pronoun and conjugate the verb correctly. Because the sentence is in the present tense ("if one adds" and "inclinations change"), we need a verb in the present tense. This eliminates choices **G** and **H**; they are in the past tense, so are both incorrect. Now it comes down to pronoun use. Most students will get this question incorrect because they will quickly bubble in **F**, but that is incorrect. The reason for this is because of the correct pronoun that is needed. Remember, a pronoun refers to something or someone that is established in the greater context. The question is: what should the pronoun refer to? Not "inclinations", but *beholder*. That is singular, and "they" is plural, which is why **F** is wrong. **J** correctly uses the singular "he or she" to refer to the singular "beholder."

**#23** We need the correct combination of words that will perfectly communicate that it is interesting that "preferences in aesthetics go beyond colors." **A** is incorrect because the colon does not follow a complete thought, which is our #1 colon rule. **B** is incorrect because it artificially inserts a comma after "preferences," which in the sentence creates an introductory phrase that turns the rest of the sentence into nonsense ("in aesthetics go far beyond colors and appear to be universal" is not an independent clause or complete thought). **C** has the problem of failing to set off the word "interestingly." It could go here, but it is nonessential in that case, and would need to be set off by commas. **D** is thus the correct answer; it properly sets off "Interestingly" as an introductory word, separated from the independent clause that is the rest of the sentence.

**#24** This is a matter of choosing the correct prepositional phrase. Is a building built "of right angles"? Unless right angles are the same thing as bricks and mortar, no. Thus, **G** is incorrect. Is a building built "in right angles"? Unless it is literally built inside of right angles somehow, then no, that is not what is trying to be said; thus, **F** is incorrect. Is a building built "for right angles"? Unless the right angles are paying for the buildings and are the new owners, then no; thus, **J** is incorrect. That leaves **H**, which correctly says that the buildings are built at 90 degree angles, meaning their shapes are rectangles and squares.

**#25** Here, a FANBOYS conjunction is underlined, and it just so happens that this conjunction comes after a comma. That means that what comes next must be an independent clause. **A** and **C** can both be eliminated on this ground; what comes after the comma is not a complete thought. As for **B** and **D**, the difference between them is what we called in Step 5 a transition; the question is which of the two is better in this context: "for" or "but." "For" implies cause and effect, but that is not the relationship between the two clauses. This is why **D** is incorrect. **B** is thus correct because it adds the pronoun "they" to create an independent clause and correctly uses the conjunction "but."

**#26** As written, what comes after "art." is an incomplete thought or, you might say, a sentence fragment. That is why **F** is incorrect. **J** is also incorrect; it isn't the art that is intense, but the way in which the art was studied. **H** has the problem of separating the prepositional phrases that are a part of the flow of the sentence away from the rest of the sentence. If the phrase "with intensity and interest over the course of a lifetime" came at the beginning of the sentence, that could work if it were set off by a comma. This is why **G** is the correct answer; it is the only choice that does not interrupt the sentence or change the author's intention.

**#27** Again, which prepositional phrase is proper in context? "Under construction" is a phrase to describe a building, not how someone consults; this is why **D** is incorrect. **B** is silly; did she consult "on top of" all of the construction (as if there's a bunch of rubble and rebar sticking from concrete and she is standing on top of it all wearing a hardhat)? No. **A** is similar; it makes it sound like she is over it all in a helicopter. This is why **C** is correct; it rightly identifies that she was a consultant in (of you could say "for") the construction.

**#28** This is a question of verbosity; all of the answer choices say the same thing, but **F, H,** and **J** are too wordy. This is why the correct answer is **G**; it says what the sentence needs in the fewest words possible.

**#29** This is a question of not only pronoun use, but you might say "sentence structure," or identifying that some words or phrases create nonsense. **B** and **D** are not grammatically incorrect, but they oddly shift the point of view of the essay to third person (he, she, them, they); but the entirety of the essay so far is in the first person. **C** creates nonsense; what must follow "although every" has to be singular (like, "although every apple..."), but here "human beings" is plural. This is why **A** is the correct answer; it uses a pronoun that is in the first person ("we") and maintains the structure of the sentence (it doesn't create nonsense).

**#30** Hopefully you can identify if the answer here is "Yes" or "No" before reading through the choices. If not, it is OK to circle a question of this type and come back to it when you are finished with the entire English test. Here, the question asks if the essay is a personal account of the theories of art and beauty and how they are fascinating. Well, yep, that is exactly what the essay is about. We can thus eliminate **H** and **J** as incorrect. **G** says that the essay is not an essay, but a letter. However, the ACT will never give you a letter, but always an essay. Even if you flip back, you'll see no "Dear Sally" to begin the essay. That is why the answer is **F**; it correctly says that the essay is in the first person (thus it is a personal account) and has examples of why art and beauty are fascinating topics of study.

**Passage III: An Inventor's Childhood**

**#31** The proposed sentence, it seems, can't be immediately dismissed. It mentions "him", which references Alexander Graham Bell (who was brought up in the first sentence), and it mentions the "triumphant invention", which references the invention of the telephone. The question is: does the rest of the paragraph have to do with his upbringing? That is the shift that is taking place in the sentence. Looking ahead, the next sentence mentions "three aspects of his childhood," so we can conclude rightfully that the answer is "Yes," this sentence belongs. That eliminates **C** and **D** as incorrect. **A** says that Alexander invented the telephone as a child, and that this fact is stated later in the paragraph. Reading ahead, there is no mention of this in the paragraph; this is why **A** is incorrect. **B** rightfully said that the subject of the essay is shifted from Bell to his childhood.

**#32** This is an example of a transition or transitional phrase; we need the best choice to bridge thoughts between sentences based on context. As written, it proposes no such transition is needed. That could be best, but we have to keep reading ahead a bit to figure it out. The next sentence begins with "Second." That is the only clue you need to determine that **H** is the correct answer. **G** and **J** unnecessarily use a transition that creates contrast, but that is not what the context calls for. **F** would work if the following sentence (instead of saying, "Second,") said, "Then, his parents..." or "Not to mention, his parents...", but it doesn't. That is why **F** is incorrect.

**#33** As written, there is something nonsensical about this. Shouldn't it say, "...his curiosities and *the* inventing spirit inside of him"? Yes, it should; that is why we can eliminate choice **A** as incorrect. The rest of the answer choices all say the same thing. The problem is that **C** and **D** are not only too wordy, but also redundant (can his "inventing spirit" be somewhere besides inside him or in his spirit?). That is why the answer is **B**: it is the least wordy and has no redundancies.

**#34** This, as written, is a run-on sentence. We are trying here to combine two independent clauses, so **F** is incorrect because it fails to do so correctly. The other three options contain punctuation that permits combining these clauses: the semi-colon, the colon, and the em dash. The correct answer hinges on this word "rather." First, that word makes no sense as a concluding word to the first independent clause ("...he had a natural genius that he refused to squander rather"); this is why we can go ahead and eliminate **G** as incorrect. Let's isolate the second clause and begin it with that word: "Rather, he used it for good." That word must be set off by a comma; it is nonessential and as a transition or "connector word" needs the comma. That is why **H** is incorrect; there is no comma. **J** is correct because it uses a semi-colon properly and correctly sets off the introductory word "rather" with a comma.

**#35** This is a classic question of verbosity (too many words). All of the options mean the same thing, but **B, C,** and **D** are all incorrect because they are too wordy compared to the less-wordy correct answer: **A**.

**#36** "Even so" implies contradiction between two sentences. For example, I might say, "I hate cartoons. Even so, I am willing to watch them with my children." While we're at it, "On the other hand" and "Be that as it may" are transitional phrases that do this exact same thing to a pair of sentences: imply contradiction. "I hate cartoons. On the other hand (or Be that as it may), I'm willing to watch them with my children" works. That is why **F, G,** and **J** are all incorrect. The sentence needs to begin with a transitional phrase that implies cause and effect (he was curious about human speaking (cause) and he developed voice talents (effect)). This is why **H** is correct; it rightly unites the two sentences.

**#37** If you read the two sentences that are being united here, which begin a few lines before with #36, it is clearly two independent clauses (complete sentences or complete thoughts, in other words). Punctuation has to be used here to correctly combine them. **B** and **C** fail to do this; these two options simply let the sentence run on and on with commas (and no FANBOYS conjunctions), so they are incorrect. The problem with **A**, which is why it is incorrect, is that it misplaces the phrase "in addition;" that phrase is supposed to be a transitional phrase between the two sentences. In its current location, it is not only awkward, but redundant (it has the same effect on the sentence that the word "and" does earlier in the sentence). That is why **D** is correct; it rightly deals with two independent clauses by ending one with a period and beginning the second, and it rightly places the transitional phrase "In addition" at the beginning of the second sentence.

**#38** Here, you must identify the proper prepositional phrase. You must rely on your *listening skills*, and by that I mean this: don't some of these simply sound awkward or nonsensical? If so, you have good instincts because you have been (presumably, though not true for everyone) listening to English your entire life. **J** is incorrect; it could be an option if the word "all" was not a part of it, but it is. **H** is a jumble of nonsense; it's incorrect. **F** is incorrect as well; have you ever heard someone say, "I'm destined of working over a hospital to help save lives." No, and for good reason; it makes no sense. That is why the correct answer is **G**; it rightly uses the verb "to work" and correctly uses the proposition "within" before "the realm."

**#39** As written, the verb is conjugated in the present tense, but the rest of the sentence is in the past tense ("encouraged"). So **A** is incorrect for this reason. If the phrase "to tinker" wasn't squeezed in there, we could identify this as the combination of two independent clauses. But, that's not what his happening here; the phrase "to tinker" *is* there, and it follows "to invent." Those two verbs are part of a sequence, and the underlined portion is the third verb to be listed in this sequence. That is why **D** is correct. **B** and **C** are incorrect because we don't need to begin a new independent clause here; doing so fails to complete the sequence of verbs set off by commas.

**#40** As written, this sentence is nonsense; you can't say "by gathering and use"; it would have to say, "by gathering and using." **F** and **G** both use "gathering," so they can be eliminated as incorrect. As for **J**, it is equally nonsensical. "...for to be commonly gather" is not a phrase you will ever hear because it simply makes no sense. For starters, if it were to make sense, it would have to say "for to be commonly gathered." Only answer choice **H** correctly ends the first independent clause with a semi-colon, then properly begins the second independent clause.

**#41** Step 5 taught you about modifying clauses and that they modify (change, alter, identify, describe) the word, noun, or subject that immediately follows the comma. As written, it makes it sound like "a flour mill" (it immediately follows the comma) grew up in Scotland...um, no. This is why **A** is incorrect. The other wrong answers are all wrong for this same reason: the modifying clause modifies the wrong subject. **B**, for example, makes it sound like Alexander ran the flour mill, but that is not true, which is why **B** is incorrect. **D** is also incorrect; this choice makes it sound like the flour mill was Alexander's neighbor, but the sentence is clearly trying to say that the Herdman family were the neighbors, and that they ran the mill. Only choice **C** has a modifying clause that works properly: it correctly says that Alexander was growing up in Scotland.

**#42** The subject that should agree with the verb here is "a dehusking device," which is singular. This makes **G** incorrect because it uses the verb "were," which is plural. **H** is incorrect because it doesn't even conjugate the verb "to be," thus it is nonsensical and overly wordy. **J** is singular ("was"), but says that the deshusking device was using the family. Besides sounding like something out of a cheaply made horror movie, it is not what the sentence is trying to imply. Only choice **F** correctly conjugates the verb and states that the family used Alexander's dehusking invention.

**#43** In this sentence, the independent clause is "he mastered the piano when he was a child." Everything else is nonessential or, according to the analogy used earlier in the book, a pitstop that slows the car. That is how we know that **A** is incorrect. Maybe you think to yourself, "I don't need to pause as I read this sentence," but remember that commas in ACT English have *deliberate use*, to set off nonessential and introductory words and phrases (among other things). **C** is also incorrect: it can be eliminated because there is not a complete thought before the colon. **D** is incorrect because of the location of the phrase "in fact." In this context, this phrase is a transition; it unites the previous sentence to the present one by helping the reader see the cause and effect nature of the two sentences. That is why **B** is correct; it positions the transitional phrase "In fact" in the proper place, and it correctly sets off "with no training" as a nonessential clause.

**#44** Whose genius? As written, the pronoun "her" makes it sound like Alexander applies his mother's genius. His mother might have been a genius, who knows, but the sentence is clearly trying to imply that Alexander's genius is that which is being applied. This is why **F** is incorrect. **H** is wrong for the same reason. **G** has the problem of being plural, but we need a singular pronoun. This is why **J** is correct; the pronoun "his" matches with Alexander and is singular.

**#45** The opening paragraph is about Alexander being the inventor of the telephone and about his childhood. **A** is about children, but not Alexander Graham Bell, so it is incorrect. **B** is about families and Alexander's ability to play the piano, but that in no way links to the first paragraph (and isn't a good way to end the essay as whole anyway). **C** links with a story earlier in the essay, but makes a claim that is not supported by the essay: Alexander's invention of the dehusking device didn't *cause* him to invent the telephone, so **C** is also incorrect. If there way any doubt about **C**, then **D** should help you get through the weeds. **D** is correct because it straightforwardly mentions Alexander's invention of the telephone. It also uses the transition "As a consequence," which fittingly ends the essay because the previous sentence is a summary of one of the essay's main points.

# Answer Explanations - Step 6 - Passages I and II

**Correct Answers:**

<u>Passage I</u>
1: C
2: F
3: D
4: H
5: A
6: H
7: D
8: G
9: C
10: J
11: A
12: J
13: C
14: G
15: B

<u>Passage II</u>
16: H
17: D
18: F
19: B
20: J
21: A
22: G
23: B
24: F
25: D
26: H
27: A
28: G
29: A
30: J

**Passage I: Mammoth Cave**

**#1** In this sentence, "located in Kentucky" is a nonessential phrase. It is sandwiched in there between the subject, "Mammoth Cave," and the verb, "is." Thus, it must be set off by commas. Only answer **C** does this, which is why it is correct. **A** has no commas setting it off, which is why it is incorrect. **B** creates a new nonessential phrase ("where it is located"), but that isn't set off by commas either, which is why it is incorrect. Lastly, **D** sets off the preposition "in Kentucky," but the clause as a whole begins with "located," which also must be set off as a part of it; that is why **D** is incorrect.

**#2** First, we can eliminate **J** because what must follow "is able" must be "to match," not "to matches;" that's nonsense, so **J** is incorrect. **G** and **H** make the same mistake: they use "it's." Remember, "it's" is a contraction meaning "it is," but that doesn't make sense in either answer choice. That is why **F** is correct; it rightly uses "its", which is possessive: the cave *possesses* a massive size, which is what the sentence is trying to communicate.

**#3** This is a question of subject/verb agreement. What is it that "estimate" or "estimates"? It is "Researchers," which is plural. That eliminates **A** and **C**, both of which conjugate the verb to match a singular subject (you can't say, "Researchers estimates..."). **B** inserts two commas, setting off "the total length" as a nonessential clause or phrase. But that is not the case; the commas are unnecessary. You can tell this because take out "the total length" from the sentence and see what happens: it turns into nonsense. The phrase is necessary, and thus the correct answer is **D**: it treats "the total length" as an essential phrase and has subject/verb agreement.

**#4** This question is a combination of Step 6 subjects! First, because we are dealing with a distance, we need *farther*, not *further*. This eliminates **F** and **G**. Second, because we are dealing with a comparison (and not a matter of time), we need *than*, not *then*. That eliminates **J**. That is why the correct answer is **H**; it correctly uses "farther" and "than."

**#5** First, because we are dealing with only one distance, we can eliminate any option that uses the plural "distances." This is why **B** and **D** are incorrect. Remember, *between* is used when referencing two objects/spaces/things, and *among* when referencing more than two. This is why *between* is correct here: Boston and Atlanta are *two* cities. Thus, **C** is incorrect because it uses "among," and **A** is correct because it uses the word "between."

**#6** Although Mammoth Cave is probably made up of multiple *caves*, it is the singular "Mammoth Cave" that the word "cave" is referencing. This is why **F** and **G** are incorrect; they put the apostrophe after the letter "s," which indicates that the passages are the possession of multiple caves. Option **J** artificially adds a comma after the word "cave's", which is incorrect; that does not need to be set off. This is why **H** is correct; it rightly denotes possession by the singular "cave" and only sets off the word "However" with a comma to start the sentence.

**#7** First, we are dealing with the past tense, so we can eliminate any option that uses the present tense "become"; thus, **A** and **B** are incorrect. That leaves a question of less vs fewer. Remember that *fewer* is used when what it references can be numbered or counted (or you might say, exist as individuals). What is being referenced in this case is "cracks," which *can* be numbered or counted, or which do exist individually. This is why **D** is correct; it rightly uses "fewer." **C** uses "less," which is reserved to refer to something that can't be numbered, or which can't exist individually (like "air," "water," "love," etc.).

**#8** This is a question of sentence structure. Remember to read the entirety of both sentences that this line overlaps. If you read only the underlined portion, "as the water moved through" might sound like a fine phrase to end a sentence with (like, "During the hurricane, I got scared in the house as the water moved through."). However, in this case, the water is moving through *the limestone*, so we can't separate the two. This eliminates **F** and **J** as they both insert periods after "through". As for **H**, it separates off "the limestone" from the preposition "through." This is unnecessary and disruptive, so **H** is incorrect. That leaves **G**, the correct answer, which rightly sets off "as the water moved through the limestone" from the independent clause "it actively dissolved minerals in the rock" with a comma.

**#9** As written, this is redundant. We don't need to say "they were now big enough" because the sentence already states that they were "large enough." That is why **A** is incorrect. **D** has a similar problem; it says "over time," but that idea is already implied by the first word in the sentence: "Eventually". Thus, **D** is incorrect because it is redundant. **B** has a couple of problems; first, it again says that these are something "large," which is redundant; second, it is overly wordy when compared to **C**. **C** is correct because if the sentence is ended with the word "into," it is already implied that what is being entered into is the cracks that are now large enough.

**#10** This is a question of who vs whom, to start. Remember the rule: rephrase the clause with "he" or "him". Here, we could say, "Was *he* the first to discover the cave?" or "Was *him* the first to discover the cave?" Putting "him" there makes no sense; it would be "he." That means that the sentence calls for *who*, not *whom*. This eliminates **F** and **H** as incorrect. The other thing to consider in this question is verb tense. In this case, we are dealing in the past tense. That means that the correct answer is **J**, which uses the past tense "were." **G** is incorrect because it uses the present tense "are."

**#11** Here, the subject of the sentence is "tribes," so the verb "to use" will need a plural conjugation. This eliminates **B** and **D**, both of which have subject/verb agreement problems. **C** has a pronoun error; it says "them", but the pronoun that follows "used" is referring to something singular ("the cave" from the previous sentence), not something plural (even though "the elements" is in the previous sentence, that is not what is being referenced here; that is not what is being "used" in the sentence). That is why **A** is correct; it rightly has subject/verb agreement and uses the singular pronoun "it" to refer to "the cave."

**#12** "They're" is a contraction representing "they are." Because "some of they are possessions" makes no sense, we can eliminate **F** as incorrect. Similar nonsense is the result when you consider choice **G**: "some of them possessions" makes no sense. What the sentence is trying to say is that the possessions were, well, *possessed* by the Native Americans; that is why the correct answer is **J**, because "their" is possessive. As for **H**, it is incorrect because "there" as reference to a place makes no sense coming before the word "possessions."

#13 First we can eliminate choices **A** and **B** because they are in the future tense and the sentence calls for past tense. Now it is simply a question of lie vs lay. Remember, "lie" is something a subject does *to itself* ("My dog will lie down (you could say, *lie itself down*) in its crate when it is tired"). Here, the body is being put down *by something/someone else*. That is why "lay" is needed (as in "I lay the dog down in the crate at night"). This means **D** is incorrect because it uses "lie;" **C** is correct because it rightly uses "lay."

#14 If you read the following sentence (the one about how surveyors have made huge leaps in understanding), it becomes clear that the sentence being referenced by the question belongs. This is because the next sentence has a little word in it: "however." This word contrasts with something, but it's not Mammoth Cave becoming a national park (sentence 1) that it contrasts with. When the sentence is inserted, it suddenly makes sense that the "huge leaps in understanding" contrasts with "only 40 miles of passageway" that at the time had been mapped out. This eliminates choices **H** and **J**. **F** says that the sentence should be kept because it is necessary to know that Mammoth Cave is the world's largest; however, that's not true, we already know that with or without the proposed sentence (see the first sentence of the essay!). This is why **G** is correct; it rightly notes that research has come a long way since 1941 by giving a number of miles that had, at the time, been mapped: 40.

#15 The proposed sentence has to do with water flowing through cracks. Hopefully that rings a bell: wasn't there a paragraph about water flowing through limestone? Even if you can't remember that, placing the sentence one at a time should help you. Choice **A** makes no sense because paragraph 1 is entirely about the large size of Mammoth Cave and mentions nothing about water. Choice **C** also makes no sense because paragraph 3 is about the use of the cave by Native Americans and also mentions nothing about water. **D** is also incorrect because the last paragraph, paragraph 4, mentions nothing about water flowing over rocks and is more about the cave's overall recent history. This is why **B** is the correct answer: paragraph 2 is all about how the caves were formed when water flowed through the cracks in the limestone.

**Passage II: Nikola Tesla**

#16 This kind of jumble of words and verb tenses is exactly what the ACT English section likes to throw at you. Try one at a time and trust your *listening judgment*; some should, hopefully, *sound* like nonsense. **F** says, "as if Nikola Tesla," but when read in the context of the sentence, it makes you want to ask, "as if Nikola Tesla...what?" It feels incomplete because the phrase "as if" is always followed by a complete thought, like "as if Nikola Tesla really cared." **G** should sound funny because the verb "have" is a plural conjugation, so there is no subject/verb agreement; we need singular because "Nikola Tesla" is singular. **H** is correct because it rightly does this. **J** is a nonsense jumble of words; it makes it sound like other inventors tried to be like Nikola Tesla, but that is not the purpose of the sentence.

#17 You should recognize that the phrase "overall more work" makes no sense. Maybe in some contexts you could have it look like this: "Overall, more work...", or like this: "Overall, work...". This is why **A** is incorrect. **B** is also incorrect because the sentence calls for the word "work" to be used as a noun (it is the object of the verb "indicates"), not as a verb, but **B** turns it into a verb (that, even still, doesn't make sense). This leaves you to discern if we need "good" or "well" to describe "work." "Well," though, is an adverb, and would be proper if we needed to describe the verb "to work" (as in, "I worked well on the yard today"). But, as we said, "work" here is a noun, so what is needed is an adjective: "good." This is why **D** is correct and **C** is incorrect.

#18 All four of these choices have modifying clauses. **G** says that "science and technological pursuits" were dedicated, but it is Tesla who is supposed to be described that way, so **G** is incorrect. **H** says that "technological pursuits" are "a scientist" (because they follow the comma), so it is incorrect. **J** says that "pursuits" had a career in science, so it is incorrect. **F** is the only option that correctly uses a modifying clause; it rightly modifies "Tesla" (after the comma) with the clause "Throughout his life".

**#19** At first, it seems like nothing is wrong with the way this is written. But, to be technical, the FANBOYS conjunction "so" is not the *best choice* here. Why? Because "so" implies cause and effect. Did Tesla's humble beginnings cause his mother to run the farm? No; both of them probably have the same cause. This is why **B** is correct; it combines these two independent clauses in the *best* way. **C** is incorrect for a couple of reasons, but the primary reason is because it uses the pronoun "she," but there is no woman yet identified that the pronoun can refer to (who is "she"?). **D** is incorrect because, although it uses the FANBOYS conjunction "and," there is no comma after the word "beginnings."

**#20** In Step 6, I introduced you to the idea that, actually, semi-colons technically have a second use. The odds of you needing to know that semi-colons are used to combine independent clauses on ACT English? 100%. The odds of you needing to know that semi-colons can be used like commas in a series? Closer to 0% than 1%, which is why this is the only question in this book that tests your knowledge of it. All you need to remember, though, is that if semi-colons are being used in a series, you can't replace one of them with a comma or some other punctuation; you have to be consistent. This is why **J** is the correct answer; the series already uses semi-colons, so it must be finished that way. **F, G**, and **H** all use commas after "Graz," but like we said, it must be a semi-colon because a semi-colon is used to begin the setting off of the list of three clauses earlier in the sentence (after the word "student").

**#21** The paragraph that precedes this possible sentence placement begins to tell a story about how Edison undervalued Tesla. Then, it says that Edison offered Tesla $50,000...doesn't sound like he's being undervalued to me! This is why the sentence does, indeed, belong. Choices **C** and **D** can be eliminated for this reason. Of the other two options, **B** is incorrect because it seems to say that the essay (or maybe the paragraph) is about American humor, but that's not true. **A** is correct because, without the sentence, there is no way to understand how Tesla was undervalued.

**#22** This is strictly a question of apostrophe use. Two people are possessing something, but the thing that is possessed (in this case, "rivalry") is possessed by the both of them. If we were to leave the sentence as it's written, it means that Tesla had a rivalry, and then Edison had a rivalry as well that he didn't share with Tesla. But that's not the case, which is why **F** is incorrect. **J** can be eliminated because there are no apostrophes to denote possession. **H** is incorrect because it pluralizes "Tesla" and "Edison" as if there were multiple of both, like a family feud. That is why the answer is **G**; because only "Edison" contains the apostrophe and then the s, what is signified is that the pair shared a rivalry, which is what the sentence is attempting to say.

**#23** Is there a kind of rivalry that two people can have that's not "against each other"? No, which means that **A** is redundant and incorrect. **C** is incorrect for the same reason; the clause in the commas simply restates what is already stated about the pair being rivals. **D** replaces the word "rivalry" with a definition of rivalry; of course this isn't grammatically incorrect, nor is it redundant, but it is *verbose* (too wordy). That is why the answer is **B**; everything that is needed be said is summed up in the word "rivalry."

**#24** Even if you don't know what a "magnate" is, hopefully you can eliminate the other answer choices. **G** is incorrect because I don't think Tesla is partnering with a magnet. **H** and **J** are incorrect for the same reason: Tesla wouldn't be partnering with a "manage" or the color magenta either. Because a magnate is a wealthy business person, that is the word that fits; thus, **F** is the correct answer.

**#25** Remember our who vs whom rule (restate the clause with *he* or *him*): did *he* see Tesla's potential, or did *him* see Tesla's potential? *He* makes sense there, so "who" is the word we are looking for. That eliminates **A** and **B**, both of which use "whom." **C** puts the pronoun "he" before "saw," but we don't need that pronoun; we already know that it is Westinghouse "who saw" the potential. That is why **D** is correct: it correctly uses "who" in place of "whom" and does not unnecessarily insert a pronoun.

**#26** The question says that the correct phrase will show that the inventions have "had a lasting effect." This is why **H** is correct; it is the only option that says that derivatives of his inventions are still being used today. **F, G**, and **J** make no mention of this, which is why they are all incorrect. **G** makes mention of the inventions being used for a time, but then they were "phased out," which contradicts the requirement that the inventions have a *lasting effect*.

**#27** If **C** were to be correct, there would need to be some kind of clause after the comma; either that or the sentence would need an overall change to make it make sense. **B** is incorrect because it wrongly replaces the preposition "to" with "too." As I just said, "to" here is being used to start a prepositional phrase. **D**, though still a prepositional phrase, strangely puts in the word "the" before homes; this has the effect of *specifying* certain homes and businesses, but this is meant to be a general statement. For that reason, **A** is correct in that "to" is used as a preposition and creates a phrase that remains general.

**#28** Each of these four options has the pronoun "he" or "they." The first thing to do is to figure out which of those is proper. What, exactly, is this pronoun supposed to refer to? Though it may be tempting, the answer to that question is not *eccentricities*, but rather "Tesla"; *he* is the one having a difficult time finding funding. This eliminates **F** and **H** as incorrect. **J** would only work if "having found it..." were the beginning of a nonessential phrase set off by commas, but neither of those things is true here. That is why **G** is correct; it uses the correct pronoun "he" to replace "Tesla" and it uses the correct verb tense.

**#29** "One thing is for sure" is an independent clause, and so is the clause that comes next: "Nikola Tesla was one of the foremost brilliant people of his day and age." What is needed is a proper way to combine two independent clauses. We can thus eliminate choices **C** and **D** as neither does so. Although **B** has a comma plus a FANBOYS conjunction, there is another problem: have you ever heard anyone say, "One thing is to be for sure"? While there is nothing incorrect here grammatically speaking, it changes the *idiom* (remember, a group of words that always goes together?) "On thing is for sure." Thus, **B** is incorrect. **A** is correct because it keeps the idiom correct (and less wordy) and it properly combines independent clauses.

**#30** All four of these options are synonyms; they all say the exact same thing. None of them is *grammatically* superior to any other. Simply, **F, G,** and **J** are too wordy. That is why **J** is the correct answer.

# Answer Explanations - Step 7 - Practice Test #1

**Correct Answers:**

| Passage I | Passage II | Passage III | Passage IV | Passage V |
|---|---|---|---|---|
| 1: C | 16: F | 31: A | 46: G | 61: B |
| 2: F | 17: B | 32: J | 47: A | 62: F |
| 3: D | 18: J | 33: C | 48: G | 63: A |
| 4: J | 19: C | 34: J | 49: B | 64: F |
| 5: A | 20: F | 35: A | 50: G | 65: D |
| 6: H | 21: A | 36: H | 51: B | 66: H |
| 7: D | 22: H | 37: A | 52: J | 67: D |
| 8: J | 23: A | 38: F | 53: D | 68: G |
| 9: B | 24: F | 39: B | 54: H | 69: A |
| 10: H | 25: C | 40: J | 55: B | 70: G |
| 11: B | 26: G | 41: C | 56: F | 71: C |
| 12: J | 27: C | 42: H | 57: C | 72: J |
| 13: C | 28: H | 43: C | 58: H | 73: D |
| 14: G | 29: D | 44: G | 59: B | 74: F |
| 15: D | 30: G | 45: A | 60: G | 75: C |

**Passage I: Fallingwater**

**#1** This is a question of verb tense and subject verb agreement. Because the sentence is in the present tense ("Most would agree"), we need a verb in the present that fits with the subject ("boulder," singular). **B** can be eliminated because it is in the past tense. **A** and **D** can also both be eliminated because they are conjugated to fit with a plural subject; in other words, they would work if "boulders" were bulging through the floor, but not "boulder." That is why the correct answer is **C**; "is" is both singular and present tense.

**#2** This is a comma question of setting off a nonessential clause. Remember that a nonessential clause can be spied by it being lifted from the sentence. Here, we can see that the main clause of the sentence (or independent clause or main thought you might say) is this: "there is very little practical use for a large rock." The large nonessential clause in the middle is just that: one (not two) large clause. That is why it must be set off by commas, and why **F** is the correct answer. **G** is incorrect because it never sets off the phrase with a comma. **H** is incorrect because it wrongly creates a nonessential clause within a nonessential clause. **J** is incorrect because it it also fails to set off the nonessential clause at the correct place.

**#3** Due to the wordiness of the words underlined and before this, it seems like commas would be a good idea, but they are not. I know that "famous American architect Frank Lloyd Wright" is pretty wordy. However, there is no need for commas here. "Famous American architect" is essentially one large adjective describing the one person "Frank Lloyd Wright." Thus, **D** is the correct answer. **B** sets off Wright's name as if it is a nonessential phrase, but that is incorrect. **C** is incorrect because it artificially inserts a semi-colon into the sentence, but that would only work if we were linking two independent clauses. **A** separates "for the famous American architect Frank Lloyd Wright" off as its own nonessential clause, which would be OK if it weren't for "and his client Edgar Kauffman" that follows, because those 5 words are also a part of the same clause. In other words, they can't be set off. That is why **A** is incorrect.

**#4** Based on the context of the sentence, it is clear that a noun is needed here. **F, G,** and **H** are all verbs of some kind. This is why the correct answer is **J**; "effect" is a noun and properly works.

**#5** Answer choices **B, C,** and **D** all create a new independent clause that ends with the word "Pennsylvania." However, all that comes after "Pennsylvania" is a comma; there is no FANBOYS conjunction after it. That means that **B, C,** and **D** are all incorrect; only **A** rightly creates an introductory phrase that can be set off with a comma.

**#6** What is needed is an option that stresses Fallingwater's *importance*. **F** is incorrect because having a nice view doesn't stress the importance of the home. **G** and **J** are wrong for the same reasons; those are all nice things about the home, but they don't stress or highlight the home's importance. That is why **H** is correct; having "historic and cultural significance" stresses the home's importance.

**#7** Here you are asked for the order of sentences in the paragraph. Look at sentence 2: "Fallingwater is the name of this home" is a phrase that introduces the name *for the first time*. It makes no sense coming after sentence 1, which is written assuming that you already know that the name of the home is Fallingwater ("Fallingwater draws over 100,000..."). So we know for sure that sentence 2 comes before sentence 1. Out of all four options, only one has this: **D**, which is the correct answer. **A, B,** and **C** are all incorrect because they put sentence 2 after sentence 1.

**#8** We already know that the plans called for a home above the falls. We learned that the home is over the waterfall in the last paragraph. That means **F** is incorrect because it is redundant. **G** is also redundant; it says Kauffman wasn't thrilled with the plans, and then later in the sentence it says the plans didn't suit his desires. **H** is wrong for the exact same reason; it says Kauffman lost the view he wanted, which is what is stated later in the same sentence. That is why **J** is correct; it is the only choice without a redundancy.

**#9** Here, we need the correct transition linking the two sentences. The sentence previous states that Kauffman did not like the initial plans. The sentence following says that Kauffman "came around" to the idea. That's contrasting, which is why **B** is correct; "However" properly contrasts the two sentences because a change has taken place. **A** and **C** would both imply cause and effect, but that's not the case. **D** does not work either; "Otherwise" is used to mean something like "Or else," like this: "It's a good thing my dog is cute. Otherwise, I would have gotten rid of it long ago."

**#10** Here, "At one point" is an introductory phrase, so it must be set off with a comma. That is why **H** is correct. **G** is incorrect because it is nonsensical to switch the words "Kauffman" and "point." **F** is incorrect because, as written, there is a comma after Kauffman, which separates him from the word "thought." **J** is incorrect because it sets off "At one point" with an em dash (—); that would only be acceptable in this circumstance if that was the beginning of a nonessential clause also closed off later in the sentence with an em dash, but that never happens.

**#11** The easiest way to think about the correct answer here is to reimagine the independent clause without the very long nonessential or dependent clause in the middle. That would mean this: "Kauffman thought the space set out for his personal desk that was too small." **A** would only work if the beginning of the clause said something like, "Kauffman had a desk that was too small." But that's not the case, and hopefully you can *listen* and hear that this makes no sense as written. **C** is incorrect because it creates a new independent clause, and the sentence and its punctuation do not account for that. **D** is incorrect; "Kauffman thought the space set out for his personal desk too small" is missing something: what did he think? That is why **B** is correct; it rightly says that he thought the space "to be too small."

**#12** There's nothing grammatically incorrect here, but it is contradictory. How can he read the plans that he had sealed up in the wall? This is why **F** is incorrect. Other problems besides, **G** and **H** imply the same thing. That is why **J** is correct; it is the only choice that rightly concludes that the plans put into the wall were not read again (which is why they were put into the wall in the first place).

**#13** This should strike you as only loosely connected to the previous paragraph. In other words, it's not a fitting conclusion to a paragraph about the disagreements between Kauffman and Wright. Thus, it does not belong, and that is why **A** and **B** are incorrect. As for **D**, it correctly says "No," but it implies that the sentence contradicts earlier statements, but there have been no statements so far about the sturdiness of the home. That is why **C** is correct; it rightly says "No," giving a true reason: the information is not relevant.

**#14** Starting the sentence with "Having been used" implies that the sentence is being lead off with an introductory phrase. However, if you read the entire sentence this way, you will notice that never happens; what should be an introductory phrase is ended with a period as opposed to set off by a comma before an independent clause. This is why **F, H,** and **J** are all incorrect; any of these three options creates an incomplete sentence for the same reason. **G** is the correct answer because it is the only option that creates an independent clause that can be ended with a period.

**#15** As always, there are clues in this sentence that can help place it correctly. The sentence is about writing a check. Unless you remember exactly where the sentence may go (which is certainly great!), then we need to go back and check this idea in the context of all four choices (or at least enough possibilities until we can be sure of the correct answer). **A** is not a good fit; the previous sentence is about a boulder, and the sentence following references this boulder as "such a feature," so inserting a sentence about writing a check would be disruptive. **B** is also not a good fit; the first paragraph already has a fitting sentence to end it, and inserting a random sentence here about writing a check would be irrelevant. **C** is probably the most tempting wrong answer; the sentence before is about Kauffman's dislike of the plans, and so the idea of inserting a sentence that implies that Kauffman wouldn't pay Wright seems fitting. However, the sentence is about the *space* needed to write a check, not about how Kauffman was angry with Wright. This is why **D** is the correct answer; it rightly follows a sentence about Kauffman's desk being "too small," meaning there might not be enough space on it to write a check.

**Passage II: Turn Out the Lights!**

**#16** What we have here is two independent clauses, and what is underlined is the link between them. There are only a handful of ways to properly join independent clauses into a single sentence (comma+FANBOYS conjunction, semi-colon, — (em dash), or colon). Letters **G, H,** and **J** do none of these things, and thus they are all incorrect. **F** rightly separates the two independent clauses into their own sentences.

**#17** This is a great time to illustrate again our main comma rule: commas in English are *deliberate*; they don't belong just because a pause "sounds" good. If you're reading this, I'm guessing that you most likely put **A** because a pause kind of sounds nice after "operate." However, the comma does not belong; it interrupts the flow of the sentence, which is also why options **D** and **C** are incorrect. Only **B** correctly leaves out any commas and allows the sentence to flow as it is intended.

**#18** As written, the word "clarify" is in the present tense. The paragraph however is written in the past tense, describing an event that already happened. This is why **F** and **H** are incorrect. "Were to clarify" implies a time the clarifying should be done, like "They were to clarify where they had been when they got home." This is why **G** is incorrect. That is why the answer is **J**; it rightly conjugates the verb in the past tense.

**#19** Here, the verb tense has shifted to the present to describe the hatching of sea turtle eggs. This is one reason why **A** and **D** are both incorrect. **B** would only be correct if a new nonessential clause was being introduced, but if you keep reading, the sentence would then end abruptly. That is why **C** is correct; it rightly begins the nonessential clause with "which" after a comma and uses the verb "has," which is present tense.

**#20** After the word "change" there is a comma, and then an independent clause (but not FANBOYS conjunction). This means that whatever comes before the comma can't be an independent clause.

However, when you insert options **G, H,** or **J**, that is what you get, which is why they are all incorrect. Only **F** leaves the opening clause as a dependent clause or introductory phrase.

**#21** Every one of these options says the same thing: that the beach is dark. As you can see, **B, C,** and **D** are all very wordy, which is why **A** is the correct answer: it says what the sentence needs without being overly wordy.

**#22** This is a question of "further" vs "farther." "Further" refers to something growing or extending that isn't distance, like "Further research is necessary." "Farther" refers to distance, and that is what we have here. Thus, we can eliminate **F** and **G** because both use "further." **J** is too wordy, and it also says that the lights "went" farther inland as if they can walk themselves farther. That is why **H** is the correct answer; it rightly uses "farther" to refer to distance in the least wordy way possible.

**#23** All four of these options essentially say the exact same thing, and none of them contains grammar errors. You know what that means: you need the option that is the least wordy. That is why **B, C,** and **D** are all incorrect; they are all too wordy. That leaves **A**, which is correct because it says what the sentence needs without being overly wordy.

**#24** Remember: "lie" is something I do to myself (or a subject does to itself): "I lie down for a nap," or, "The cat lied down in the middle of the road" (I had a cat that used to do that...RIP Mittens!). "Lay" is something a subject does to something else, like "I laid the book on the shelf." Here, cash is being put on the table by someone else: that's what we need "laid." That eliminates **G** and **J** because they say "lied." **H** has the problem of being in the present tense when the greater context is in the past tense...so it's out. That is why the correct answer is **F**.

**#25** The key to this question is to leave off the sentence and reread at least the previous sentence. In this case, if we did that, the paragraph would leave off with the people telling the story leaving money on the tabletop. You could probably fill in the blank and guess that the next thing they did was rush to the beach, but the sentence that is there gives you that detail. **A** says something about people all over the world taking care of animals, but there is none of that in the sentence, so it is incorrect. **B** says that there's a restating of a fact about sea turtle eggs, but that isn't in the sentence, so it's out. **D** says that the sentence helps humans love animals more, but that is not in the sentence either. That is why **C** is correct: the sentence simply provides a detail in the flow of the story.

**#26** This is an example of an idiom: a group of words that always goes together in English. We say that people arrive "just in time." It's as simple as that. That's why **G** is correct. It's not that there's grammar issues with **F, H,** and **J**, but rather, in English, those things don't have any meaning whatsoever.

**#27** We need to try the phrase in question in all of the locations to see which fits. **A** is tempting because the current placement isn't terrible, but there is something a bit off about it (the question asks for the *best* placement, not any placement that works). **B** is incorrect because "Some to darken bait lights" makes no sense. **C** fits well; it puts the preposition "to darken bait lights" immediately behind the action of using black garbage bags, and this is why it is correct. **D** is incorrect because "nearby to darken bait lights piers" is also nonsensical.

**#28** Here, "like the baby turtles" is a nonessential phrase that has to be set off by commas, so we definitely need a comma after "turtles." This eliminates **G** and **J** as incorrect. **F** has the problem of artificially placing a comma after "drawn," which separates the prepositional phrase "to it myself" apart from the rest of the clause. This is why **H** is correct: it properly sets off the nonessential phrase and uses no other commas that do not belong.

**#29** This sentence ought not be too difficult to place because it is a simple sentence in the narrative about the turtles hatching. We just need to look back at the proposed locations and ask, "Does a sentence about turtles walking to the ocean belong here?" **A** can't work; the detail of the turtles is too soon and disrupts the paragraph. **B** is probably the most tempting wrong answer because this paragraph is about turtles hatching. However, this paragraph is more scientific and is in the present tense; the sentence we are trying to place is a part of the story and is in the past tense. **C** is also tempting because at this point we are back into the story. However, placing the sentence here is premature; the person telling the story hasn't made it down to the beach yet and would have no perspective as to how many turtles there are or if they've hatched or what they're doing. That is why the correct answer is **D**; only at this point does the perspective of the hundreds of baby turtles walking make sense because the previous sentence says that they arrived to the beach just in time.

**#30** Again, we want to know if the answer is "Yes" or "No" before reading the answer choices. The question asks if the essay gives the scientific background to a personal experience, and yes, that is exactly what this essay does. It is a personal story, but it also tells us scientifically about the hatching of sea turtle eggs. That eliminates **H** and **J**. **F** states that the essay is about the author's interest in marine biology, however, that is never mentioned in the essay, so it is incorrect. **G** rightly says that a personal story is bolstered or supported by the science of turtle eggs hatching.

**Passage III: Jefferson and Lewis**

**#31** Here, **C** is nonsensical when read in the context of the entire sentence, so it is incorrect. **B** does not work because "which" is a word applied to non-human things, but here we are dealing with a person; thus, "who" would be more appropriate. **D** is also nonsensical; you wouldn't say he's a "president knowing for." You say he is "known for" something if he is famous for something. That is why **A** is correct.

**#32** There are a lot of words here, but again, that does not mean that a comma is necessarily required. In ACT English, commas are used *deliberately*, not to create artificial pauses to break up long stretches of words. In this sentence, there are no nonessential clauses that sidetrack the sentence; there are also no introductory phrases to begin the sentence or any dependent clauses of any kind. That is why **J** is the correct answer. **H** is probably the most tempting wrong answer because it "seems" like a pause would be good where a comma is, but that is unnecessary, so it is incorrect. **F** and **G** have the same problem; they put commas in places they don't belong.

**#33** Here, notice what comes before and after the comma: independent clauses. Again, there are a handful of ways to unite these clauses. One way is to simply create two separate sentences, but that is not an option. The other options are to use a comma and a FANBOYS conjunction, an em dash (—), a colon, or a semi-colon. Here, though there is a comma, there is no FANBOYS conjunction, so **A** is incorrect. **B** has no punctuation at all, so it is incorrect as well. **D** is very tempting; it rightly uses a semi-colon. However, the second clause is started with the word "because," which would then turn the second half into an introductory phrase that would need to be set off from more information with a comma (in other words, what comes after the semi-colon is no longer an independent clause). That is why **C** is correct; it rightly uses a colon to separate two independent clauses.

**#34** We need a sentence that introduces us to the idea that Jefferson chose Lewis to go to the Pacific Ocean. **F** talks of the West Coast, but that has nothing to do with choosing a person to lead the expedition, so it is incorrect. The same can be said for **H**. Choice **G** mentions Thomas Jefferson, but it is about Jefferson being busy, not about Jefferson choosing a person to go West. That is why **J** is the correct answer: Jefferson needed to choose "the right man for the job" (as the question says, we need a sentence that transitions to Jefferson choosing Lewis).

**#35** Again, check what comes before and after what is underlined (read in the context of the entire sentence!). What we have is two independent clauses, from "Jefferson" to "expedition" is one, and "he" to "leader" is another. There are a few ways to join these together. We could make them two sentences, use a comma and a FANBOYS conjunction, use an em-dash (—), use a colon, or use a semi-colon. There is only one answer choice that does any of these, and that is answer choice **A**; it rightly has a FANBOYS conjunction ("and") after the comma between the two clauses. **B, C,** and **D** not only fail to properly combine these two independent clauses, but they are all nonsensical as well for various reasons.

**#36** Although there are multiple words underlined here, this is a question of choosing the proper transition. "Because" implies cause and effect, but there is no cause and effect between him having qualities necessary and him not knowing much; what is needed is a transition that creates contrast. This is why **F** is incorrect. **G** makes the least sense; why would he have to explain his qualities? That is why **G** is incorrect. As for **J**, it creates one long sentence with two independent clauses, but there is no proper punctuation to join them. **H** is correct because it creates the proper contrast between the two clauses in the sentence.

**#37** There is nothing grammatically incorrect with any of the answer choices, which must mean that there is a *best* answer. In this case, three of these answer choices are redundant. **B** says "experts were needed," but the sentence says later that he was sent to experts (thus, it's redundant). **C** has a redundancy within it; "because of this" and "having been caused by this" mean the same thing. **D** says "there were many things Lewis did not know", but the sentence before said that already. **A** is the shortest, but more importantly, it contains no redundancies.

**#38** The question asks for the answer that stresses the seriousness of the training. As written, choice **F**, it says that the skills could prove "life-saving." That's pretty serious. Is **G**, proving he's a Renaissance man, more important than that? No, so **G** is incorrect. Is **H**, proving his critics wrong, more important than saving lives? No, so **H** is incorrect. Is **J**, proving a fun entry into knowledge, more important than saving lives? No, so **J** is incorrect. That is why the correct answer is **F**, it is the choice that makes his training with experts the most important.

**#39** As written, there is something very short about the sentence; it ends very abruptly, especially compared to the rest of the essay. Because it is an opening sentence, it establishes the tone of the rest of the paragraph, and it's hard to imagine the paragraph continuing with short abrupt sentences like these. Those are some reasons why the answer is "Yes," but even if you're unsure and read the answer choices **C** and **D**, their reasons why the answer is "No" aren't good enough. Now, as for **A**, it says that we need to know that Lewis studied medicine, but we already know that. This is why **B** is correct. Yes, it gives credibility to his study, but if you read on in the paragraph, all of the other people that Lewis studied under are named, which is what the proposed phrase does here.

**#40** We are trying to place the word "under," so we must try them out one at a time. Thinking of **F**, there's nothing grammatically incorrect, but there is something funny about the sentence as written; for starters, it says that Lewis is tutoring Andrew Ellicot, but shouldn't it be the other way around? That is why the answer is **J**, it rightly places "under" after "tutored," which makes it clear that Lewis is the one being tutored. The other answer choices, **F, G,** and **H** do not solve the problems that exist with the sentence as written.

**#41** The introductory clause in this sentence ("Though capable of learning such a vast array of knowledge") is a *modifying clause*. That means that it is going to describe or modify or refer to whatever comes after the comma. In this case, the question is, what is "capable of learning"? **A** says that "Lewis's intellect" is capable of learning. However, that doesn't sound exactly right…isn't an intellect the result of learning? **B** says that "Lewis's willingness" is capable of learning, but that's not what we're looking for either. **D** says that "multiple subjects" are capable of learning; again, close but no cigar. **C** rightly says that "Lewis" was capable of learning, and thus that is the correct answer.

**#42** This is an example of an idiom. There's nothing wrong grammatically with any of these answers, but only one of them is *best*. What do we do with time? We *spend* it. That is why **H** is correct. **F, G,** and **J** are fine, but not better than saying that Lewis "spent" hours in the library.

**#43** The previous sentence said that Lewis was willing and eager to learn, and then the sentence in question highlights that by saying that Lewis spent time in Jefferson's library. What this sentence does is it gives evidence for the sentence before it, or proves it, you might say. Let's look for an option that says something like that. **A** talks about Jefferson's jealousy, but there is no indication of that, so it is incorrect. **B** says that libraries should be in all homes, but there's no indication of that not only in the sentence, but the paragraph or even the essay, so it too is incorrect. **D** says that the library demonstrates Jefferson's love of learning. Now, while that is *probably true*, the question isn't asking for any statement that might be true, but for what the sentence does to this particular paragraph. **C** rightly says that Lewis went above and beyond in his learning, which is exactly what the sentence shows.

**#44** The sentence before this one mentions how dangerous the journey is, and then the sentence of which the underlined is a part is about how an explorer lost his life. **F**, or "conversely," implies contradiction between two sentences, but we don't have that here, so it is incorrect. **H**, or "suspiciously," implies mystery, and would introduce a mysterious element to the paragraph, but that is not what the paragraph needs, so it is incorrect. **J**, or "uniquely," implies that something is unique, but a person dying on an expedition that is dangerous is not unique. **G**, which says "Miraculously," works because it implies that there could have been many more deaths on an expedition as dangerous as that one (it also links well with the word "only" that is in the sentence).

**#45** If we are looking for a phrase to end a paragraph, it needs to wrap up the paragraph, but if we are looking for a phrase to end an essay, it needs to wrap up the essay as a whole quite nicely. Was the essay as a whole about the Louisiana Purchase? Although this purchase of land is mentioned, that is not the topic of the essay, so **B** is incorrect. Is the essay about Jefferson's library (choice **C**) or learning (choice **D**)? No and no. Rather, the essay is about the Lewis and Clark expedition, which is why **A** is correct. Another way to get at the proper answer here is to read before the colon: "Jefferson got his wish." And what was that? To get to the Pacific Ocean, which is what choice **A** says.

**Passage IV: The Eastern Indigo Snake**

**#46** We need a phrase that most contrasts the author with her friends. As for the author, it says she finds "them fascinating." Looking over the answer choices, **D** says that the friends are "enamored by" snakes, which essentially means the same thing as finding them fascinating. This is why **D** is incorrect. As for the other choices, all of them communicate the same idea, which is that her friends do not like snakes. That being said, **F** and **H** are incorrect because they are not as strongly worded as **G**, which is the correct answer.

**#47** Here what is needed is a phrase that, according to the question, sets up the next question. In this case, the next sentence is about "visiting him in his office." **B** is incorrect because it is about camping, and I doubt that her father has an office at a campsite. **D** is incorrect because it mentions stories her father told, but the next sentence mentions nothing about stories. **C** is the most tempting incorrect choice. However, if **C** ("my father had a book of snakes that he kept on the bookshelf…") were to be correct, then we would expect the following sentence to say something like this: "One of those books showed pictures of snakes from around the world." But, **A** is correct because it communicates the the father was a professor at a university, and this links perfectly well with the fact that she visited him in his office (not to mention that the sentence after the phrase in question also mentions "campus").

**#48** Because a semi-colon is underlined, the essential thing to look for here is whether or not two independent clauses are being linked in this sentence. After the semi-colon we have "I was honored…", which is an independent clause. However, before the semi-colon, we have "This is why, when finally allowed as a teenager to be his intern," which is not an independent clause (it can't stand on its own as a sentence). For this reason, **F** is incorrect; a semi-colon can only be used to link two independent clauses. **H** is wrong for the exact same reason. As for **J**, apart from other problems, "then" does the same thing for the sentence as the word "when" earlier in the sentence; both of them specify a time that something happened or was done. That is why the answer is **G**; this answer rightly finishes setting off the nonessential clause ("when finally allowed as a teenager to be his intern") with a comma without any additional awkward phrasing or redundancies.

**#49** "I'm eager" is present tense, but the story being told is in the past tense; this is why **A** is incorrect. Let's simplify this sentence by wiping away prepositional phrases; which of these is correct? "I was honored… and eagerly to help" or "I was honored…and eager to help"? It is the second, which is why **C** is incorrect. Now, both **B** and **D** rightly say "eager," but **D** adds "in my desire." However, that's redundant: if you're eager to do something, you have the desire to do it. That is why **B** is the correct answer.

**#50** Commas in ACT English, again, are used *deliberately*. In this case, the introductory clause "The Eastern Indigo Snake is not only the longest species of snake native to the United States" is one long clause, and within it there is no derailing nonessential clause. Thus, **F, H,** and **J** are all incorrect because they all wrongly insert commas into places they don't belong. **G** is correct because it rightly leaves out the commas and lets the phrase flow uninterrupted.

**#51** "Those" is a plural pronoun that has to refer to something that has already been established as plural. However, there is nothing in the sentence or the previous sentence for that, or any other pronoun, to reasonably refer to. In other words, we're left asking, "The snake plays a role in the balance of life in… what?" **B** is the correct answer because it rightly answers this question; **A, C,** and **D** all use a pronoun in the aforementioned way, and thus they are all incorrect.

**#52** The question asks for a relevant phrase, which means one that fits into the flow of the paragraph in a deliberate way. The previous sentence is about the states the snake is found in; the sentence after is about how rarely they have been spotted. **F** is incorrect because we don't need to know they have never been found in Arkansas; we already know that by deduction based on where they *are* found in the previous sentence. **G** seems OK because it is a fact that points to how they help the balance of life in forests. However, that does not, in a deliberate way, connect the previous and following sentences. **H** is a fact we already know, so it too is incorrect. **J** says the species is endangered; this phrase fits well with the transition "However" that begins the sentence and explains why the next sentence discusses how rarely the snake has been seen.

**#53** As written, there is a comma after "endeavor," which signals that what is being begun is a nonessential phrase. However, there is no comma to finish such a phrase and we are left with an incomplete sentence (The new endeavor…what? We need a verb to have a complete thought or independent clause). That is why **A** and **B** are incorrect; neither of them creates a complete sentence. The only difference between **C** and **D** is verb tense. The verb "had been" implies that something existed and then changed. This seems tempting because the next sentence even has the phrase "had been" in it. However, it is incorrect. It would only be correct if the author were trying to say, "The new endeavor had been a collaborative effort, but we ended up going solo." That's not the case, which is why **C** is incorrect. **D** correctly puts the effort in the past with "was" without implying change of the project.

**#54** Let's eliminate **G** as nonsensical; plug it in, and the sentence becomes nonsense. As for **J**, the word "which" at this point in a sentence is always going to come after a comma; besides, the word that goes here refers to people ("biologists"), which means we need who or whom; this is why **J** is incorrect. Remember our who/whom rule: *who* goes where *he* goes, and *whom* goes where *him* goes. Does it make more sense to say that *he* shared the urgency or that *him* shared the urgency? Of course, it is *he*; "him shared" makes no sense. That is why **F** is incorrect and why **H** is correct.

**#55** This is obviously a question of commas…do we need commas or not in the underlined portion? No, we don't; remember, commas in ACT English are *deliberate*, not just thrown in to make artificial pauses. Because **A, C,** and **D** use a comma, they are all incorrect. **B** is correct because it has no commas to interrupt it.

**#56** These questions always are the trickiest; you've got to read the question, understand it, and then choose the correct answer in context. Here, the question is asking for a shift in focus from research to actual release of the snake, which is implied by the next sentence. **G** is too broad; it doesn't transition the paragraph to something specific; besides, it is redundant, so incorrect. **H** delays getting to the specific release; it implies that there is more looking to do. **J** shifts the focus of the essay to to the Longleaf Pine, as if the next sentence is going to tell us more about that kind of tree. This is why the correct answer is **F**; the forest is selected, thus things are getting specific. Having a forest in which to let the snakes go shifts the focus, as the question requires, to the "actual release" of the snakes.

**#57** I hope that the sentence preceding this one seems like the kind of one to end a paragraph; the one being proposed is random, and unfitting for this point in the essay. Besides, it says something we already know about the father. That is why the answer is "No," it doesn't belong. Thus, **A** and **B** are incorrect. **D** says that the sentence doesn't belong because it suggests the writer was a part of the project, but that is true. Thus, **C** is correct because it rightly says that the information has already been said.

**#58** All four of these say the same thing, that the snake got away. This is an example of a question that needs the *best* answer. That is why the answer is **H**. As for **F, G,** and **J**, they are all grammatically fine, but too wordy compared to "escaped."

**#59** This sentence is a factual sentence about the look of the snake; take a look back at all four choices and see which fits. **A** is incorrect because it is premature; it's not yet time to physically describe the snake. **B** is in a spot in which the snake has begun to be described, which is why it is the correct answer. **C** is incorrect because it is too late; same with **D**. By this point in the essay, the snake is no longer being physically described.

**#60** Does this essay talk about an author's meaningful participation in a project? Yes, it sure does. That is why **H** and **J** are incorrect. As for **F**, it indicates that the author herself organized the project, but that's not true. **G** is correct because it rightly says that she helped in the project to release the endangered snake.

**Passage V: Fred "Nall" Hollis**

**#61** If there is no comma after "Hollis," the sentence sounds like Fred Hollis gives a nickname to a person named "Nall." However, it is clear that "Nall" is Hollis's nickname. Thus, **A** and **C** are incorrect on those grounds alone. However, "When Fred Hollis" is not an introductory phrase (which is why **D** is incorrect); the phrase here that needs to be set off by commas is "nicknamed Nall," which is a nonessential phrase. We know it is nonessential because, if eliminated from the sentence, the sentence carries on just fine. This is why **B** is the correct answer.

**#62** The word "foresee" means to see into the future. **G** then is redundant. **J** has a problem as well; this option says "back then," but we already know this is in the past, meaning the "back then" is unnecessary. **H** is also redundant; we already know that Fred Hollis came from a small town. Thus the correct answer is **F**; all we need is the word "foresee" because the other options are all redundant.

**#63** The question states that all options are accurate, so again we need the *best* answer. In this case, which option states that Nall's art is both unique and beautiful? **B** is incorrect because the generic word "area" does not portray his art in any kind of positive light. **C** and **D**, as a matter of fact, both have this same problem: they are both bland and boring. **A** is the correct answer because calling someone's work a piece of "artistic genius" means it is unique and beautiful.

**#64** Choice **J** can be quickly eliminated; "they are" makes no sense in the context of the paragraph. **H** is not a word in the English language, so it is out. **G** is incorrect because the underlined portion is not meant to claim possession (remember, "its" is possessive, like, "Its name is Fluffy"). That is why **F** is correct; "it's" is a contraction that means "it is," which is appropriate for the sentence.

**#65** The sentence is communicating that most people have to stop to contemplate a work of Nall because there is beauty and purpose in it. If the phrase were eliminated, it would make it simply say, "It's almost impossible to pass by one of Nall's pieces…." **A** says that the underlined portion gives people a reason not to stop for one of Nall's pieces, but that is the opposite of what the sentence already says. **B** says something we already know and in simpler terms: that Nall's work is beautiful, which is why it is incorrect. **C** wrongly says that the detail adds irony, but that is incorrect. That leaves **D**, which is correct because it rightly says that the underlined portion gives a reason why people stop to contemplate his work. The first part of the sentence implies we want to stop for Nall's work, and the underlined portion tells us why.

**#66** Before the comma, there is an independent clause (again, that means that the clause could stand alone as a sentence): "Nall was admitted to the School of Fine Arts in Paris." This is also true for what comes after the comma; it too is an independent clause: "Here he learned to further harness his artistic ability." Thus, we have to join the two in a proper way. **F** is incorrect because, though there is a comma, it is missing a FANBOYS (for, and, nor, but, or, yet, so) conjunction to link the two independent clauses. **G** has the opposite problem; there is a FANBOYS conjunction, but no comma, so it too is incorrect. **J** makes no attempt to link the two independent clauses with punctuation, so it is incorrect. **H** is correct because it is the only one to link the two independent clauses properly; in this case, it is with a semi-colon.

**#67** When read in the context of the sentence, the only way that "being" or "those being" could ever fit in this sentence is if it were to begin some kind of nonessential clause set off by a comma. However, there is no comma here to set off such a dependent clause, so **A** and **B** are incorrect. That leaves us with two words that rhyme, but only one of them fits. "much as" is a combination of words that works if you were to say "as much as," but that is not the case here. That is why **C** is incorrect. **D** is correct because "such as" properly introduces the examples of cultures that follow.

**#68** This is an example of choosing the proper vocabulary word; the ACT is trusting that you can recognize which word is proper, like much else on the ACT, based on context. If something is "incorporated," it becomes a part of something else; but this sentence isn't trying to say that Nall's pieces became a part of America and Europe, so **F** is incorrect. **G** is incorrect because, to me at least, "seasoned" sounds like Nall brought some art to American and Europe and then the Americans and Europeans seasoned them with salt, pepper, etc. **J** sounds like Nall's pieces didn't do well ("underwhelmed"), meaning people weren't attracted to them or found them boring. However, based on the context of the essay as a whole, that would be strange; the essay is a praise of Nall and his work. That is why **G** is correct; "featured" means that they were shown in America and Europe.

**#69** What is needed here is something like a transition, but in the form of a sentence. The sentence before speaks of Dalí's influence on Nall's work. The sentence following describes a human character in his art as being in black/white with hints of lovely color. **B** implies that Dalí did some of Nall's art; that does not transition to the example in the next sentence, so it is incorrect. **C** speaks of Nall's art going to Europe, but that would only make sense if the rest of the paragraph were about the various art galleries or locations in Europe his art was featured, so it too is incorrect. **D** simply contradicts the previous sentence, which, if it were put in the paragraph, would derail the paragraph that had been already introduced. **A** is the correct answer because it begins to transition from Dalí's influence to what Nall himself was capable of in his own art; it also makes sense of the phrase "For example" that begins the following sentence.

**#70** As written, there is an em-dash (—) uniting two words. Em dashes can work in two situations: to link independent clauses or in a pair to act as parentheses. However, though what comes before the em dash is an independent clause, what follows is not; there is also not another dash anywhere. This is why **F** is incorrect. **H** inserts a colon and removes the word "with." Though what comes before the colon is an independent clause, what follows after the colon puts emphasis on "black and white," thus making it sound like "black and white" are "lovely hints of color." But that is contradictory and makes no sense, which is why **H** is incorrect. **J** artificially inserts a comma, which awkwardly separates "with" from the words that "with" is trying to connect to. This is why **G** is the correct answer; only **G** allows the sentence to flow properly without interruption from punctuation.

**#71** If you read through the options, it becomes clear that all four of these sentences are attempting to say the same thing. That simply means that three of them will have errors, and one won't. **A** seems fine, but it is problematic because it says that the person looking at the art is a "distorted observer." **B** looks pretty good as well until you get to the end: is the observer's sense of wonder "out of proportion"? That's not right, which is why **B** is also incorrect. **D** also makes the mistake of saying that the observer is "out of proportion and distorted." This is why **C** is correct; it is the only option that rightly says the art is out of proportion and that the observer has a sense of wonder.

**#72** The underlined portion of this sentence is an independent clause, but so is the clause that comes after the comma ("Nall has not forgotten his small town roots"). But a comma isn't sufficient to link the two independent clauses, which is why **F** is incorrect. **G** and **H** do the exact same thing: introduce an independent clause that isn't properly linked to the independent clause that follows the comma. This is why **J** is correct; it is the only option to insert an introductory phrase (dependent clause) that can properly be set off by a comma from the main independent clause of the sentence.

**#73** What is needed here is the proper pronoun to agree with the verb "owns." **B** is not a pronoun and makes no sense, and is incorrect. Clearly, the sentence is trying to say that Nall still owns and operates a studio. This is why the correct answer is **D**; it replaces Nall with the correct pronoun "he." **C** has "he" in it, but "he or she" is used to refer to a singular person whose sex is unknown (like this: "A person robbed the bank. He or she stole a billion dollars."). Of course, Nall is not a "they," which is why **A** is incorrect.

**#74** All of these options essentially say the exact same thing: that Nall still makes art. This means we are looking for the best answer. In this case, that would be the least wordy option. **G, H,** and **J** are all too wordy when compared to **F**, which is the correct answer.

**#75** Again, give it your best shot to know if the answer is "Yes" or "No" before reading the answer choices. If that is a struggle, you could usually circle this kind of question and return to it if you have time at the end; that way, you give yourself a chance to read over the essay to find the right answer. With this being #75 though, this *is* the end, so do what you need to do to get the question correct, and balance that against any other questions you wanted to go back to. Here, the question asks if the essay is about the circumstances of Nall's art being displayed in museums around the world. That is not the central purpose of the essay, so the answer is "No." This eliminates **A** and **B** as incorrect. **D** says that the answer is "No" because the essay never mentions that Nall's work gained international attention. But the essay *does* mention that he had work shown in Europe (particularly Italy) in the first paragraph. This is why **C** is the correct answer; it rightly says that though Nall is mentioned as receiving international attention, that isn't the focus of the essay as a whole.

# Answer Explanations - Step 7 - Practice Test #2

**Correct Answers:**

| Passage I | Passage II | Passage III | Passage IV | Passage V |
|---|---|---|---|---|
| 1: A | 16: F | 31: C | 46: J | 61: B |
| 2: J | 17: C | 32: J | 47: C | 62: J |
| 3: B | 18: H | 33: A | 48: H | 63: B |
| 4: G | 19: A | 34: F | 49: C | 64: H |
| 5: D | 20: H | 35: C | 50: G | 65: C |
| 6: G | 21: A | 36: H | 51: D | 66: G |
| 7: D | 22: H | 37: D | 52: F | 67: D |
| 8: G | 23: C | 38: F | 53: A | 68: F |
| 9: D | 24: J | 39: D | 54: J | 69: A |
| 10: F | 25: A | 40: J | 55: D | 70: G |
| 11: D | 26: J | 41: B | 56: G | 71: C |
| 12: F | 27: A | 42: J | 57: B | 72: H |
| 13: B | 28: G | 43: C | 58: F | 73: D |
| 14: H | 29: A | 44: H | 59: B | 74: F |
| 15: A | 30: H | 45: B | 60: G | 75: B |

**Passage I: Goodall and the Chimps**

**#1** **C** and **D** are both redundant (they both say things already stated in the sentence) and can both be eliminated. **B** is not only too wordy, but "and that she did earn a spot in history" is not a functioning dependent clause. **A** is correct because the word "did" is not only grammatically correct, but implies that she earned a spot in history as she intended.

**#2** There is a semi-colon in the underlined portion. This should prompt you to check if the sentence is attempting to combine two independent clauses. However, the first clause ("While she is known...mostly by men") is not an independent clause, but rather a dependent, introductory clause. This means that it simply needs to be set off from the rest of the sentence (or the independent clause you could say) by only a comma. Thus, **F** is incorrect. **H** uses a comma and a FANBOYS conjunction ("but" in this case), and for the same reason as the semi-colon (comma+FANBOYS is used to combine independent clauses just like a semi-colon) is incorrect. **G** is incorrect because beginning this clause with the word "preferring" creates another dependent or nonessential clause, and that would leave the sentence without an independent clause at all, which is impossible in English. This is why the answer is **J**; it rightly sets off the introductory clause with a comma and creates an independent clause after the comma.

**#3** The question asks for a choice that stresses her difficulty and strife. While the reader be able to imply that there was difficulty and strife involved if the answer choices were **A, C,** or **D**, none of those three is as strongly worded as choice **B**, which is the correct answer.

**#4** As written, what could "it" possibly refer to? There is no obvious answer, so choice **F** incorrect. It seems pretty clear that the "groundbreaking observation" is trying to be attributed to Goodall, who is a singular female. Choices **H** and **J** are incorrect because they are plural pronouns. That is why the correct answer is **G**: "hers" is singular and refers to Goodall herself.

**#5** A look over the four options makes it pretty clear that they are all attempting to say the same thing. Thus, three of them will have some kind of error. **A** has such a problem: beginning with "inserting" turns the underlined part into a dependent clause, making an incomplete sentence. **B** begins with "over and over insert," but isn't the more common phrasing "insert over and over"? Besides, the ending of the sentence, "into where the termites lived" is a little wordy compared to other options. For these reasons, **B** is incorrect. **C** also creates an incomplete sentence; in addition, it uses the designation "there" and then attempts to say where "there" is instead of simply saying "termite mounds" in the first place. **D** rightly creates a complete sentence that is not overly wordy.

**#6** Letter **J** insinuates that the underlined portion shifts the focus of the paragraph, but that isn't the case; the focus is still on the chimpanzees eating termites, so it is incorrect. **H** says that the underlined portion is repetitive, but it has not yet been said that the next step in the process is for the chimpanzee to remove the stalk, so **H** is also incorrect. **F** says that the phrase is necessary for us to know what kind of ape is being observed, but that's not true; we already know that it is chimpanzees with or without the phrase, so **F** is incorrect. That leaves **G**, which rightly says that it simply provides a step in the chimpanzee's process of eating termites; thus it is the correct answer.

**#7** We need a choice that emphasizes that the chimpanzee is a *hunter*. **A** doesn't emphasize that at all; it just says that the termites were eaten. This is also true for **B** and **C**; neither emphasizes the chimp as a hunter. **D**, however, uses the word "predator" to describe the chimpanzee, thus stating strongly that the chimp is a hunter; this is why it is the correct answer.

**#8** This is one of those unique questions where the correct answer is the only choice that is wrong. "Consumption" of course means "eating." Because **F** and **H** are synonyms of "consumption," they would both work in the sentence, so they are (as far as the question is concerned) incorrect. **J** is an interesting option and needs exploring. What happens when the underlined portion is deleted? Well, the sentence then says this: "…it was believed that chimps ate a mostly vegetarian diet supplemented by some insects." This implies that the insects were eaten along with a vegetarian diet, which means that **J** would work in the sentence. Thus, **J** (because it works) is incorrect. This is why **G** is the right answer; "combustion" means explosion, and I don't think the chimps are blowing up termites.

**#9** A comma would only be needed after "tree" if we were setting off items or actions in a list or setting off a nonessential clause. While this happens elsewhere in the sentence, it does not need to happen here. Because **A, B,** and **C** all use this comma, they are all incorrect. **D** is correct because it rightly leaves out this comma and keeps the compound verb (climb and surround) together.

**#10** We simply need a past tense verb that indicates that the chimps shared the carcass with each other. Well, "shared" happens to perfectly do this, which is why the correct answer is **F**. **G** is grammatically incorrect and does not work in the sentence; this is also true of **H**; both of those are thus incorrect. **J** is present tense, which is why it is incorrect.

**#11** Read the sentence at a normal pace. Does anything stick out to you as unnecessary or nonessential? Any introductory phrases or dependent clauses? Don't try to convince yourself that the prepositional phrase "with the chimpanzees" is some kind of nonessential phrase that sounds good when set off by commas. That is not the case. There is no need for the *deliberate* use of a comma in this sentence. For this reason, **A, B,** and **C** are all incorrect because they insert commas where none belong. **D** is correct because it lets the sentence flow as it is intended to do.

**#12** All of these four options mean essentially the same thing, and they all grammatically fit within the sentence. That means what is needed is the *best* answer. In this case, **G, H,** and **J** are all too wordy, and are thus incorrect, when compared to the short and simple **F**, which is correct.

**#13** "Goliath" is not the chimp's title, which is why **A** is incorrect. It also isn't his "designation;" that word is too informal and not applied to names, which is why **D** is correct. **C**, or "known by," may be tempting, but when referring to someone's name, it would be more proper to say "known as." This is why **C** is incorrect. **B** is correct because it rightly says that the chimp is "named" Goliath because, well, that's his name.

#14 "Mike" refers to a chimp, and this chimp takes over some other chimp's job. This is what can be gleamed from the sentence that needs placing. Simply apply that idea to all four options. **F** does not work because that would insert the sentence about Mike in the middle of the story about the chimps hunting another monkey. **G** doesn't work either; though the sentence before mentions the names of apes, it doesn't set up the paragraph to state that one of these apes had a job that could be taken over by another named Mike. **H**, on the other hand, is the correct answer; this is because the preceding sentence says that a chimp named "Goliath" was the alpha male: this is the position that Mike takes over. **J** also does not work, of course; this is because it would be the concluding sentence of the essay, but the essay is already concluded nicely with a reference to Goodall, not the chimps.

#15 Again, give it your best shot to know if the answer is "Yes" or "No" before reading the answer choices. If that is a struggle, circle this question and return to it if you have time at the end; that way, you can give yourself a chance to read over the essay to find the right answer. In this case, the answer is "Yes," the essay does highlight one scientist (Jane Goodall) and her contribution to the knowledge of animals (chimpanzees). Thus, **C** and **D** are incorrect since they both say "No." **B** says that the essay compares and contrasts scientists, but the essay is only about one scientist, which is why **B** is incorrect. **A** rightly says "Yes," giving the true reason that the essay centers on the work of one scientist: Jane Goodall.

**Passage II: A Fishing Memory**

#16 Remove the "yet urgent" and what do you get? A sentence that flows smoothly, uniting the adjective "gentle" with the noun "fashion." That means that the phrase "yet urgent" is nonessential and must be set off by commas. **G, H,** and **J** all fail to fully set off the phrase with commas. This is why **F** is the correct answer.

#17 Here we need the correct prepositional phrase. If he were to stare "from" the dark morning he would have to be *in* the dark morning. But, he's not; he is inside the bedroom looking outside the window. This is why **A** is incorrect. If he were to stare "behind" the dark morning, he would have to see to the other side of it, or something like that; this is why **B** is incorrect. **D** has the same problem; how could he possibly see "above" the dark morning? That makes little sense. That is why the correct answer is **C**: he stares from his room *into* the dark morning that is outside the window.

#18 All of the choices are grammatically correct and true, and the question asks for the one that best transitions into the next paragraph. **F, G, H** and **J** could all end this paragraph fairly well, so the question is, what is the next paragraph about? Reading ahead, it's about rigging the fishing poles the evening prior. Because **F, G,** and **J** all fail to mention this, they are all incorrect. **H** is correct because it rightly mentions that the tackle and poles were already prepared.

#19 ""Can I help, Grandpa?" I'd ask" is an independent clause, and so is "even though he never needed it, he'd let me be his assistant." We have to join these in a proper way: a comma+FANBOYS, a semi-colon, a colon, an em-dash, or separate them into two separate sentences. Only one of them does that, and that's **A**, which is the correct answer because it uses a comma and a FANBOYS conjunction. As for **B, C,** and **D**, they all fail to properly link independent clauses.

#20 The opening paragraph is about the boy waking up while it's still dark to go fishing. **H** mentions "before first light," which means it is the correct answer. **F** and **J** both mention the previous paragraph, but don't refer back to the opening paragraph. **G** says something about weather, but there is no mention of bad weather in the first paragraph.

#21 There are a couple of things going on here, so let's address them one at a time. First question: is a comma necessary after the word "large"? Technically, there are two adjectives describing the word "rig": "large" and "oil." However, the rule is this: if the adjectives can be reversed, use a comma to set them off.

Does "oil, large rig" make any sense? No, because an "oil rig" is its own noun. So, we do not need a comma after the word "large," which means that choice **D** is incorrect. I think it's also safe to eliminate **C** because it separates "oil" from "rig" with an unnecessary comma. The next question is this: do we need to set off "about a mile off the coast of the island" from the rest of the sentence? No, it is not a dependent or nonessential clause; it fits perfectly well in the flow of the sentence. This is why we can now eliminate **B**. Only **A** leaves out all commas, which makes it the correct answer.

#22 "he was simply tying" would only work if the sentence went on to say, "he was simply tying a rope *when* a shark came....". In other words, the "when" is missing to properly continue the flow of the story, which is why **F** is incorrect. **G** is strange because it seems to want to say, "to tie simply he would do this or that." But it never does so; this is why **G** is incorrect. **J** is an example of nonsense; it should recognized as too strangely worded to be correct. **H** is correct because it uses words in their proper order to put the tying of the rope in the past tense.

#23 The question says we need a choice that shows the grandfather's delight. **A** says "Carefully," but there is no joy or delight implied in that word, which means it is incorrect. The exact same thing can be said for **B** ("Unexpectedly") and **D** ("Dutifully"). **C** uses an adverb that implies delight and joy: "Excitedly," which is why **C** is the correct answer.

#24 The topic of the paragraph is how the pair would get their boat to the rig, tie it up, and start fishing. The sentence proposed is about the thousands of species of shrimp. Does that fit in? No, which is why **F** and **G** are incorrect. **H** wrongly says that the sentence implies that they will catch fish (because the sentence says that shrimp are eaten by a variety of fish), but that is not *why* it is wrong. **J** correctly says "No," giving a valid reason: the proposed sentence detracts from the purpose of the story and interrupts its progress.

#25 Let's start with **D**, and let's rule it out as incorrect because it is nonsensical. **B** can also be ruled out because it uses the pronoun "they"...but who are "they", the fish? I don't think the fish will fill up ice chests with themselves, thus **B** is incorrect. **C** is too strange to be correct...who would say "we were to be filling" an ice chest when there is a simpler way to communicate the idea that the ice chest became filled up with fish? That is why **A** is correct: it says in the most simple way that the ice chest became filled with fish.

#26 As written (choice **F**) should sound a little odd; the sentence makes it sound like they can name every kind of fish they caught except for one; this is also true of choice **H**. Their strange nature makes them both incorrect because we are looking for a good or normal fit at this point in the sentence. **G** has a problem because it sort of contradicts the rest of the sentence; it sounds like they caught a lot of different kinds of delicious fish, not a "lack" of them. This option is also incorrect. **J** is correct because it simply fits the best in the sentence; you might say it is normal or not-strange like the other options.

#27 Here is yet another example of a nonessential clause. Again, the test as to whether or not it actually is a nonessential clause is to remove it from the sentence and see if the sentence flows well without it. In this case, removing "quality time not included" results in the sentence saying this: "...my favorite part was never knowing what we would pull from the water." Clearly, the "quality time not included" is a nonessential phrase and must be set off by commas from the rest of the sentence. **A** is the correct answer because it is the only choice to do this. **B, C,** and **D** are all incorrect because they are missing at least one comma (or two, as in choice **D**) to completely set off the nonessential phrase.

#28 If you are struggling putting these three sentences in order, there are some clues to follow. As always, look for references to other sentences that serve as signposts, allowing you to see that a certain sentence comes before or after another. Sentence 1 begins with "In other words." That is a strange way to begin a paragraph because it is a clarifying phrase, and what it attempts to clarify usually comes in the sentence before. This would mean that **F** and **H** are both incorrect because they put sentence 1 first. Another clue can be found in sentence 3, which includes the phrase "any one of these." The question is: any one of what? Well, it is clear from the paragraph that this means "any one of these fish," as in the list of fish listed off in sentence 2. This means that sentence 3 must follow sentence 2, but sentence 1 can't come before sentence 2. That leaves only one possible order: 2, 3, 1. This is why **G** is correct. **J** wrongly puts sentence 3 before sentence 2; this would make the phrase "any one of these" have no point of reference.

**#29** The word "battle" certainly doesn't fail to transition the sentence to the next one; this is why **D** is incorrect. It is clear as well that **C** is also incorrect; this is because the word "battle" doesn't *understate* how tiresome the fight with the fish was. **B** is also incorrect because the theme of battling is nowhere to be found in the first paragraph. This is why **A** is correct; the word "battle" puts emphasis on the fact that the angler had to fight the fish long and hard.

**#30** We already know that the kid had the fish on the line for a long time; look at the first sentence of the paragraph: "…for what seemed like hours…" That means the underlined portion is redundant and does not belong. This means of course that **F** and **G** are both incorrect. **H** rightly says that the idea has already been stated, and is thus redundant, making it the correct answer. **J**, though it says the phrase should be deleted, gives an incorrect reason for its being deleted: who cares about the reaction of the workers in the last sentence of an essay about a grandfather taking his grandson fishing?

**Passage III: The Sailing Stones**

**#31** What comes before the comma (from "Visitors" to "visit") is an independent clause, and so is that which comes after the comma (from "from lively cities" to "too short"). This means we need punctuation that accounts for that. **A** is incorrect because, though there is a comma, there is no FANBOYS conjunction to go with it. **B** is incorrect for this same reason, but it also has the comma in a strange place. **D** is also incorrect because it has no punctuation at all. **C** is correct because it separates the two independent clauses into two sentences.

**#32** What we have here are four options that all grammatically work. Because we need the best answer, one thing to do would be to try out the shortest answer of them all, which is choice **J**. Because this option works, let's think about if the other choices add anything we need. **F** says "as one may experience," but that is unnecessary to say; if a person is on vacation to this area, or course he or she might experience it. **G** is also redundant; if it is "sure" to be too short, we don't need to also say "most definitely." **H** adds a phrase that adds nothing to the sentence at all; it is simply too wordy.

**#33** This is an example of an idiom: a group of words in the English language that always go together. The "receiving end" means the "recipient of," which is exactly the context that the sentence calls for. This is why **A** is the correct answer. **B, C,** and **D** do not create a series of words that is purposefully used in the English language, and are thus incorrect.

**#34** The question asks for a phrase that suggests two things about the sailing stones: a) not man-made, and b) difficult to explain. **G** is lacking in both of these, and is thus incorrect. **H** is contradictory; if something happens "logically" it is probably pretty easy to explain. **J** calls them an "event," but still it falls short in both categories. This is why the answer is **F**; if the stones are "natural" then they are not "man-made," and if the stones are a "phenomenon" then they are not easy to explain.

**#35** As written, we have an incomplete sentence, which is why **A** is incorrect. **B** seems to work OK until you get to the verb "cut" (plural) which would have to attach to the subject "movement" (singular), which is grammatically incorrect, so **B** is incorrect. **D** is problematic because the verb "to create" could only come after "movement" if it were the beginning of a new nonessential clause, but because there is no comma, this is not happening, which is why **D** is incorrect. **C** correctly says that the movement "creates trails", and that the trails "cut." In other words, **C** creates subject-verb agreement to the extent that what it creates is a functioning sentence.

**#36** Each of the four choices has "giving the" at the beginning of it, so this is merely a question of correct vocabulary. An image that deceives is an "illusion," which is why **H** is the correct answer. **F, G,** and **J** are incorrect because they simply use the incorrect words.

**#37** Choice **A** has to be incorrect because the previous sentence said this exact same thing already: that the stones appear to have been moving of their own accord. Choice **B** has the same problem; the last sentence of the previous paragraph says that the stones have been "on the receiving end of growing interest." **C** is also redundant; the first sentence of this paragraph says that this is "natural." That is why the answer is **D**: there should be none of these other sentences here because they are all redundant, repeating facts that have already been stated.

**#38** "The stones are" means that a verb ending in "ing" must follow "are." This eliminates **H** and **J** as incorrect. As for **G**, it is wrong because when the word "across" is removed, it makes it sound like the stones have the ability to move the desert itself, which isn't possible. This is why the answer is **F**; it rightly uses a verb ending in "ing" after "are" and says that the stones are moving across the desert, not moving the desert itself.

**#39** Well, it is pretty clear that this previous sentence doesn't describe every detail in the water cycle, and this is why **A** is incorrect. Since the previous sentence is the beginning of a scientific explanation as to how the stones move across the desert, it isn't a distraction and shouldn't be deleted, which is why **B** is incorrect. **C** is a tempting answer, but still it is incorrect because it says nothing about "hot days." This is why **D** is the correct answer; this choice says that the sentence explains how ice could end up in the desert, which is exactly what the sentence does when it says that the ice forms during "cold nights."

**#40** When something is "accompanied," it is usually "accompanied *by*"; we have to know what accompanies that certain thing. This is why **J** is the correct answer; it is the only choice that puts the preposition "by" behind "accompanied." The other choices, **F, G,** and **H** are all incorrect because none of them does this. Specifically, **F** doesn't work because it is, as written, nonsensical. **G** makes no sense: how could the stones be accompanied *through* the wind? **H** is incorrect because it creates a nonsensical sentence ("When this breakup is accompanied with the ice is pushed…").

**#41** Again, em dashes (these things: —) can be used to either combined independent clauses or take the place of parentheses. Notice that, a few words later, there is another em dash, which has to be serving one of these two purposes. It just so happens that between the underlined portion and the next em dash is a nonessential phrase, which must mean that the em dashes are being used like parentheses. This is why **B** is the correct answer; it rightly opens the nonessential phrase with an em dash. **A, C,** and **D** all fail to do so: if an em dash is used to "close" a phrase later, it must be used to begin a phrase at some point. It can't be that the later em dash is used for separating independent clauses because what comes before is a dependent or introductory clause.

**#42** If the word "though" were to be put in before the word "technically" here, it would need to be set off somehow as a nonessential clause. That is not the case, which is why **F** is incorrect. As for the other choices, it is clear that **G** and **H** are incorrect because they are too wordy. **J** is correct because it is less wordy and gives what the sentence needs.

**#43** "movement of mud was to blame the others"? This makes it sound like mud, while moving, tried to blame people for something. This is why **A** is incorrect. **B** puts a comma and adds, "and though others"; the problem with this is that this begins a new nonessential clause, and because the sentence ends shortly thereafter with a period, we are left with an incomplete sentence. **D** is wrong because it is nonsensical; "was to blame theorized that something…" makes no sense at all and is missing words, punctuation, or both to form a complete thought. This is why **C** is the correct answer; it correctly adds a dependent clause to the end of an independent clause.

**#44** Let's eliminate **J** as incorrect because the pronoun "they" is in a place that makes the sentence nonsensical. **G** can also be eliminated because it is strangely worded. Now we are left with a simple who vs whom distinction. The rule is this: put *who* where *he* goes, and put *whom* where *him* goes. Is it better to say "he travels far to catch a glimpse" or "him travels far to catch a glimpse"? It is the former, *he*, which is why **H** is correct and **F** is incorrect.

**#45** As written, there is no clear reason why it ought to be deleted. The sentence preceding it about the scientists seeking explanation isn't as good a fit to end a paragraph or the essay as a whole compared to the one present here. **C** is incorrect because it says that the sentence shifts the focus, but that is not true; the focus is supposed to be on the stones, not on the tourists. **D** falsely claims that the sentence assumes that everyone will get to see the stones, but that is not implied in the sentence, and thus this option is incorrect. **A** rightly says that the sentence should be kept, but the reason is strange: because it stresses that scientists should do research? That's not the purpose of the sentence. **B** is the correct answer because it rightly says that the sentence should be kept for a good reason: that it links with the first paragraph (because the first paragraph is about visitors to the stones, which is mentioned in this sentence as well).

**Passage IV: The Moai of Easter Island**

**#46** The underlined portion here contains a semi-colon. Again, the main purpose of a semi-colon is to link independent clauses. In this case, what comes before the semi-colon is an independent clause, but what comes after is a dependent clause. This means that **F** is incorrect. Such a clause must simply set off from the independent clause of the sentence by a comma, which eliminates answer choice **G** as incorrect. As for **H**, because there is a comma and a FANBOYS conjunction, the only way this could work (like the semi-colon) is if what comes after is independent. However, this is not the case. This is why **J** is the correct answer: it rightly sets off the dependent clause "of which it is a special territory" from the independent clause of the sentence with a comma.

**#47** This question is extremely similar to the one that precedes it. There is an independent clause to begin the sentence, followed by a dependent clause that must be set off with a simple comma. This is why **C** is the correct answer. Choices **A** and **B** are incorrect because they wrongly insert commas into the dependent clause without deliberate purpose. **D** is incorrect because it fails to set off the dependent clause ("which occurred on Easter Sunday") with a comma.

**#48** Remember the #1 colon rule: a colon must always follow a complete thought. Although there are lots of words before the colon, there is no complete thought (which is why **F** is incorrect). The sentence begins with a long introductory phrase, then begins the independent clause ("the most academically appealing aspect of the island") without ever attaching a verb to the subject within it. This is because a nonessential phrase is inserted. This phrase is this: "not to mention its most mysterious." As a nonessential phrase, it must be set off by commas. This is why **H** is correct. **J** is incorrect because it fails to close off the nonessential phrase with a comma. **G** is incorrect because it unnecessarily inserts a comma after the word "its."

**#49** We only need one noun to possess "height and weight." As written, there are two: "stone" and "it," which are linked with an "and" and are both shown to possess the height and weight. But both of these refer to the same thing: a stone. This is why **A** and **B** are both incorrect (though **B** also has the added problem of putting the apostrophe after the 's', which means that multiple stones possess it). **D** neglects to insert an apostrophe, but the apostrophe is necessary because the sentence is attempting to denote possession. This is why **C** is the correct answer: it rightly uses an apostrophe before the 's' to denote that the stone possesses height and weight.

**#50** Because a semi-colon is present in the underlined portion, the first question is whether or not two independent clauses are being linked. Here, the answer is no, and thus **F** is incorrect. **J** does something similar: it uses a comma and a FANBOYS conjunction, but again, this is incorrect because independent clauses are not being linked. **H** is incorrect because it fails to close off the word "respectively" with a comma. **G** is the correct answer because it rightly closes off the word "respectively" (technically a nonessential phrase; you can tell this because if the word is removed from the sentence, the sentence flows freely) with a comma.

**#51** "They carve" (choice **A**) can be eliminated because it is in the present tense. As a matter of fact, this is also true of **B** and **C**: both of these choices are also in the present tense. **D** then is correct because, consistent with the essay, it is in the past tense.

**#52** When multiple adjectives are describing a noun, as is the case here, the question is this: can the adjectives be reversed? If so, a comma will be needed after the first adjective. If not, no such comma is needed. It makes sense to talk of an "inactive volcanic crater," but does it make sense to talk of a "volcanic inactive crater"? No, because the word "volcanic" must come immediately before "crater." This means that no comma is necessary after "inactive," which is why **G** and **H** are incorrect. As for **J**, it makes the mistake of unnecessarily putting a comma after "crater," which separates the prepositional phrase beginning with "on" from the rest of the sentence when it ought to flow smoothly. This is why **F** is the correct answer: it inserts no commas because none are needed.

**#53** Choices **B** and **C** can't be correct because both assume that two independent clauses are being linked. But, that is not the case; the first clause (beginning with "While"), is not independent. **D** is incorrect because it fails to set off the introductory clause from the independent clause of the sentence with a comma. This is why **A** is correct; as written, this choice properly sets off the opening clause from the independent clause beginning with "hundreds of statues."

**#54** This essay has the tone of formality; it sounds like something out of a history textbook. This is why **F** is incorrect; "pillow talk" is not only informal, but it is more synonymous with "gossip." There's nothing grammatically incorrect about it; there must simply be a *better* answer. Of the remaining choices, **G** and **H** are too wordy. This is why **J** is correct; it provides the idea needed by the sentence with the fewest words possible.

**#55** This question is tricky because you must read the question stem first: we need a choice that is NOT acceptable. Of the answers, all of the following are more or less synonymous with "arrived", and are thus incorrect: "landed" (choice **A**), "came" (choice **B**), and "reached the shore" (choice **C**). This is why choice **D** is the correct answer: "glanced" is not a synonym of "arrived."

**#56** This is a great example of a question that requires you to read the entire sentence to get the question correct. The sentence is saying that there is teamwork involved in this process of moving the stones, and that they are happening at the same time: some men lift logs from the back of the line to the front **while** men pull on the stones by rope. This is why **G** is the correct answer; it uses "while" to indicate that the two actions are happening at the same time. **F** can't be correct because it implies contrast, but that isn't the relationship between the two actions. **J** simply does not belong, and besides, it would probably need to be set off from the rest of the sentence by a comma. **H** uses "However" to begin the sentence, but that changes the meaning of the opening clause; instead of it being an action that men are doing, it creates a phrase that fails to link with the clause that comes after about the men lifting logs from the back of the line.

**#57** Without the information being added, the sentence sounds like a random scientific fact about the island. This eliminates **C** and **D** as incorrect. **A** correctly says that the sentence belongs, but wrongly says the reason that this is so is because the new information tells the reader that the island is wooded. This is wrong because that is the purpose of the sentence already there, not of the information being proposed. This is why **B** is the correct answer: it links the fact to the theory being proposed.

**#58** Choices **G** and **H** do not work because they are plural conjugations of a verb, but we need a singular option ("A second hypothesis" is singular). Because the sentence is trying to say that a hypothesis has been growing in popularity, **J** is incorrect. Only choice **F** rightly denotes that the hypothesis continues to get more and more popular by conjugating the verb to match the singular subject.

#59 Choices **A, C,** and **D** are all not only saying that the "ropes were tied to" statues, but that the statues had been previously carved. However, this is redundant: if a statue is made of stone, isn't it already carved (otherwise, it's not a statue but just a big piece of rock)? Thus all three of those options are incorrect. **B** is correct because it is not redundant.

#60 Hopefully it "sounds" strange for the pronoun "them" to be put in this situation (this is why **F** is incorrect). It would be good instincts if you thought to yourself, "not *them* but *they*." Unfortunately, "they" is not one of our choices. While **J** ("all they") may be tempting for this reason, don't be fooled: "all of them" would be appropriate here, not "all they." **H** uses a singular pronoun, "it," but we are attempting to describe a plural subject: the "statues." This is why **G** is the only acceptable answer; instead of a pronoun, the title of the stone statues can fit in this place just fine.

**Passage V: John Hart, Unsung Hero**

#61 Reading through the four options, they are all attempting to say the same thing. However, **A, C,** and **D** are all too wordy and don't quite hit the mark, which is why they are all incorrect. **B** is correct because it is the *best* answer, and it is best because it is the least wordy.

#62 Three of these options (**F, G,** and **H**) all begin the sentence with some kind of transition, meaning it creates a special or specific relationship with the sentence that came before. **F** is incorrect because "On the contrary" implies contrast or a stark difference between the two sentences, but the second sentence doesn't have this relationship with the first. **G** and **H** are synonymous; both of them imply that the second sentence is a conclusion or flows in logical order from the first; but that is not the case (the fact that they are exact synonyms is a clue that they are both incorrect as well). All of this means that the sentence doesn't need a transition, or at least any of these three. Beginning the sentence with "Most" works perfectly well, especially if you read the entire sentence (as you should). This is why **J** is the correct answer.

#63 First, let's eliminate **D** because "rather" on its own here is nonsensical because the word "than" needs to follow it to make any sense. Clearly the sentence is trying to say that Jefferson, Washington, etc. took risks *for* the USA. **A** and **C** both mean something different than that, and they are both incorrect. Because choice **B** is synonymous with "for" ("…they are not the only ones who took risks on behalf of/for so great a nation."), it is the correct answer.

#64 The first requirement of the question is that the correct answer "fit the tone" of the essay. This is enough to eliminate **F** as the incorrect answer; "some person" is too informal. The second requirement of the question is that the right answer emphasize that the subject of the essay (meaning the person who the essay is about) have a story worth telling. **G** can be eliminated as incorrect because "a man" is too bland. **J** is much closer to what the question requires, but what is required is the *best* answer. This is why **H** is correct. The story of "an unsung hero" is a story more worthy of telling than that of "a great citizen."

#65 The paragraph already ended on a good note with a sentence that makes you want to ask: "Who is this unsung hero?" That is why a random fact about George Washington, though neat and historically important, does not belong here. This eliminates options **A** and **B**, which for this reason are both incorrect. **D** claims that the first paragraph never mentions George Washington, but that's not true; his name comes up in the second sentence of the opening paragraph. This is why **C** is correct; it rightly says "No" and says that the information is only loosely tied to the first paragraph, which is true.

#66 Because a semi-colon is underlined, the first question must be whether or not two independent clauses are being linked. However, the first clause ("As a politician…American colonies") is not independent; in other words, it couldn't stand alone as a sentence. This is why **F** is incorrect; a semi-colon is used to link two independent clauses. Looking at the rest of the answer choices, **H** and **J** both make attempts at linking independent clauses (comma+FANBOYS and a period, respectively), which is why they are both incorrect as well. This is why **G** is the correct answer; it rightly separates the introductory phrase (or dependent clause) from the rest of the sentence with a simple comma.

**#67** None of these four answer choices contains grammar errors, and all of them mean the same thing. That means, of course, that what is required is the *best* answer. None of them are redundant (meaning none of them are repeating information already stated or implied), but one of them is less wordy than the others. This is why **D** is the correct answer; it says what the sentence requires in the least words possible. As for **A, B,** and **C**, they are all simply unnecessarily wordy.

**#68** For **G** to work, it would have to say something like, "where he *was* to hide," but as it is written it is nonsensical, and thus it is incorrect. **H** sounds like some kind of slang, but grammatically speaking, "he be hiding" is incorrect and nonsensical. **J** is incorrect because "were" is a plural conjugation, but we need a singular conjugation to link with "he." This is why **F** is correct: it is singular and grammatically sound.

**#69** The question asks for the choice that gives the most drama. Thus, you need to compare and contrast the options and see which is the most dramatic. Each of the options has an element of drama. **B** mentions that "the troops searched." **C** speaks of "enemy forces." **D** mentions "soldiers in red uniforms." However, all of these are incorrect because they are not as dramatic as choice **A**. "…the British hunted him like an animal" is the best answer.

**#70** "after living in terrible conditions for such a long time" is a modifying clause, which means it describes or it will modify what comes immediately after the comma. Did "the relief of returning home" live in terrible conditions? No, which is why **F** is incorrect. Did "home" live in terrible conditions? No, which is why **H** is incorrect. Did "the caves" live in terrible conditions? No, which is why **J** is incorrect. Did "Hart" live in terrible conditions? Yes, which is why **G** is the correct answer.

**#71** Who are "they"? The only people this pronoun could refer to is Washington's patriot army, but it's not them that said that about Washington, which is why **B** is incorrect. **D** ("its'") is not a word in the English language, and thus is incorrect. **A** is possessive, which is incorrect in this context. This is why **C** is correct; *it's* is a contraction meaning "it is," which is proper in this context.

**#72** There are clues to help you place sentence 4. The biggest of them is that sentence 2 begins with "For example." If this sentence were in the right place, based on the content of sentence 1, you would expect sentence 2 to give an example of how relieved John Hart was when he returned home. Instead, the sentence is about how Hart's land was used during the war. This is why **H** is the correct answer; by inserting the sentence there, it gives sentence 2 an example of Hart "doing his part." **F, G,** and **J** all fail to properly transition the paragraph.

**#73** As written, what does "there" refer to? There is nothing in this or the previous sentence that designates a place for him to have passed away. This is why **A** is incorrect. **B** creates a second independent clause, but gives no punctuation to combine the clause that would have to end with "1779" and the clause that would now begin with "there," so **B** is also incorrect. As for **C**, it is incorrect simply because it is too wordy; there is a simpler way to word what is needed here. This is why **D** is the correct answer; not only is it grammatically correct, but it is less wordy compared to other options.

**#74** After "the land" there is the verb "to build" and then the prepositional phrase "in the first place." It makes no sense to set off any of it with a comma, which is why **F** is the correct answer. Remember: commas aren't thrown into sentences to create a pause because it kind of sounds nice to create a pause there. Rather, they are deliberate, and in this sentence, the clause from "Since" to "place" is one long introductory clause. **G, H,** and **J** are all incorrect because they insert commas in places where they do not belong.

**#75** This is a biographical fact about John Hart's life. Simply look at the four options and determine if a biographical fact is appropriate or not. Choice **A** is incorrect because the first paragraph is not yet about John Hart, but the country as a whole. Choice **C** is incorrect because, by this point, the story has shifted to be that of his hiding out in the mountains. Choice **D** is incorrect because a biographical fact about John Hart's wife is not an appropriate way to end the paragraph about his hiding in the mountains. Choice **B** is correct because this paragraph, the second paragraph in the essay, is primarily focused on biographical details.

# Score Conversion

| Raw Score | Scale Score |
|---|---|
| **73-75** | **36** |
| 71-72 | 35 |
| **69-70** | **34** |
| 68 | 33 |
| **67** | **32** |
| 66 | 31 |
| **65** | **30** |
| 64 | 29 |
| **63** | **28** |
| 61-62 | 27 |
| **60** | **26** |
| 57-59 | 25 |
| **55-56** | **24** |
| 52-54 | 23 |
| **49-51** | **22** |
| 46-48 | 21 |
| **43-45** | **20** |
| 41-42 | 19 |
| **40** | **18** |
| 37-39 | 17 |
| **34-36** | **16** |
| 30-33 | 15 |
| **27-29** | **14** |
| 25-26 | 13 |
| **23-24** | **12** |
| 20-22 | 11 |
| **17-19** | **10** |
| 14-16 | 9 |
| **12-13** | **8** |
| 10-11 | 7 |
| **8-9** | **6** |
| 6-7 | 5 |
| **5** | **4** |
| 3-4 | 3 |
| **2** | **2** |
| 0-1 | 1 |

Here is a chart to give you an idea of how you might score on an actual ACT English exam. To figure this out, first find your "raw score," which is simply how many questions you got correct out of 75, for either or both of the full length practice tests of Step 7. The second step is to convert that into an ACT score on a scale of 1-36, which is what this chart is for. Follow the line from the Raw Score column to the Scale Score column to determine your approximate ACT English grade.

This chart assumes that the environment you created for yourself when you took the two practice tests was as authentic as possible. Did you take it on a Saturday morning? Did you time yourself with exactly 45 minutes? Did you take it in a quiet room? Did you put your phone away? The more realistic the test experience, the more accurate the outcome.

Remember: this is *approximate;* even the ACT itself uses different charts for different tests! Do not count on this for perfect accuracy.

## About the Author

Philip J Martin studied Industrial and Systems Engineering and Philosophy at Auburn University before earning his Master's Degree in Theology from the Franciscan University of Steubenville. He has been a classroom teacher for more than a decade, and in addition has taught (as of publication) nearly 600 hours of ACT prep in person to hundreds of different students. Along the way, he has earned multiple awards for his short fiction and has published poetry, non fiction, and fiction in print. Today, he lives and writes from beautiful Daphne, AL with his lovely wife and children.

Made in the USA
Monee, IL
05 September 2022